RESHAPING AUSTRALIA'
Growth with Equity and Sustainability

Reshaping Australia's Economy draws together some of the best economists and public policy analysts in Australia to provide a major 'audit' of the economy. The book evaluates the impact of recent economic reform and restructuring in Australia and then pinpoints what is required to ensure vigorous growth with socially and environmentally acceptable outcomes for the future. Leading economists write on Australia's productivity growth, international trade orientation, unemployment, labour market reform, capital market efficiency, immigration and education policies and the impact of the ageing population. Other writers consider the social, regional and environmental dimensions of growth, with probing assessments of Australia's performance in the 'new economy', public sector reform and an evaluation of how corporate governance impacts on growth.

John Nieuwenhuysen is the Chief Executive of CEDA, the Committee for Economic Development of Australia.

Peter Lloyd is a Professor in the Department of Economics at the University of Melbourne.

Margaret Mead is CEDA's Deputy Director of Research.

RESHAPING AUSTRALIA'S ECONOMY

Growth with Equity and Sustainability

EDITED BY

JOHN NIEUWENHUYSEN

Committee for Economic Development of Australia

PETER LLOYD

University of Melbourne

MARGARET MEAD

Committee for Economic Development of Australia

CAMBRIDGE
UNIVERSITY PRESS

PUBLISHED BY THE PRESS SYNDICATE OF THE UNIVERSITY OF CAMBRIDGE
The Pitt Building, Trumpington Street, Cambridge, United Kingdom

CAMBRIDGE UNIVERSITY PRESS
The Edinburgh Building, Cambridge CB2 2RU, UK
40 West 20th Street, New York, NY 10011–4211, USA
10 Stamford Road, Oakleigh, VIC 3166, Australia
Ruiz de Alarcón 13, 28014 Madrid, Spain
Dock House, The Waterfront, Cape Town 8001, South Africa

http://www.cambridge.org

First published 2001

Printed in Australia by Brown Prior Anderson

Typeface New Baskerville 10/12 pt. *System* QuarkXPress® [PH]

A catalogue record for this book is available from the British Library

National Library of Australia Cataloguing in Publication data
Reshaping Australia's economy: growth with equity and sustainability.
Bibliography.
Includes index.
ISBN 0521 81219 4.
ISBN 0 521 01120 5 (pbk.).
1. Australia – Economic conditions – 1990–. I. Mead,
Margaret. II. Nieuwenhuysen, J. P. (John Peter)
III. Lloyd, Peter J. (Peter John).
330.994

ISBN 0 521 81219 4 hardback
ISBN 0 521 01120 5 paperback

Foreword

By Sir Zelman Cowen AK GCMG GCVO QC DCL

This volume is published in 2001, as CEDA celebrates the fortieth anniversary of its first annual general meeting. During these four decades, CEDA has created a quite remarkable range of independent published work. Almost every topic that is relevant to economics, as well as social development, has been covered.

Specially high on the agenda have been trade, immigration, labour market, industrial relations and taxation issues. However, there is virtually nothing that has been neglected – poverty, equity, unemployment, Indigenous Australia, international comparisons, downsizing, ageing, demography and regional growth are among the many subjects included.

This volume, *Reshaping Australia's Economy*, is a particularly appropriate publication, through a distinguished press, with an outstanding group of authors, to mark CEDA's fortieth anniversary. Its topics encompass several of the many themes pertinent to Australian economic and social development that feature in CEDA's previous contributions: trade, Australia in the international economy, equity, capital and labour market efficiency, productivity and innovation, education, new growth frontiers, governance, and sustainable development.

As one of the members of CEDA's original Board of Trustees, I find it heartening to look back and see how the ideas of the man who inspired the formation of CEDA – Sir Douglas Copland – have been carried into practice. Sir Douglas saw how essential it was to establish the conditions for searching debate – a debate in which people of goodwill, but with occasionally differing, indeed strongly opposed views, would come together to explore issues relevant to Australia's economic and social development in the international context.

CEDA, through its extensive conference program, its international linkages, and its independent research output, has fulfilled the Copland mission. In its 40-year history, CEDA has helped to ensure that policy judgements have been made on the basis of enlightened and informed discussion. In doing so, it has had an effect on the welfare of the entire Australian community.

I welcome this volume as a celebration of that achievement, and as a contribution to continuing debate on matters of importance to all Australians.

Contents

Tables

Figures

Contributors

KYM ANDERSON is Professor of Economics and Executive Director of the Centre for International Economic Studies at Adelaide University, where he has been affiliated since 1984. Previously he was a Research Fellow in Economics at ANU's Research School of Pacific and Asian Studies (1977 to 1983), following doctoral studies at the University of Chicago and Stanford University (1974 to 1977). During periods of leave he has spent time in Korea (1980–81), Stockholm (1988) and at the GATT (now WTO) Secretariat in Geneva (1990 to 1992). His research interests and publications are in the areas of international trade and development, and agricultural and environmental/resource economics.

FRED ARGY is a former Canberra policy adviser. He was honoured for his contributions to public policy by both the Coalition government in 1982 and Labor government in 1992. After retiring in 1991 he contributed to several CEDA research papers and actively participated in public policy debate. He has several publications to his name, including a book, *Australia at the Crossroads: Radical Free Market or Progressive Liberalism?* (1998). He is currently a Visiting Fellow, Australian National University, and Adjunct Professor, Queensland University.

SCOTT BAUM is a Research Fellow at the University of Queensland. Trained in sociology and economics, his research interests are in the socioeconomic aspects of urban and regional transformation, including distributional equity, housing choice and preferences, residential mobility and global city functions. He holds a Bachelor degree in Economics and a PhD in Sociology from Flinders University in Adelaide, South Australia.

JEFF BORLAND is Professor of Economics at the University of Melbourne. He has also held visiting positions at the Centre for Economic Policy Research at ANU, University of Iowa and University of Wisconsin, Madison. His main research interests are analysis of the operation of labour markets in Australia, and applications of microeconomic theory to labour markets. In 1997 he was awarded the Academy of Social Sciences Medal for Excellence in Scholarship in the Social Sciences. He is currently Managing Editor of the *Economic Record*.

BRUCE CHAPMAN is a Professor of Economics and Director of the Centre for Economic Policy Research at the Australian National University. He has a PhD from Yale University and is a labour economist with expertise in the areas of training, wage determination, higher education financing, unemployment, labour market program evaluation and the economics of cricket. He has published over 100 articles and has had extensive direct policy experience, which includes motivating and helping to design the Higher Education Contribution Scheme in 1988, as a senior economic adviser to Prime Minister Paul Keating from 1994 to 1996, and to the governments of around 10 countries. He was made a Member of the Order of Australia in 2001 for services to Australian economic, labour market and social policy.

TERRY CUTLER is the principal of Cutler & Company, a consulting firm specialising in the information and communications sector. Before establishing his advisory practice, he was Executive Director Corporate Strategy with Telecom Australia. He has served on numerous government boards, including chairing the Industry Research and Development Board. He is currently a member of the International Advisory Panel of Malaysia's Multimedia Supercorridor, and is Chairman of the Australia Council.

STEVE DOWRICK dropped out of his first degree in Science to get involved in community action projects before returning to Cambridge as an undergraduate in Economics. His PhD and his early research papers were in the field of union bargaining as the interface between non-competitive product and labour markets. Since then he has published extensively in the field of economic growth, particularly the forces of convergence and divergence across countries, and in the development of index number theory to make sense of cross-country comparisons of real incomes. He is currently Professor of Economics and Australian Research Council Senior Fellow at the Australian National University in Canberra.

VINCE FITZGERALD has been Executive Director of The Allen Consulting Group Pty Ltd since 1989. The Allen Consulting Group Pty Ltd consults across a wide range of economic and public-policy issues. Before 1989 he was a senior official in Canberra. Positions held included Head of Economic Division, Prime Minister and Cabinet; Deputy Secretary, Finance, including responsibility for Budget coordination; Secretary, Trade; and Secretary, Employment, Education and Training.

He is probably best known for his work on saving, superannuation and retirement issues, particularly his 1993 report *National Saving: A Report to the Treasurer*. His other studies in these areas include *Superannuation 2000: A Study of the Development of Superannuation and its Context over the 1990s* (1990); *Cultural, Social and Institutional Influences on Saving: Asia Viewed from Australia* (1996); *An Assessment of Current Superannuation Arrangements* (1996); and *Rethinking Work and Retirement: Better Balance, Better Choices for Australians* (1999).

Dr FitzGerald also specialises in the assessment of government policies and programs. He chaired the Queensland Commission of Audit in 1996, which extensively reviewed the performance of that government overall and in each major area of activity, not only in financial and efficiency terms but also in effectiveness terms.

BRIAN HOWE has been a Professorial Associate at the Centre for Public Policy at the University of Melbourne since 1996. He was a member of Australia's federal parliament from 1977 to 1996, and a minister in five successive Labor governments from 1983 to 1996. He was Deputy Prime Minister of Australia from 1991 to 1996. Mr Howe, who was Social Security Minister from 1984 to 1990, was responsible for a number of important social policy reforms in Australia during his time as a minister. His principal interests continue to centre on social reform and social policy issues. He is a member of the boards of the Brotherhood of St Laurence, Victorian Council of Social Service and the Australian Theological Forum. He is currently undertaking research on the future directions of social policy in Australia. He was made a Member of the Order of Australia in 2001 for his contribution to policy and legislative reform in the areas of social justice, health and urban development.

MICHAEL KEATING is currently a company director and a Visiting Fellow in the Economics Program in the Research School of Social Sciences at the Australian National University, and an Adjunct Professor in the School of Politics and Public Policy at Griffith University. He has played a leading role in public policy and reform of public administration. His previous appointment was as Head of the Australian Public Service and as Secretary to the Department of Prime Minister and Cabinet (1991 to 1996). Prior to that he was Head of the Department of Employment and Industrial Relations (1983 to 1986), and Head of the Department of Finance (1986 to 1991). Dr Keating has published various economic and employment-related articles and co-authored a book on Australian economic policy. He has also published extensively in Australia and overseas on public-sector management reform, and most recently he has edited two books on the capacity of our system of governance and the policy choices we are facing.

IAN MANNING has carried out research covering a wide range of topics in Applied Economics. He has worked on macroeconomic policy, social and regional economics, public finance, household, urban and industry economics. His core areas of interest include regional economic structure, transport economics and income distribution. Specific projects have ranged from relationships between Aboriginal people and the mining industry to the effect of different insurance schemes on the costs of motor vehicle smash repairs. Dr Manning is Deputy Executive Director of the National Institute of Economic and Industry Research.

JANE MARCEAU is Pro-Vice-Chancellor (Research) at the University of Western Sydney and Director of the Australian Expert Group in Industry Studies (AEGIS), specialising in the analysis of innovation and strategies for industry development. She has published widely on industrial, technological and organisational innovation. She led the team that produced *The High Road or the Low Road? Alternatives for Australia's Future* (1997), which has been highly influential in both business and public policy-making circles. Professor Marceau has undertaken much of the research behind the development and implementation of the federal government's Action Agendas.

KEVIN O'CONNOR has a Master of Commerce from the University of Melbourne, and a PhD from McMaster University, Canada. Associate Professor O'Connor's teaching and research focus at Monash University is on the links between the economic system (particularly manufacturing and services), and the growth and internal structure of cities. A current project explores changes in the patterns of travel to work that have been associated with the change in the location of jobs and housing in Melbourne.

BILL SHIELDS, at the time of writing, was Chief Economist and an Executive Director of Macquarie Bank Limited. He has had wide experience in economic analysis and policy advice, including with the Reserve Bank of Australia, the International Monetary Fund and the Australian Treasury, and in 1998 was a member of the Prime Minister's Task Force on International Financial Reform. He is currently a Professorial Fellow and teaches in the MBA program at the Macquarie Graduate School of Management, Macquarie University.

ROBERT STIMSON is Professor of Geographical Sciences and Planning at the University of Queensland, where he coordinates a research group in Urban and Regional Analysis, and teaches in the fields of urban and regional development, planning and human spatial behaviour. He is a former director of the Australian Housing and Urban Research Institute at both the University of Queensland and Queensland University of Technology, and has held academic positions as Head of the School of Management at the University of Canberra, and Senior Lecturer in geography at the Flinders University of South Australia. He has been a Fulbright Senior Scholar and is a Life Member of the Regional Science Association International, Australia and New Zealand Section.

DAVID THROSBY is Professor of Economics at Macquarie University in Sydney. His research interests include the theory of public goods, cultural economics and the economics of sustainable development. His most recent book is entitled *Economics and Culture*, and is published by Cambridge University Press. He is currently editing (with Victor Ginsburgh) a *Handbook of the Economics of Art and Culture* for North Holland's Handbooks in Economics series.

GREG TURNIDGE holds a Master of Economics (Hons) degree from Macquarie University. He worked as an economist for the Reserve Bank of Australia, the Victorian Chamber of Manufactures, and the Victorian Government's Office of Management and Budget prior to being appointed Managing Director of Aluminium Smelters of Victoria in 1984.

He has been a company director for the last seventeen years, and participated in the Australian Quality Council's corporate governance benchmarking study in 1998. He is a Fellow of the Australian Institute of Company Directors.

Greg Turnidge is currently a consultant to start-up businesses on corporate strategy and organisational development.

GLENN WITHERS is Professor of Public Policy in the Asia-Pacific School of Economics and Management at the Australian National University. He was previously Commissioner of the Economic Planning Advisory Commission. Professor Withers has a masters and a doctorate in business economics from Harvard. He was made an Officer of the Order of Australia in 1992 for services to Applied Economics. He is Vice-President of the Committee for Economic Development of Australia (CEDA).

MARK WOODEN is a Professorial Fellow with the Melbourne Institute of Applied Economic and Social Research, the University of Melbourne. He was previously Professor and Acting Director at the National Institute of Labour Studies, Flinders University, where he had been employed for 19 years. His main area of research interest has been the operation of labour markets in Australia and, in particular, how they are affected by institutions. He is the author of four books, including most recently, *The Transformation of Australian Industrial Relations*, and a large number of academic journal articles.

Acknowledgement

The editors wish to thank Yvonne Holland of CEDA for her efficient assistance in organising the two authors' meetings at which draft chapters of this book were reviewed and for her excellent administrative help with this project.

Introduction

John Nieuwenhuysen, Peter Lloyd and Margaret Mead

Australian economic growth over the decade of the 1990s was consistent, sustained and strong. Along with the United States and Ireland, Australia enjoyed the strongest economic performance of all nations in the 10 years from 1990. From the low point in the early 1990s recession to the third quarter of 2000, Australia's quarterly real gross domestic product (GDP) increased by nearly half (46 per cent). Over each of the 14 quarters to September 2000, real year-end growth exceeded 4 per cent – the first time that this scale of expansion has been experienced since the ABS began recording quarterly data in 1959. In addition, a combination of low inflation, strong productivity growth and a weak Australian dollar significantly increased the economy's international competitiveness (Stammer 2001: 16).

But continued growth is not guaranteed, and at the time of writing it is faltering. Claims that economic cycles have disappeared, and that investment and other markets are set to move along smooth trend lines seemed to grow stronger just as cycles re-emerged. Growth in an economy cannot be without interruption, and is influenced by many factors, including swings of investor confidence and consumer expectations. Moreover, Australia's impressive recent growth has not overcome socioeconomic disparities, and environmental sustainability remains threatened.

This book documents Australia's recent growth performance. It analyses the causes of growth and the challenges to it; and identifies the major policy initiatives required to secure socially acceptable and environmentally sustainable growth for the future.

Explanations of growth are as complex as the process of development itself. In previous decades, as Jeffrey Sachs notes, '. . . many economic models . . . attributed economic growth essentially to the accumulation of more capital per person' (1999: 21). Yet, emphasis on capital accumulation did not succeed in raising living standards, for example, in the centrally planned economies, where policy-makers neglected other labour market, social and institutional reforms on which economic development depends. These simple ideas of the genesis of growth are now discounted, since they failed to give sufficient prominence to the importance of other factors such as human capital accumulation and innovation and to social transformation. Growth must also be viewed in an international context as factors of production and technologies are mobile between countries.

A more accurate explanation of differences in the rates of growth among countries required new theories. There was a flurry of output of economic growth models in the 1960s based on the work of Trevor Swan (1956) and Robert Solow (1956). Their models tried to explain the long-run rate of growth, but took as given (or exogenous) the rates of technological progress and of growth of the population and labour force. They left unexplained some of the main variables in the growth process. Consequently, from the mid-1980s, there has been further interest in the causes of growth. New (endogenous) theories have emerged emphasising the role of technical progress, population growth, innovation and human capital formation in determining the rate of growth of the real output of economies.

This new theory was accompanied by much empirical testing of the growth experiences of different countries. This empirical literature on the causes of economic growth has not, however, unearthed a magic formula that can be used to ensure consistent and sustained progress. There are, as Michael Mussa remarked, 'few uncontested conclusions' (Mussa 1999: 34).

Understanding the causes of growth requires a knowledge of the institutions that shape it. These include the nature of markets; the degree of government intervention; the scope for mobility of the factors of production – land, labour and capital; the openness of the economy to international competition; and the level of competition in the domestic economy. All of these features depend on the institutions, laws, habits and customs of a country's society and political structure.

Also of significance are mobility and adaptability between economic sectors; that is, the capacity of the economy to adapt to changing consumer needs and domestic and externally induced pressures. Central to this adaptability is the scope for extended divisions of specialisation in the labour force; the capacity to continually acquire new skills; and the deepening of human capital assets through education and training. These are closely related to the role of innovation. As Sachs notes: 'the more specialisation, the more ideas; the more ideas, the more new ideas; the more new ideas, the more innovation; and the more innovation, the faster economic growth' (1999: 22).

In recent decades, the scale of innovation and the rapidity of productivity improvements in certain sectors of the economy have accelerated dramatically. For example, if there had been the same kind of technological change in motor vehicle production as has occurred in computers, a car costing \$20 000 in 1980 would have cost \$2 in 1999 (Jensen 1999: 143).

One result of this very rapid change is that substantial resources have moved swiftly from one segment of the economy to another. In addition, downsizing and contracting out have altered the nature of company work-forces, creating new patterns of employment in a different industrial relations environment. And the international implications of the technological revolution for business organisation and structure have been immense.

Of critical importance in assessing growth and its consequences are, there-fore, equity considerations related to changing patterns of work and job security. As well, environmental sustainability issues have become extremely sensitive.

Relative poverty and unemployment are concentrated in certain economic sectors and geographic regions, and much unemployment is long term. Income distribution is heavily skewed. Social stability can be threatened where, especially in cyclical downturns, these differences are quickly accentu-ated. Economic institutions and policies require continual attention, and, frequently, fresh design.

Economic growth imposes heavy demands on the environment. Australia's ecosystem is increasingly strained, and a large and respectable body of scien-tific opinion is pointing to dependence on fossil fuels as a cause of climate change. Species extinction, land degradation and forest depletion raise serious doubts about the capacity of the environment to sustain further growth. Is environmental harmony compatible with increasing living standards? Can imaginative solutions be found to reconcile economic growth with environ-mental sustainability?

Another important issue related to the growth process is the changing nature and age distribution of the population. Welfare arrangements for yes-terday's population structure, designed 20 or 30 years ago, may not be appro-priate today. Fiscal strains will be severe as the baby-boomer generation moves to old age, and the proportion of the population over 65 increases. Declining birth rates mean that (in the absence of immigration) population size may stagnate and decline, as reproduction rates fall below the levels necessary to maintain existing population numbers into the future.

For all these reasons a study of the policy environment for Australia's economic growth is important. This book deals with many (but not all) of these issues.

Patterns of growth

Part 1 examines aspects of Australia's recent pattern of economic growth. In Chapter 1 Steve Dowrick assesses Australia's growth record over the last few decades. The trend decline in growth that occurred during the 1970s was reversed in the mid to late 1980s. Growth recovered even further in the 1990s, with per capita GDP growing at an average of 3 per cent a year – a level 'not recorded since the golden growth years of the 1960s', and outperforming the OECD decade average.

Dowrick notes that the recovery between 1985 and 1990 was led by strong growth in employment, but underlying productivity growth was weak and the contribution of investment was small. In contrast, the recovery of the 1990s was driven by productivity growth and investment. 'It is interesting to note that the Australian productivity surge was stronger and began earlier than the much-heralded surge of productivity in the US "new economy".'

Australia's recent productivity growth rates have indeed been impressive, with trend productivity growth now at a 25-year high. Over the 1990s Australia became one of the top 10 OECD performers in multi-factor productivity (MFP) growth. According to Dowrick, this remarkable performance was not just the result of cyclical recovery. The most likely explanations appear to be the adoption of new information and communication technologies, the effects of microeconomic reform, development of skills and intensification of work, and the reduction of barriers to trade.

However, Dowrick warns that these changes to the workings of the economy have substantial welfare implications – tending to worsen the lot of those who are less skilled, most subject to work intensification and employed in sectors where the terms of trade are declining. Nevertheless, he concludes, the widespread adoption of information and communications technology (ICT) and the reduction of trade barriers augur well for future economic growth.

In Chapter 2 Kym Anderson examines the increasing integration of the Australian and international economies. He ascribes Australia's good growth performance in the 1990s to economic reforms, in particular 'the belated opening of the Australian economy to the rest of the world'. This has changed the structure of trade as new market opportunities abroad have arisen, and non-governmental trade barriers (especially resulting from the information technology revolution) have been reduced.

Anderson notes several factors that will influence strongly Australia's future growth:

- the extent and speed with which economic events abroad are transmitted to domestic markets will increase inexorably and governments will be ever more unable to isolate their economies from the interactions of a globalised world
- Australia will benefit from further international trade liberalisation, not just for agricultural products, but for skill-intensive products and services as well
- Australia has adapted quickly to the digital revolution, and its impact effectively reduces the country's long distance from other markets.

Regional disparities (of which much has been heard in Australia recently) are dealt with in Chapter 3 by Kevin O'Connor, Robert Stimson and Scott Baum. The analysis of these authors is central to understanding the political economy of Australia today. In particular, they conclude that there is a great divergence between 'people prosperity' and 'place prosperity'. The modern economy has lifted incomes, and created more and diversified employment. However, not all regions have enjoyed this tide of prosperity. Instead, there has been a widening gap between the high-income, diverse consumption clusters, and those with high unemployment and social security dependence. The visibility of this gap has been a potent source of electoral dissatisfaction among communities that feel left behind by rising affluence in other regions.

Growth in the global economy has a major city bias but the economic divides in Australia are far more complex than simply between country and city. They include gaps between the inner city and outer suburbs, and between large and small rural settlements. O'Connor, Stimson and Baum offer no easy answer to the dilemma: it is difficult for policy to encourage a greater geographic spread or participation in people prosperity, since the causes propelling this are inherently bound up with strong forces of unbalanced growth. The intensity of feeling in rural electorates may well be a call to action by governments, but resolving the issue will require, as the authors say, 'a long-term perspective and some innovative thinking'. Moreover, much rural and regional hardship is a result of the unrelenting decline in the prices of agricultural products.

Growth and equity

The income distribution implications of development are extremely important. In Part 2 relationships between the growth of real income and the equity of its distribution are examined, including environmental aspects of growth.

This section starts with Fred Argy's chapter on Liberalism and Economic Policy. It is essential to consider the philosophies or ideologies that have influenced recent policies. In the past 20 years policy has been underpinned by a belief in broad economic liberalism – the switch to hard liberalism is a recent phenomenon. Policies have emphasised as their goal the attainment of the efficiency properties of markets – enabling factors and assets to flow to where their marginal productivity is greatest, and serving to aggregate information and make it widely available throughout the economy.

There is little doubt that this commitment to freely operating markets has substantially increased productivity, competitiveness and living standards. However, Argy emphasises that economic liberalism tries only to alter methods of policy intervention, not policy goals. Social and environmental objectives and the range of government services considered necessary should not be abandoned, in Argy's view, under economic liberalism.

The scope for governments to pursue change through reform and increasing reliance on the market (through sale of public-owned enterprises, deregulation and avoidance of budget deficits) is indeed limited. The extent to which the consequent social and economic changes – and the shifting relative fortunes of segments of the population – are acceptable politically will determine the fortitude of governments in promoting reform. This is clearly an issue of central policy importance, and the ability of governments to manage the tricky path of reform, and at the same time retain power, is never assured.

In his chapter, Equity and Growth, Ian Manning is critical of the distributional outcomes of Australia's recent growth performance. The economy, he considers, is 'providing serious inequalities of educational opportunity . . . is failing to provide paid work opportunities for all who want them . . . (and) from an egalitarian point of view, it is generating too wide a spread of income and wealth'. In Manning's view, 'the equity-fix approach of letting the market rip and attending to equity concerns solely through redistribution is inadequate . . .'.

Manning argues that the 'hard liberalism' currently underpinning economic policy should be questioned. Growth in the longer term requires, he considers, an investment composition and direction different from that of the last decade. For example, the 'hype' should be taken out of casinos, so as to help rebuild household savings; the 'financial theatre' should be calmed, so as to help corporate savings expansion; and a surge of long-term investment should be generated. According to Manning; 'both redistribution, and markets themselves, work best within legal frameworks that express equitable requirements much more strongly than the laws envisaged by hard liberalism'.

The theme of unequal social and economic power is continued in Brian Howe's chapter, Economic Growth and the Ethical State: Refashioning an Australian Settlement. Howe takes a long-term view of growth and equity. The term 'Australian Settlement', borrowed from Paul Kelly, refers to an interlocking set of policies adopted soon after Federation to effect an equitable distribution of income without sacrificing growth. One plank was the wage arbitration system. As reform of the labour market has proceeded, and the nature of industrial relations has changed, Howe sees a 'critical convergence' of issues regarding the balance of work, family and community responsibilities. The key question, therefore, becomes the integration of new patterns of household participation in work with a labour market that lacks the protective regulation of past decades.

As the labour force participation of women increases, and the proportion of casual jobs in total employment rises, it becomes important to reconcile the demands of the workplace with those of the home. Unless this reconciliation is achieved, gender inequality may well continue as the burdens of domestic and caring tasks are not evenly shared.

While many factors drive the growth process, no subject has such fundamental importance as the sustainability of the environment. This is discussed in David Throsby's chapter on sustainable economic development.

Throsby outlines the principal aspects of environmental concern, notably land and water use; other natural resource use (mining, forestry and fisheries);

atmospheric pollution; waste management; and nature conservation. The picture painted is not encouraging. Indeed, it documents a growing environmental crisis, one which Australia shares with the rest of the world. While the principle of environmentally sustainable development (ESD) is accepted by governments, this recognition is seldom translated into practice.

Throsby discusses how the concept of sustainability can be incorporated into the definition of economic growth. However, he notes (including the 'sharp illustration' of the climate change debate) that rhetoric is in the ascendancy over action. Throsby concludes that fundamental questions are being raised about economic growth and its consequences, and argues that a broader concept of sustainability is needed, embracing cultural and social dimensions alongside environmental and economic concerns.

The equity questions discussed in Part 2 are in the context of the rapid pace of recent economic change. The achievement of greater equity itself depends, however, on further growth, and the creation of an environment that will encourage it. This requires participation in the new economy, effective innovation systems, and appropriate institutions of governance. These issues are examined in Part 3.

New frontiers, innovation and governance

The pivotal role of the ICT industries in facilitating industrial development and economic growth in the new information economy is described by Terry Cutler in Chapter 8. The digital revolution has transformed the way companies, markets and economies function, and 'the main opportunity for new wealth creation lies in the emerging, information-intensive, knowledge industries', he says.

According to Cutler, 'Australia is seriously behind the game in building the industries that are, around the world, creating the new jobs and the new wealth'. While we may have relatively high levels of technology consumption, this is not matched by production capability. Australia's information and communications industry 'is dominated by a few multinationals (only one or two Australian owned), and a huge tail of sub-scale, undercapitalised small and medium enterprises with a domestic market focus in the areas of product distribution and support services'.

Cutler is also critical of Australia's research and innovation record. Business investment in research and development has been falling substantially, and there has been a downward trend in higher education funding, particularly for postgraduate research. Investment in information technology is 24 times greater per capita in the United States than in Australia.

What can be done to improve Australia's performance in the new economy? Cutler proposes the development of a national strategy for the information industries. 'What is needed is an Australia-wide web of innovation linking businesses, research institutes and governments within a creative part-nership . . . The government's role in funding R&D and high-level skills devel-opment is fundamental . . . Without serious government funding there is little prospect for the necessary structural adjustment in Australia's economy and industrial landscape.'

The critical importance of innovation in determining a nation's competitive advantage is explored further by Jane Marceau in Chapter 9. She notes that successful economies have well-functioning innovation systems with effective linkages between firms, public-sector research institutions and government.

Marceau states that Australia has not done well recently in the innovation field, and lags behind many other OECD countries on indicators of innova-tion. Improving Australia's innovation performance will require putting into place a range of mutually supporting policies, including measures aimed at improving R&D, education and training, intellectual property protection, and access to development finance.

Effective approaches to encouraging innovation will require a sophisticated understanding of industry dynamics, which recognises differences between industries and sectors, and the complex linkages between firms and institutions that determine industry development. 'This . . . means a move away from simply improving the macro environment as though all industries needed the same things . . . Each industry may well need different elements [of assistance] . . . in different proportions at different times, or in different ways . . . It is only by understanding the need for many points of assistance for any one sector that innovation encouragement can succeed.'

Recent policies, such as the R&D tax concession and the training levy, while effective in the short term, failed to change the permanent behaviour of firms. Rates of investment in R&D dropped sharply after the tax concession was reduced in 1996–97, and investment in training also declined after the training levy was abolished.

Marceau says the federal government's current Action Agenda, developed after the National Innovation Summit in 2000, is a step in the right direction. The Action Agenda brings together government and industry in a range of sectors to examine collectively what is needed to improve the competitiveness of individual industry sectors. But, she says, there remains an urgent need for a package of policies aimed specifically at developing Australia's IT sector.

The ability of financial markets to mobilise and allocate capital efficiently is a fundamental driver of the growth process. As the Asian financial crisis of 1997–98 showed, inefficient financial markets can seriously disrupt growth. In Chapter 10, Bill Shields assesses the relative efficiency of Australia's capital markets.

Shields describes the rapid expansion of the Australian financial sector over the past decade, with all market segments growing faster than GDP since 1985. This expansion was driven by the relatively intense deregulation of

Australian capital markets occurring from the late 1970s to the mid-1980s, combined with the effects of technological innovation, globalisation and changing demographics and consumer needs.

The result has been the establishment of a diversified and well-developed financial structure in Australia, with a significantly reduced cost of capital to borrowers. Shields notes that another important consequence of deregulation and innovation has been the development of a more responsive regulatory framework. But he also points out that deregulation did not come without some costs; in particular, an increase in financial market volatility, although this appears to be declining, particularly for the domestic capital markets.

Shields uses three criteria to judge the relative efficiency of Australia's capital markets: empirical testing of the efficient market hypothesis against the actual behaviour of asset prices; the ability of Australia's financial markets to withstand unexpected shocks (such as the Asian financial crisis); and a comparison of the cost of capital in Australia with that in markets generally accepted as being efficient, such as the United States. According to Shields, most of the evidence supports the view that capital markets in Australia appear to be efficient, at least relative to other global markets.

Can government do more to enhance financial market efficiency? Shields suggests improvements to 'the quality and timeliness of major economic and financial data', and 'greater transparency in the conduct of economic policy, particularly monetary and taxation policies that have a direct impact on the markets'. Shields also notes some market deficiencies; namely, difficulties faced by new ventures in obtaining adequate capital and the limited market for corporate debt in Australia. But, he concludes, 'this does not alter the overall conclusion that capital markets in Australia are efficient and, importantly, operate in a framework that generally encourages competition and innovation'.

In Chapter 11, Michael Keating examines the relationship between the structure of government and economic growth. He is sceptical of the view that '. . . the system of governance must influence the rate of economic growth'. He sees 'little objective proof that one set of governance arrangements in a market economy are inherently superior to another in this respect'. Keating concludes that the changes proposed in Australia towards an 'even more majoritarian form of government' (such as referral of powers to the Commonwealth, lengthened parliamentary terms, and reduced Senate powers) will not necessarily lead to better economic growth.

Keating notes that in the last 20 years, governance arrangements in Australia have evolved in favour of a greater role for competitive markets. There have been significant alterations in the way government services are delivered in Australia, with the introduction of wider choice and competition. Microeconomic reform has also involved greater competition and a change in the nature of regulation in favour of more use of market instruments. Significant reforms along these lines, in Keating's view, were achieved by joint action by governments under collaborative federalism, and were not seriously hindered by the nature of Australia's federal structure.

But Keating concludes that governments are finding it difficult to meet all the expectations they are facing and to mediate the variety of competing claims. 'New approaches to seeking cooperation and consultation will, therefore, need to be part of Australian public governance. The trick will be to respond most effectively to the circumstances of individuals and communities while not becoming captured by vested interests.'

Corporate governance is another important factor in creating a climate conducive to growth. Greg Turnidge observes in Chapter 12 that calls for improved corporate governance in Australia in the 1990s first occurred after incidents of unethical business practice, but were subsequently based on a perception that company performance, and overall economic prosperity, depended upon it.

The legal accountability of company directors and their consequent liability for company actions have enlarged the risk of directors. Corporate governance incentives have therefore increasingly focused on satisfying statutory obligations – that is, the duty of care and diligence – and conformance and compliance objectives have been stressed, imposing a high level of conservatism on management. This has led to the fear that too little time is spent on the business issues that need to be confronted to ensure profitability.

In contrast, as Turnidge shows, the conservative approach induced by these pressures for diligence is different from the institutional investor influence, which emphasises swift shareholder returns. This influence is augmented by share schemes effectively encouraging directors and management to strive for short-term financial performance and reward.

Another theme in Turnidge's chapter is the contrast between government promotion of the market mechanism and a prescriptive approach to business behaviour, due to public concern about the outcomes of an unregulated private sector. In Turnidge's view, policy trends are inimical to economic growth, since effective leadership requires reduced fear of failure, through changed board behaviour and a longer term institutional investment perspective.

Clearly, these unsettled issues of corporate governance, and the role of legislation in influencing them, are key factors in the future economic progress of the private sector.

Labour markets, human resources and demography

Despite Australia's recent record of strong economic growth, unemployment has remained stubbornly high, and is sensitive to economic downswings. There are also concerns that the workforce is not sufficiently skilled or flexible to compete successfully in the global knowledge economy. As well, the ageing of the population, coupled with a poor national savings rate, raises questions about government's ability to fund future growth. These issues are discussed in Part 4.

As Jeff Borland observes in Chapter 13, unemployment in Australia has risen dramatically over the last three decades. Although the rate of unemployment fell to just over 6 per cent at the end of 2000, this was after nine years of economic expansion. Should that expansion be reversed, says Borland, it seems quite likely that the rate of unemployment would return rapidly to double-digit levels. What has caused this worrying trend in unemployment and what are the policy options for dealing with it?

Much of the increase in Australia's unemployment rate can be explained by a significant increase in joblessness that occurred between the mid- to late 1970s and was not subsequently reversed. This was followed by sharp cyclical increases in unemployment between 1981 and 1983, and between 1989 and 1993 (both of which were reversed by 1989 and 2000, respectively). According to Borland, periods of rising unemployment in Australia are associated primarily with reductions in the rate of output growth, or with very high rates of wage inflation. Institutional change does not seem to have been an important causal factor.

Borland also notes that Australia's persistently high rate of unemployment during periods of economic expansion seems partly related to declines in the search efficiency of the unemployed. The duration of unemployment lengthens with each period of recession, reducing the 'job readiness' and skills of the unemployed, impeding their employment prospects as the economy recovers.

Economists generally agree that the primary policy mechanism for reducing unemployment is to maintain high rates of economic growth, and avoid recessions. But, as Borland points out, there is disagreement about how high a rate of growth is sustainable in Australia while keeping price inflation within the target range of the RBA; and about the relative importance of policies designed to improve 'employment absorption' from output growth, such as changes to the wage structure and the role of labour market programs.

Maintaining a moderate rate of wage inflation is critical in fighting unemployment. Here, Borland notes that wage outcomes under the new decentralised wage-setting system (described in Chapter 14) will have important implications for unemployment. But he doubts the efficacy of proposals for a freeze on safety-net wage adjustments to stimulate employment growth. He also notes that, despite the potential benefits of labour market programs, evidence on their effectiveness is mixed.

Borland concludes that the challenge facing government in reducing unemployment is not to devise new policy solutions, but to implement existing policies – particularly high rates of output growth – for sustained periods.

In Chapter 14, Mark Wooden focuses on the impact of recent reforms to Australia's industrial relations system. Since the late 1980s Australian governments of all persuasions have emphasised the role of workplace relations in improving productivity growth and overall economic efficiency. A flexible workforce, unfettered by the constraints of a centralised wage-fixing and arbitration system, has been seen as an essential requirement for sustained economic growth in the new global environment. To achieve this, a significant program of industrial relations reform was enacted.

Prior to the 1990s, employment conditions for the majority of Australian employees were governed by highly prescriptive, multi-employer awards, determined by tribunal-based systems of conciliation and arbitration. Today, however, enterprise bargaining has replaced arbitration as the dominant industrial relations method. Most awards now provide only a 'safety net' above which wages and other conditions can be negotiated. The role of trade unions in the bargaining process has declined; scope for employers to use individually negotiated employment agreements instead of awards has increased, and the powers of industrial tribunals have been significantly curtailed.

Have these changes resulted in improved productivity? Wooden notes the marked pick-up in Australia's productivity growth during the 1990s, but suggests that there is no conclusive proof that this was driven by industrial relations changes alone. Other factors such as microeconomic reform initiatives, particularly changes to the delivery of government services, may also have played a part. According to Wooden, it is yet to be shown that enterprise bargaining has enhanced the productive performance of Australian enterprises. On the other hand, he finds little evidence to support claims by critics of enterprise bargaining that it has exacerbated trends in job insecurity, increased working hours and wage inequality.

Two important factors in building national capability – education and immigration policies – are discussed by Chapman and Withers in Chapter 15. According to the authors, 'smart' growth in human capital formation, driven by formal education and skilled migration, is a key determinant of economic growth in today's competitive environment.

Chapman and Withers find that, in the education system over the last two decades, there has been:

- a significant increase in school retention rates for both girls and boys over the period 1980 to 2000, but small declines in recent years, particularly for boys
- a large increase in TAFE vocational enrolments over the same period, particularly for girls
- a 50 per cent expansion in university enrolments since 1990 (despite the introduction of the Higher Education Contribution Scheme (HECS) in 1989).

Have these changes in the *quantity* of education been associated with improvements to the *quality* of education? Taking expenditure per student as an indicator of quality, the authors note:

- a very small increase in government outlays per school student over the last two decades
- a consistent decline in real government outlays per university student since the mid-1990s.

As well, there has been a four-fold increase in private-sector expenditure on education over the last 20 years and a large increase in enrolments in non-Catholic private schools.

It is not clear if these trends have led to an overall decline in the quality of education but they raise a number of policy issues. Importantly, the move away from public to private financing of education – and in particular a tendency to impose up-front student fees in the tertiary education sector – has implications for inter-generational opportunities and intra-generational social justice. According to the authors: 'Income-contingent charging mechanisms, such as HECS . . . should be given policy priority'.

Chapman and Withers also review the contribution of migration to human capital formation and economic growth. There is evidence that Australia's population expansion has been a major source of technological change – one of the key drivers of growth. And considerable research has shown a significant pay-off in terms of growth per capita from skilled migration.

Despite these potential benefits, Australia has been steadily reducing the rate of migration, while at the same time the rate of emigration, particularly for high-skilled workers, has increased. The authors observe that the skilled entry migration program prevents a major 'brain-drain' occurring from Australia.

In the authors' view a declining fertility rate means that an increase in migration levels (to around 250 000 per year by mid-century) is required to achieve a population growth rate sufficient to generate per capita income growth. The policy challenges will be how to achieve such an inflow without reducing the skill quality of the intake, and the need to develop complementary investment in education, innovation, infrastructure and environmental sustainability so as to maximise the potential gains.

In Chapter 16, Vince FitzGerald discusses how changes to Australia's demographic structure could constrain future growth if an appropriate national savings policy is not put in place. He notes several trends including:

- a decline in the fertility rate over recent decades to a level now below the replacement rate
- a strong rise in female participation in the workforce, attributable almost exclusively to increased participation by married women
- a decline in workforce participation by males, reflecting almost entirely increased early retirement by older males, most of which is involuntary.

Other significant trends are the progressive retirement of the 'baby-boomer' generation from the workforce (the oldest 'boomers' now being around age 55) and projected increases in the aged dependency ratio. Meeting the future cost of income support, health care and other aged care for the elderly population will pose a significant fiscal challenge for government.

According to FitzGerald, recent superannuation initiatives have reduced concerns about the future cost of the age pension. 'It is becoming increasingly clear that the biggest area of concern for future affordability is health and related expenditure', he says. While some health care costs are met privately, currently around 70 per cent of all health care costs are met by government. 'Plausible estimates for total health costs in the 2030s and 2040s range from 13 per cent of GDP upwards – implying an increase in aged health care costs of at least 3 per cent of GDP to the Commonwealth Budget alone', says Fitzgerald.

Strong savings flows will be needed to meet these increased expenditures, and to minimise the extent to which growth-inhibiting higher taxes will be required. While FitzGerald considers the possibility of increasing voluntary savings to meet growing health care costs, he also advocates increased *public* saving. But the way in which increased national saving will be put to use is critical. Increased saving will have greatest effect on growth if it is invested in additional physical capital within the economy – rather than used to reduce external liabilities – and if it occurs in combination with other sustainable measures to lift productivity growth. 'The threat to growth from demographic change can be made into an opportunity – the choice is ours', he concludes.

Conclusions

The evidence of growth in the past decade is easier to produce than an analysis of its causes. However, the directions on which future success depends clearly include embracing new technology and encouraging innovation; investing in human resources and skills development; further opening Australia to world markets; and reforming those institutions and practices that inhibit development.

Growth, however, carries costs that need to be monitored and, where possible, reduced and contained. The impact of growth on regional income and other aspects of distribution is uneven, and, on the environment, it is destructive to the extent that large tracts of the nation and its resources may be lost permanently to use or cultivation; for example, through the spread of salinity.

These aspects – equity and sustainability – are major issues, requiring policy attention and care. Ironically, however, where growth slows or the economy stagnates or contracts, the degree of inequality can be increased and the scope for restraining environmental damage reduced. Consequently, with or without growth, equity and sustainability remain important issues. The best opportunity to improve equity in income distribution, to maximise employment and to develop policies for sustainable development, comes when wealth is generated by growth, and a portion of the newly created income can be directed to these purposes.

Collectively, these chapters highlight a number of unresolved debates about growth and equity. Hard liberalism is still the dominant approach to economic policy-making in Australia, as discussed by Fred Argy. This is reflected in several of the chapters in this book but some commentators put forward alternative policies. Argy wants to discard the ideological baggage that often comes with economic liberalism and pleads for a closer integration of economic and social policy. Ian Manning and Brian Howe are representative of more interventionist views.

In relation to particular policies or reforms, differences emerged among the authors. For example, Dowrick attributes part of the increase in the rate of productivity growth during the 1990s to the adoption of new ICT technologies whereas Cutler has a less sanguine view of Australia's ICT sector. Some authors are unsure of the economic benefits from recent policy reforms; according to Wooden, it is still not clear what benefits we have received from the introduction of enterprise bargaining, and Turnidge concludes that changes to corporate governance designed to increase the accountability of company directors may have discouraged risk-taking.

The regional divide outlined by O'Connor, Stimson and Baum is changing the political landscape of rural and regional Australia. The trick, as Michael Keating concludes, is to accommodate these concerns without allowing public policy to be captured by vested interests. Another issue, on which little progress has been made, is the conflict in some sectors of the economy between achieving higher rates of growth of real output and the maintenance of environmental balance. These unresolved conflicts illustrate the need for a political consensus – a new Australian settlement – appropriate for an era of rapid technological change and global competition.

The pursuit of growth with equity and sustainability, therefore, remains a primary policy objective for Australia. To this end the issues raised in this volume are crucial:

- the attainment of efficiency in capital, labour and other markets
- the creation of effective systems of corporate and public governance
- a policy environment conducive to innovation and technological change in the new frontiers of growth
- suitable incentives and institutions to encourage saving and other changes necessary to prepare Australia for the consequences of demographic shifts
- flexible and creative measures to ensure human resources development and the minimisation of unemployment
- stronger commitment to environmentally sustainable development
- a set of general policies that promote reform.

At the same time measures should be adopted that cushion the effects of growth on those segments of the economy that are made worse off by the processes of change and structural adjustment.

References

Jensen, M.D. (1999) 'Ownership and Economic Growth', in *Creating an Environment for Growth*, SNS Centre for Business and Policy Studies, Stockholm.

Mussa, M. (1999) 'Changing Growth Patterns in the World Economy', in *Creating an Environment for Growth*, SNS Centre for Business and Policy Studies, Stockholm.

Sachs, J.D. (1999) 'Why Economies Grow', in *Creating an Environment for Growth*, SNS Centre for Business and Policy Studies, Stockholm.

Solow, R.M. (1956) 'A Contribution to the Theory of Growth', *Quarterly Journal of Economics*, 70, February, pp. 65–94.

Stammer, D. (2001) 'Prepare to Slow Down', *Deutsche Bank Solutions*, Autumn, p. 16.

Swan, T.W. (1956) 'Economic Growth and Capital Accumulation', *Economic Record*, 32, November, pp. 334–61.

PART 1

Patterns of Growth

1

Productivity Boom: Miracle or Mirage?

Steve Dowrick

Introduction

Bill Gates sparked off heated discussion with his allegations in September 1999 that Australia had failed to convert to the 'new economy' based on information technology. His remarks displayed remarkable ignorance of both economic principles and the facts of the Australian economy. While it is true that Australia is not a major producer of IT hardware or software, we are intensive users of these products – and the gains from the new IT, as has been the case with previous technological advances, are likely to accrue to both users and producers. Furthermore, the Australian economy has experienced a major and sustained surge in productivity growth since 1992 – of equal magnitude to, and of longer duration than, the IT-driven surge in US productivity that began only in 1996.

There are, in fact, good reasons to think that the Australian economy is in a favourable position for further strong growth based on a modern economy that makes productive use of IT developments and that has been substantially purged of inefficiencies due to trade barriers. In this chapter we examine the recent growth performance of the Australian economy, comparing it with performance over previous decades and also with the performance of other industrialised economies in order to identify factors likely to sustain growth.

Investigating the Australian productivity 'miracle' of the 1990s

The Industry Commission (1997) drew attention to the fact that underlying productivity growth had increased substantially during the 1990s. They noted that, by the mid-1990s, multi-factor productivity growth in the market sector of the economy was running at around 2 per cent per year – a rate of growth not seen since the golden growth years of the 1960s.

One explanation for the Industry Commission's findings is that the successive introduction of macro- and micro-economic reforms over the previous decade, including a series of deregulations and privatisations, had started to show up in improved productivity growth. While the Commission's paper is careful not to claim proof of such a link, their evidence is suggestive. More recently, Forsyth (2000) has reviewed reform and productivity in various sectors of the economy, expressing the view that 'both the magnitude and timing are consistent with the view that microeconomic reform has been a primary contributor to the productivity boom' (p. 236). He comes to the conclusion that 'there is scope for the process of microeconomic reform to continue, albeit at a slower pace than in the 1990s, and some further gains, though of a smaller order of magnitude than before, can be expected' (p. 265).

Alternatively, and contrary to the prognostications of the Microsoft chairman, is it the 'new economy' that is driving the resurgence of productivity growth in Australia? With regard to the recent surge of one percentage point in annual US labour productivity growth, Oliner and Sichel (2000) argue that two-thirds is attributable to information technology production and usage. On the other hand, Gordon (2000) argues that much of the US productivity resurgence is attributable to cyclical factors and that the 'new economy' miracle is largely confined to productivity growth in the production of IT hardware and software.

Gordon's emphasis on the cyclical nature of productivity growth is clearly important for analysis of the Australian situation. We know that productivity growth tends to be pro-cyclical, rising in the recovery phase of the business cycle as under-utilised capital and hoarded labour are brought back into full production. Was the productivity surge of the mid-1990s merely a cyclical increase in productivity growth as the economy climbed out of the depths of the 1991 recession? If that were the case, we would expect the productivity miracle to be fading away by now.

Four years on from the Industry Commission's announcement, we are in a position to investigate whether or not the productivity resurgence of the mid-1990s was purely a cyclical event, or short-lived for other reasons. Figure 1.1 graphs the growth of labour and multi-factor productivity in the market sector over the past three decades. Because the growth rates are fairly volatile (see Table 1.1 for the annual data), I have smoothed the series by using a three-year moving average. Annual multi-factor productivity (MFP) growth shows a trend decline from around 2 per cent in the 1960s to stagnate at levels under 1 per cent for the 14-year period 1978 to 1992. Since then, however, MFP growth has returned close to 2 per cent.

Labour productivity growth is typically just over one percentage point higher than MFP growth, due to increasing capital intensity. It has followed much the same path as MFP, except that the recovery in labour productivity began earlier, in 1988. A clear conclusion is that Australian productivity growth recovered remarkably well from a long period of stagnation. Although

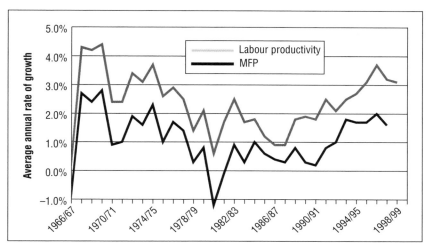

Figure 1.1 Market sector productivity growth (three-year moving average)

there was a slight dip towards the end of the 1990s, the recovery appears to have been sustained.

These estimates refer only to the market sector of the economy, excluding the following industries, which account for around one-quarter of GDP:

- property and business services
- government administration and defence
- education

Table 1.1 Average rates of growth of real GDP and productivity (% per year)

	1980–85	1985–90	1990–95	1995–2000
Whole economy				
GDP	3.2	3.5	2.6	4.4
GDP per capita	1.7	2.0	1.5	3.1
Hours worked	1.1	3.4	0.8	1.7
GDP per hour worked	2.0	0.1	1.9	2.8
Market sector				
GDP market sector	2.7	3.5	2.2	4.9
Hours worked market sector	0.4	3.0	0.0	1.2
GDP per hour worked market sector	2.3	0.5	2.2	3.7
Multi-factor productivity	0.5	0.2	0.7	2.0
US non-farm business sector				
Output			2.7	4.8
Labour productivity			1.9	2.3
Multi-factor productivity			0.5	1.2

Source: ABS Cat. nos 5204.0 and 5206.0, June 2000 and Oliner and Sichel (2000).

- health and community services and
- personal and other services.

Since the Australian Bureau of Statistics cannot properly measure the real output of these industries, where services are not traded and where quality changes are difficult to quantify, its convention is to ascribe zero productivity growth. So estimates of productivity growth in the whole economy, including these sectors, are biased downwards.

The growth of real GDP and real GDP *per capita* for the whole economy are shown in Figure 1.2, again using a three-year moving average. The vertical distance between the two lines is the rate of population growth that slowed from 2 per cent per year in the 1960s to 1.2 per cent per year in the 1990s. The *per capita* measure is more closely related to economic welfare. It is conceptually quite different from measures of labour productivity in the market sector, since it divides real output not by actual labour used in production but by population. It is therefore influenced by changes in demographic structure, participation and unemployment rates.

As observed in the market sector, a trend decline in growth set in during the 1970s. The growth recovery starts earlier than in the market sector with growth of per capita GDP averaging $2^{1}/_{2}$ per cent during the mid to late 1980s.

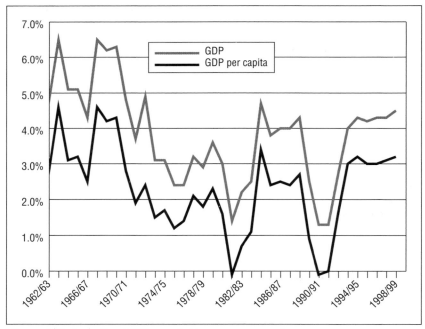

Figure 1.2 Australian GDP growth (three-year average)

Most of this GDP recovery was due to rapidly rising employment in the period of the Prices and Income Accord.

Overall *per capita* economic growth in the 1990s recovered even further – reaching levels not recorded since the golden growth years of the 1960s. Growth of GDP *per capita* has also been remarkably stable in the 1990s, averaging 3 per cent and never falling below $2^1/_2$ per cent for an unprecedented eight successive years (see Table 1.2).

Table 1.1 shows rates of growth of output, labour productivity and multi-factor productivity averaged over five-year periods, enabling a comparison of the economic recoveries following the recessions of the early 1980s and early 1990s. The recovery between 1985 and 1990 was led by strong growth in employment, with hours of work growing 3.4% per year. But underlying productivity growth was weak and the contribution of investment was small.

In contrast, the growth recovery of the 1990s was driven by productivity and investment: MFP growth averaged 2 per cent per year between 1995 and 2000, with the remaining 1.7 per cent of labour productivity growth coming from increasing capital intensity.

It is interesting to note that the Australian productivity surge was stronger and began earlier than the much-heralded surge of productivity in the US 'new economy'.

The fact that the surge in Australian productivity continued beyond the immediate recovery years of the mid-1990s suggests that it is not a purely cyclical phenomenon. In order to check this hypothesis, I estimate trends in market sector productivity growth using a standard error-correction model. I begin with a Cobb–Douglas aggregate production function with constant returns to the net capital stock (K_t) and the level of employment (L_t), and an exponential time trend, λ representing the rate of exogenous technical progress. This enables us to write the long-run relationship, at time T, between the log of hourly labour productivity, $\ln(Y/L) \equiv y-$, and log capital intensity $\ln(K/L) \equiv k$, as:

$$y_T = a + \alpha k_T + \lambda T \tag{1}$$

This is a long-run relationship in the sense that it holds only when both capital and labour are fully and efficiently employed. Long-run multi-factor productivity is defined as $MFP_T \equiv y_T -\!- \alpha k_T = a + \lambda T$.

In the short run, when shocks to demand are unanticipated, it is likely that labour productivity, y, will lie below the technically efficient level defined by (1), primarily because employment is sticky in the short run. A firm considering whether to lay off workers immediately will anticipate direct lay-off costs such as contractual redundancy payments and further costs of recruitment and retraining as and when demand recovers. A negative shock to demand will result, in the short term, in some degree of labour hoarding. We also expect that adjustment and information costs will prevent the immediate adjustment of capital. Hence the common observation that productivity moves pro-cyclically.

Table 1.2 Annual rates of growth of GDP and market sector

	Market sector		Whole economy	
	MFP	Labour productivity	GDP	GDP per capita
1965–66	−3.8%	−2.8%	2.1%	0.1%
1966–67	1.4%	2.0%	6.9%	5.1%
1967–68	−0.6%	1.3%	4.1%	2.3%
1968–69	7.3%	9.5%	8.4%	6.4%
1969–70	0.5%	1.9%	6.0%	3.9%
1970–71	0.5%	1.9%	4.4%	2.4%
1971–72	1.6%	3.3%	4.1%	2.1%
1972–73	0.9%	2.1%	2.8%	1.2%
1973–74	4.5%	5.3%	5.3%	3.8%
1974–75	0.5%	2.8%	1.1%	−0.4%
1975–76	0.6%	2.1%	2.8%	1.7%
1976–77	3.6%	4.7%	3.5%	2.4%
1977–78	−0.6%	0.8%	1.1%	−0.1%
1978–79	3.0%	4.1%	5.1%	4.0%
1979–80	−0.5%	0.4%	2.5%	1.3%
1980–81	−0.8%	0.4%	3.1%	1.6%
1981–82	1.6%	3.5%	3.6%	2.0%
1982–83	−5.0%	−2.1%	−2.4%	−4.0%
1983–84	3.9%	5.0%	5.4%	4.2%
1984–85	2.9%	3.7%	4.5%	3.2%
1985–86	−0.4%	0.3%	4.1%	2.7%
1986–87	−2.4%	−1.8%	2.7%	1.2%
1987–88	2.3%	2.6%	5.2%	3.6%
1988–89	2.0%	2.7%	4.0%	2.3%
1989–90	−0.6%	0.0%	3.6%	2.1%
1990–91	−0.7%	1.9%	−0.2%	−1.6%
1991–92	0.3%	2.9%	0.4%	−0.9%
1992–93	1.5%	2.5%	3.6%	2.5%
1993–94	2.1%	2.6%	4.0%	3.0%
1994–95	0.1%	0.3%	4.4%	3.3%
1995–96	3.4%	4.4%	4.4%	3.1%
1996–97	1.4%	3.3%	3.7%	2.5%
1997–98	2.0%	4.4%	4.6%	3.5%
1998–99	1.3%	2.8%	4.4%	3.2%
1999–2000	N/A	2.2%	4.3%	2.9%

Source: ABS Cat. no. 5204.0, 1998–99, updated with Cat. no. 5206.0, June 2000.

Note: Shaded areas indicate periods over which GDP per capita grew at a rate above 2.5% in successive years.

If adverse demand shocks prove to be more than temporary, we expect firms to revise expectations and adjust their output and inputs to long-run profit-maximising levels, implying that the relationship between y and k returns to the technically efficient levels defined by equation (1). To the extent that the previous period's labour productivity was below the efficient level, productivity will increase. A dynamic error-correction model (ECM) captures this process (see Wickens and Breusch 1988 for discussion on specifications of the ECM):

$$\Delta y_t = [\theta_1 \Delta k_t + \theta_2 \lambda] + \theta_3 [\alpha k_{t-1} + \lambda(t-1) - y_{t-1}] + \epsilon_t \qquad (2)$$

The first term in square brackets explains a portion of current growth in labour productivity as a function of the concurrent growth in capital intensity and technical progress. The second square-bracketed term represents the extent to which previous period output fell below its long-run level. The co-efficient θ_3 captures the speed of adjustment – the proportion of the gap that is corrected in the subsequent period. A value of zero for θ_3 would imply no adjustment. A negative value implies that after a shock productivity moves back towards its long-run level (in statistical terminology, there is a co-integrating relationship). Estimation of equation (2) is reported in Table 1.3.

The negative coefficient on lagged y confirms the existence of a long-run co-integrating relationship between labour productivity (y) and capital intensity (k). The error correction coefficient of –0.97 implies that almost all of the adjustment is carried out in the year following a shock. The estimated long-run elasticity of output with respect to capital is 0.27.

Table 1.3 Estimation of labour productivity in the market sector, 1964–65 to 1998–99

Explanatory variables	Coefficient	t-ratio	Long-run coefficients (t-ratio)
y_{-1}	−0.97	−5.9	
k_{-1}	0.27	2.0	0.274 (2.1)
$T64_{-1}$	0.023	3.8	0.024 (4.4)
$T74_{-1}$	−0.016	−5.6	−0.017 (−6.5)
$T90_{-1}$	0.014	4.5	0.014 (5.5)
Δk	0.138	0.8	
$\Delta T74$	−0.002	0.1	
$\Delta T90$	−0.004	−0.3	
constant	−0.47	−2.8	

$R^2 = 0.6548$ R^2–adj. $= 0.5444$ s.e. $= 0.016$

k is log (capital stock per hour worked)

Txx is a time trend variable, which is zero up to 19xx and increments by one every year thereafter

x_{-1} is lag(x) and Δx is $(x - x_{-1})$

Data source: ABS cat. no. 5204.0 'Australian System of National Accounts', 1998–99, Table 1.17.

The coefficients on the time trends should be interpreted as measures of underlying multi-factor productivity growth, purged of cyclical effects. Trend MFP growth started at 2.1 per cent per year in the 1960s, fell by 1.7 percentage points from 1974 and recovered by 1.4 percentage points from 1990. These estimates confirm the impression derived from inspecting the smoothed productivity data in Figure 1.1: trend productivity growth is now at a 25-year high.

International comparisons of the productivity resurgence

The Australian experience of a growth slowdown since the mid-1970s was an international phenomenon, shared by all of the advanced industrial economies. Explanations range from oil price shocks to the exhaustion of post-war technological catch-up. Both the United States and Australia have experienced a surge in productivity growth in the 1990s. Is it the case that the return to pre-1974 growth levels is a general international phenomenon?

To answer this question I turn to a quasi-growth accounting approach, estimating production function parameters for a panel of 25 countries and four decades. The underlying model is of an aggregate production function where capital, labour and technology are the inputs: $Y_i = e^{\tau i} F(K_i , L_i)$ with constant returns to capital and labour.

I follow previous work such as Dowrick and Nguyen (1989) and Barro (1991) in supposing that technical progress may be influenced by the opportunity to import or copy from more advanced economies. This suggests that there should be a negative relationship between income levels and subsequent growth. Technical progress, τ, is assumed to be a function of the productivity gap between country i and the United States at the beginning of decade t, and a random exogenous country component, z_{it}:

$$\tau_{it} = \gamma_1 \ln[(Y/L)^0_{it} / (Y/L)^0_{US, t}] + z_{it} \qquad (3)$$

where Y/L measures initial GDP per member of the labour force and the final term captures residual cyclical and other factors – including the effects of economic policies – to the extent that their effects are not captured through other explanatory variables such as investment and employment.

This approach leads to the following relationship for the growth of GDP *per head of population*, g(Y/P):

$$g(Y/P)_{it} = (1-\alpha) g(K/P)_{it} + \alpha g(L/P)_{it} + \gamma_1 \ln[(Y/L)^0_{it} / (Y/L)^0_{US, t}] + z_{it} \quad (4)$$

Lacking full data for the capital–population ratios, I use the share of gross investment in GDP, I/Y, as a proxy for the first of the explanatory variables.[1]

Table 1.4 reports the preferred regression estimates of equation (4). Tests for fixed period and fixed country effects show neither to be statistically significant at the 10 per cent level. The coefficient on initial income levels is negative, confirming technology catch-up. The investment coefficient suggests a gross rate of return of 9 per cent, perhaps lower than one might expect, but in line with that found in other applied studies such as Barro and Sala i Martin (1995). The estimated employment–output elasticity is 0.51.

These regression coefficients can be used to decompose Australia's growth performance relative to that of the OECD. The decomposition is shown in Table 1.5. Everything is expressed relative to the OECD mean over the whole period. The mean growth rate of real GDP *per capita* for OECD countries was 2.8 per cent per year, so the entry of 0.4 per cent for growth 1960–69 indicates that Australian growth over that period averaged 3.2 per cent.

The final row of Table 1.5 shows the growth decomposition for the 25 countries in the 1990s. Average *per capita* growth was down nearly 1 percentage point from the 40-year average, largely due to the diminishing capacity for technological catch-up with the United States after the narrowing of productivity gaps over the previous 30 years.

Over the 1990s, Australian GDP *per capita* outperformed the OECD decade average by 0.4 percentage points. The principal contribution to that performance came from a turnaround in (MFP) technical progress. In previous decades Australia had been an MFP laggard, but over the 1990s became one of the top performers – as shown in Table 1.6.

These panel data estimates suggest that the rate of technical progress in the Australian economy has switched from 0.9 percentage points below to 0.7 percentage points above the 40-year OECD average, a turnaround in the 1990s of 1.6 percentage points. This estimate is very close to the 1.4 percentage point increase in trend MFP growth that we derived in the time series analysis of the market sector.

The conclusion is clear: there was a remarkable resurgence in Australian productivity growth over the 1990s. It was not just a result of cyclical recovery. Nor did it reflect any widespread surge in growth among the OECD economies.

Table 1.4 Panel estimation of OECD growth, 1960–99

Explanatory variable	Coefficient (t-statistic)
Initial productivity gap (Y/L)	−0.018 (−9.3)
Investment (I/Y)	0.086 (3.5)
Employment/population growth	0.516 (3.3)
adj. R^2	0.536
s.e. of estimate	0.010
Test–fixed period effects	$F_{3,91} = 1.57$, $p = 0.20$
Test–fixed country effects	$F_{23,71} = 1.40$, $p = 0.15$

Note: 97 observations on 25 countries (24 OECD +Korea), 1960–69, 1970–79, 1980–89, 1990–99.

The dependent variable is the annual growth rate of real GDP per capita (mean = 0.028).

Table 1.5 Sources of *per capita* growth over four decades
(all variables measured relative to sample mean over 25 countries and 4 decades)

		GDP p.c. growth	Catch-up	Investment	Labour force/ population ratio	MFP growth
Australia	1960–69	0.4%	0.8%	0.1%	0.1%	−0.6%
	1970–79	−1.0%	−0.5%	0.0%	0.2%	−0.6%
	1980–89	−1.1%	−0.5%	0.0%	0.3%	−0.9%
	1990–99	−0.5%	−1.0%	−0.1%	−0.1%	0.7%
average for	1960–69	1.2%	1.3%	0.1%	−0.2%	0.2%
25 countries	1970–79	−0.1%	−0.1%	0.1%	0.1%	−0.2%
	1980–89	−0.4%	−0.2%	−0.1%	0.1%	−0.2%
	1990–99	−0.8%	−1.0%	0.0%	0.0%	0.3%

Table 1.6 OECD top 10 for MFP growth in the 1990s

		1990–99	'90–99 *less* '80–89
1	Ireland	3.3%	2.9%
2	Luxembourg	2.2%	0.2%
3	Korea	1.6%	−0.3%
4	Norway	1.0%	2.0%
5	Denmark	0.8%	1.2%
6	United States	0.8%	0.4%
7	Australia	0.7%	1.6%
8	United Kingdom	0.5%	0.3%
9	Iceland	0.5%	0.9%
10	Finland	0.4%	0.3%

Explanations for the productivity surge

New technology

Can the 'new economy' explain the Australian productivity resurgence?

As far as the United States is concerned, Oliner and Sichel (2000) suggest that technical progress in production and from the use of information and communications ICT equipment accounts for two-thirds of the recent one percentage point productivity surge. Madden and Savage (1998) find that in Australia the long-run elasticity of aggregate output with respect to a measure of IT use (telephone lines) is as high as 0.18. But how advanced is Australia as a producer and user of ICT?

It seems that Australia is a very minor player on the production side of the new economy. Australia ranks fourth lowest out of the 25 industrialised countries surveyed recently by the OECD – with less than 3 per cent of business-sector employment in the ICT sector. On the other hand, the Australian economy is in the forefront in terms of ICT adoption with nearly 8 per cent of 1997 GDP being spent on ICT hardware, software and services – placing Australia in the OECD top three.

It may well be preferable to be a major user rather than producer of ICT goods and services. A prominent feature of the IT revolution has been the huge decrease in the real price of computer hardware. Gordon (2000) looks at computer price changes between 1993 and 1999. He reports that price–performance ratios fell by 94 per cent for computer processors, by 98 per cent for RAM and by 99 per cent for hard disk capacity. The huge benefits to US productivity from a large ICT production sector are substantially offset, in terms of economic welfare, by the concomitant decline in the terms of trade. At the same time, ICT importers like Australia gain substantially from falling import prices.

Which sectors of the economy are likely to benefit most from the adoption of imported ICT goods? The image of industrial ICT usage that springs first to my mind is of computer-controlled robots on production lines. But Gruen and Stevens (2000) report that although labour productivity growth in Australian manufacturing is high, it dipped slightly in the 1990s and therefore contributed nothing to the recent productivity surge. Indeed, they report that *all* of the rise in labour productivity since the 1980s can be attributed to just four sectors: wholesale trade, retail trade, construction and finance.

The impact of ICT on banking is obvious to all of us on a day-to-day basis as we use ATMs and Internet banking. But the ICT revolution in trade and construction is less obvious – until we start to think about changes in business-to-business communication and transactions. Delays on building sites are endemic, due to coordination problems between contractors, engineers and architects. These delays can be minimised when all parties are accessible by mobile phone and are linked by the Internet. Computerisation of accounts and stocks can improve the timing and efficiency of wholesaler–retailer transactions. Construction and retail and wholesale trade are sectors with a multitude of idiosyncratically interacting suppliers and customers where organisational and network externalities are likely to be large, hence areas where the industry return to ICT investment is likely to exceed the perceived individual return. If that is the case, the difference between industry returns and individual returns will be measured as MFP growth.

This argument is similar to that of De Long and Summers (1991) who explain high rates of social return to investment in equipment. They suggest that equipment investment requires a skilled and flexible workforce to adapt new technology to the specific needs of particular businesses – but individual firms do not necessarily capture the full returns to the human capital investment. We might well expect to find such complementarity between human and ICT capital investment. If so, it is not just the level of ICT investment that drives productivity growth, but also investment in skills.

Other explanations for the productivity boom

The program of economic reform over the past 20 years is another plausible candidate to explain the productivity resurgence. I have not been able to address this explanation directly, lacking the systematic modelling and measurement of 'micro-reform' that would be needed to perform direct statistical tests on the macro-productivity data. Forsyth (2000) adduces support for the reform–productivity link from the timing. As with the ICT story, the evidence for this is suggestive rather than conclusive. A challenge for proponents of this explanation is to explain the very disparate performances of other countries, most notably New Zealand, which have undergone lengthy and intensive micro-reform programs but have failed to exhibit faster productivity growth in the 1990s.

We should also take account of the arguments of Quiggin (2000) who suggests that the productivity surge of the 1990s may have been built on the backs of workers subject to work-intensification and unrecorded work hours. If that were the case, recorded productivity rises would not necessarily bear the interpretation that economic welfare was rising. Quiggin's argument does, however, rely on an untested assertion that increases in working hours and working intensity amount to an unrecorded rise of some 10 per cent in real labour input.

There are, of course, other factors that might explain the Australian productivity resurgence. I list here only some of those that have been the subject of investigation in the recent literature on economic growth.

- A better educated labour force may be an important determinant of growth – see Barro and Lee (1994) and Benhabib and Spiegel (1994).
- Changes in the rate of investment in the core public infrastructure of transport and communication and water systems. Increased public infrastructure has been found to raise private-sector productivity (as conventionally measured) in a wide range of studies, including the Aschauer (1989) study of aggregate US data, the cross-country study by Easterly and Rebelo (1993) and the study of Australian aggregate productivity by Otto and Voss (1994) . However, the fact that Australian public investment has been declining rather than increasing over the past 15 years makes it unlikely that this can explain an increase in productivity growth.
- The degree of openness of the Australian economy has increased in the 1990s – total trade averaging 33 per cent of GDP in the 1980s but increasing to around 40 per cent of GDP by the late 1990s. Openness to trade is argued by some to be a spur to technical progress through increased competition, specialisation and transfer of knowledge. For Australian manufacturing industry, Chand (1999) has found that reductions in nominal rates of protection have raised MFP growth. Bodman (1998) reports that net migration and openness tend to raise Australian growth rates, but cautions that

the magnitude of these effects is fairly small. Using the magnitude of trade effects estimated in Dowrick (1994), the recent rise in trade may have contributed around one-fifth of a percentage point to the productivity surge of the 1990s.

Conclusions

There is evidence of a remarkable resurgence in productivity growth in the Australian economy over the decade of the 1990s. Both time-series and international panel studies suggest that annual productivity growth has increased by well over one percentage point since the slowdown of the previous two decades. The most likely explanations for the productivity surge are the adoption of new information and communication technologies, the process of microeconomic reform, intensification of work and the reduction of barriers to trade. These major changes to the workings of the Australian economy have substantial implications for the distribution of economic welfare – tending to worsen the lot of those who are less skilled, most subject to work-intensification and working in sectors where the terms of trade are declining. Nevertheless, the widespread adoption of new information and communication technologies and the reduction of trade barriers augur well for future economic growth.

References

Aschauer, D.A. (1989) 'Is Public Expenditure Productive?' *Journal of Monetary Economics* 23(2): 177–200.

Barro, Robert J. (1991) 'Economic Growth in a Cross Section of Countries.' *Quarterly Journal of Economics* 106(2): 407–443.

Barro, R.J. and J.-W. Lee (1994) 'Sources of economic growth.' *Carnegie-Rochester Conference Series on Public Policy*.

Barro, R.J. and X. Sala i Martin (1995) *Economic Growth*. New York; London and Montreal, McGraw-Hill.

Benhabib, J. and M. Spiegel (1994) 'The Role of Human Capital in Economic Development: Evidence from Aggregate Cross-Country Data.' *Journal of Monetary Economics* 34(2): 143–73.

Bodman, P.M. (1998) 'A Contribution on the Empirics of Trade, Migration and Economic Growth for Australia and Canada.' *International Economic Journal* 12(3, Autumn): 41–62.

Chand, S. (1999) 'Trade Liberalization and Productivity Growth: Time-series Evidence from Australian Manufacturing.' *Economic Record* 75(228, December): 28–36.

Commission, Industry (1997) *Assessing Australia's Productivity Performance*. Canberra, Industry Commission: 1–159.

De Long, J.B. and L.H. Summers (1991) 'Equipment Investment and Economic Growth.' *Quarterly Journal of Economics* 106(2, May): 445–502.

Dowrick, S. (1994) 'Openness and Growth' in *International Integration of the Australian Economy*. P. Lowe and J. Dwyer. Sydney, Reserve Bank of Australia.

Dowrick, S. and Duc Tho Nguyen (1989) 'OECD Comparative Economic Growth 1950–85: Catch-Up and Convergence.' *American Economic Review* 79(5): 1010–30.

Easterly, W. and S. Rebelo (1993) 'Fiscal Policy and Economic Growth: An Empirical Investigation.' *Journal of Monetary Economics* 32(3): 417–58.

Forsyth, P. (2000) 'Microeconomic Policies and Structural Change' in *The Australian Economy in the 1990s*. D. Gruen and S. Shrestha. Sydney, Reserve Bank of Australia: 235–67.

Gordon, R.J. (2000) 'Does the "New Economy" Measure up to the Great Inventions of the Past?' *Journal of Economic Perspectives* 4(Fall): 49–74.

Gruen, D. and G. Stevens (2000) 'Australian Macroeconomic Performance and Policies in the 1990s' in *The Australian Economy in the 1990s*. D. Gruen and S. Shrestha. Sydney, Reserve Bank of Australia.

Madden, G. and S.J. Savage (1998) 'Sources of Australian Labour Productivity Change 1950–94.' *Economic Record* 74(227, December): 362–83.

Oliner, S.D. and D.E. Sichel (2000) 'The Resurgence of Growth in the Late 1990s: Is Information Technology the Story?' *Journal of Economic Perspectives* 14(Fall): 3–22.

Otto, G. and G.M. Voss (1994) 'Public Capital and Private Sector Productivity.' *Economic Record* 70(209, June): 121–32.

Quiggin, J. (2000) Discussion of 'Microeconomic Policies and Structural Change' in *The Australian Eeconomy in the 1990s*. D. Gruen and S. Shrestha. Sydney, Reserve Bank of Australia.

Wickens, M.R. and T.S. Breusch (1988) 'Dynamic Specification, the Long-run and the Estimation of Transformed Regressions Models'. *Economic Journal* 98(S): 189–205.

Notes

1 All the productivity data are taken from OECD *Economic Outlook* with the ratio of labour force to total population, L/P, taken from World Bank World Tables via DX.

2

Australia in the International Economy

Kym Anderson[1]

In 1900, Australia was arguably the highest income country in the world. By 1950 it was ranked third; by 1970 it was eighth; and by 1999 it was twenty-sixth, according to the World Bank Atlas method of measuring GNP per capita (or twentieth using the World Bank's Purchasing Power Parity method) – not counting several rich countries with less than one million people (World Bank 2000b). By that standard at least, the long-term performance of Australia's economy has been relatively poor over the past century.

Over the decade of the 1990s, by contrast, Australia has, according to that same source (World Bank 2000b, Tables 1, 3 and 11), outperformed all other advanced economies other than Ireland and Norway in terms of GDP per capita growth.[2]

This difference between the economy's recent and earlier relative performances is due substantially to the economic policy reforms of the past two decades and in particular the belated opening of the Australian economy to the rest of the world. Having been more protectionist towards manufacturing than all other OECD countries except New Zealand for most of the century, and having stood aside from the industrial trade policy reforms agreed to by other Contracting Parties to the General Agreement on Tariffs and Trade (GATT) in the first seven rounds of multilateral trade negotiations (1947 to 1979), Australia has undergone a remarkable degree of opening up in the late twentieth century. The fact that it was accompanied by many domestic economic reforms, and coincided with a long period of rapid global economic growth that was stimulated by the information technology revolution, added to the scope for boosting gains from trade.

This chapter first explores the extent to which the Australian economy has become more integrated into international markets in the past two decades, not just absolutely but also relative to the rest of the world. It then focuses on how the structure of our trade has changed and on the extent to which markets abroad for Australian export products have opened up, this being another potential contributor to the internationalisation of our economy. A third contributor is the reduction in non-governmental barriers to trade, most notably via the information technology revolution. The chapter concludes by examining opportunities and challenges ahead for Australian businesses and governments, assuming the recent frenetic pace of globalisation continues.

Australia sheds its protectionist past

The long history of industrial protectionism has its roots in the formation of the Australian Federation in 1901. Tariffs and other import controls were used increasingly through to the early 1970s to protect a wide range of manufacturing industries. That ensured a bigger manufacturing sector than would have emerged under free trade, but it stifled the growth of other sectors, particularly the natural resource-based ones in which the country enjoyed its strongest comparative advantage (Anderson and Garnaut 1986).

Disenchantment with the interventionist trade and related economic policies gradually spread in the 1960s, but it was not until the 1970s that major tariff reductions began. A 25 per cent across-the-board cut in 1973, preceded by some cuts in 1970–71, started the tariff reform process. It was accelerated in the 1980s and continued through the 1990s. As a result, the average effective rate of assistance to Australian manufacturing fell from 36 per cent to about 5 per cent over those three decades. In the 1990s alone, both the mean and the standard deviation of Australia's import tariffs on goods halved. This brought the average tariff for manufactures down to 4.2 per cent in 1999.[3] The only manufacturers with significant tariff protection now are motor vehicles and parts, and textiles, clothing and footwear. Excluding them, the average effective rate of assistance to Australian manufacturing is just 3 per cent (Productivity Commission 2000a).[4]

Agricultural subsidies and regulatory interventions also have been reduced. The average effective rate of assistance to the farm sector has fallen from above 25 per cent in the early 1970s to well below 10 per cent today. There were just two farm groups still benefiting significantly from government programs in the latter 1990s: tobacco and milk producers. Deregulation of tobacco marketing arrangements began in 1995 and was completed in 2000, bringing effective assistance to tobacco growing down from 30 to 2 per cent over that period. As from 1 July 2000, the remaining impediments to a free domestic market in fluid milk began to be dismantled, for which compensation to dairy farmers is to be paid over the next eight years (as provided also to tobacco producers in the late 1990s). Excluding dairy, the estimated effective rate of assistance to Australian agriculture in 1998–99 fell from 8 to 3 per cent (Productivity Commission 2000c, p. 27). Thus distortionary government assistance to both manufacturing and agriculture has now all but disappeared.

Service sectors too have not been spared reform. Banking; post and telecommunications; ports; higher education; health; and rail, air and, to some extent, sea transport have been opened up. There has been progressive out-sourcing of many government services; and substantial reforms to competition policy and practice, including the corporatisation and de-monopolisation of numerous government enterprises, are well advanced.[5] In addition, a comprehensive program of review of government regulations at all levels has been under way since the mid-1990s, with the aim of reducing/removing regulations that unjustifiably impede economic activities (Productivity Commission 2000b).

Moreover, by 1983 the Australian dollar was floating and foreign investment flows began to be freed up. That has complemented financial-sector reform and has contributed to foreign direct investment (FDI), equity and foreign currency transactions growing at more than three times the pace of Australia's GDP during the past 15 years. And even the previously highly unionised labour market has undergone considerable reform (Wooden 2001), which with higher education reforms has encouraged growth in human capital (Chapman and Withers 2001).

The freeing of markets for goods, services, capital and foreign exchange, together with domestic microeconomic reforms, has increased competitiveness in the Australian economy substantially. That, together with the greater scope it has provided to specialise in production so as to reap economies of scale, has added considerable dynamism to the Australian economy.[6] It was especially important in contributing to the flexibility with which the Australian economy was able to respond to the East Asian financial crisis in the late 1990s. Despite Australia's much greater exposure to East Asia than most other OECD countries, and the consequent decline in its terms of trade, it weathered that crisis remarkably well, in part through temporarily re-directing its trade back to Europe and North America.

How exceptional is Australia's internationalisation?

How does the opening up of the Australian economy compare with the internationalisation of the rest of the world? Exports plus imports of goods and services as a percentage of GDP rose considerably faster for Australia than for the world as a whole: between 1990 and 1999 that share for Australia rose from 34 to 42 per cent while for the rest of the world it rose from 39 to 44 per cent (World Bank 2000b). Clearly, Australia has been catching up in that sense at least. However, it still has some way to go, given that as a relatively small economy with an extreme set of factor endowment ratios, one would expect it to have a higher, not lower, trade-to-GDP ratio than the global average.

Australia's FDI stock has been growing even more dramatically than its trade. Between 1980 and 1998, that stock increased from 9 to 28 per cent of

GDP for inward FDI and from 2 to 17 per cent for outward FDI, whereas the global average rose from 5 to 14 per cent (UNCTAD 2000, Annex Table B.5). Australia is also playing an active part in the internationalisation of the global economy via cross-border mergers and acquisitions. As a purchaser during the 1990s, the nominal value of cross-border mergers and acquisitions amounted to 14 per cent of 1999 GDP for Australia compared with 9 per cent globally and 10 per cent for other developed countries, while as a seller it summed to 22 per cent of Australia's 1999 GDP (based on data in UNCTAD 2000 and World Bank 2000a). Thus, in terms of both direct and portfolio foreign investment these data suggest Australia has become much more involved in international capital flows than the average developed or developing country. That capital opening may have been a substitute for product trade growth to some extent, but more likely it has complemented trade in goods and services (Markusen 1983). An obvious example is the FDI in a wide range of services, which has lowered the cost of producing, marketing and distributing many of Australia's exportables.[7]

What has reform done to the structure of Australia's production and trade?

Economic growth of advanced economies typically is accompanied by declines in the relative importance of the primary and manufacturing sectors and relatively rapid growth in the services sectors. That has certainly been the pattern in Australia too. However, the reduction in manufacturing protection enabled the GDP shares of the primary sectors to increase slightly in the 1990s as resources were freed up to allow those more internationally competitive sectors to expand faster (see Table 2.1). Manufacturing now accounts for just one-eighth of Australia's GDP and employment, compared with services' share of around four-fifths.

Australia's trade and other economic policy reforms, together with the slow growth in world agricultural trade, have contributed to a much more dramatic transformation of the structure of its exports. Australia is very abundantly endowed with natural resources per worker relative to the rest of the world, so it is not surprising that it has always been a net exporter of primary products and a net importer of manufactures. The contribution of various sectors to exports has changed considerably during the postwar period though. As Table 2.2 shows, the share of rural products has fallen steadily from more than 80 per cent in the early 1950s to under 40 per cent in the early 1980s and to barely 20 per cent today. Much of that decline was because of the growth of minerals and energy exports from the 1960s to the early 1980s. Since then, however, manufacturing and services exports have grown to the point where they each slightly exceed the one-fifth share of rural products today.

The growth in the share of manufactures in exports may seem ironic, given

Table 2.1 Composition of Australia's GDP and employment, 1900–01 to 1999–2000 (%)

(a) Share of GDP at factor cost

	Agriculture	Mining	Manufacturing	Services	Total
1900–01	19.3	10.3	12.1	58.3	100
1955–56	15.9	2.3	28.0	53.8	100
1968–69	9.6	2.4	26.1	61.9	100
1980–81	5.4	6.5	20.6	67.5	100
1991–92	3.1	4.4	15.3	77.2	100
1999–2000	3.3	4.6	13.1	79.0	100

(b) Share of employment

	Agriculture	Mining	Manufacturing	Services	Total
1962–63	10	1	26	63	100
1972–73	7	1	24	68	100
1982–83	6	1	19	74	100
1991–92	5	1	15	79	100
1999–2000	5	1	12	82	100

Source: Anderson (1995, Table 1.9), updated using the same ABS statistical series.

Table 2.2 Composition of Australia's exports, 1950–51 to 1999–2000 (%)

	Rural products	Mining products	Other merchandise	Services	Total
1950–51	86	6	3	5	100
1960–61	66	8	13	13	100
1970–71	44	28	12	16	100
1980–81	39	34	11	16	100
1989–90	26	41	14	19	100
1999–2000	21	35	22	22	100

Source: Anderson (1995, Table 1.1), updated using the same series from ABARE (2000).

that the past two decades has been a period of cuts in government assistance to manufacturers. Its explanation in large part is that the cutting of tariffs that protect Australia's least competitive manufacturers has allowed resources to move to other activities – including other industrial sub-sectors – that can compete better in international markets. For example, not all vehicle parts manufacturing firms have survived, but many of those that have now adopt a global rather than national market perspective and have thereby achieved economies of scale through specialising in producing and now also exporting what they do best. Technological changes in the late twentieth century have aided that process, increasing the scope to subdivide the processes of production and distribution into parts that can be relocated anywhere in the world according to changes in comparative advantages over time (Jones and Kierzkowski 1997, Feenstra 1998). Such out-sourcing can be via various means including sub-contracting, licensing, joint ventures, and direct foreign investment by multi-national corporations (Markusen 1995, Markusen et al. 1996).

The growth in services exports since the mid-1980s is due only in part to domestic policy reforms; also important are technological change (particularly the digital revolution that has made many more services internationally tradable), the growth in international tourism, and the opening up of services trade abroad, to which the Uruguay Round's General Agreement on Trade in Services has begun to contribute.

The direction of Australia's trade continues to trend away from traditional markets in Europe and North America and even Japan, as developing East Asian economies expand. Notwithstanding the latter region's financial crisis in the past three years, their share of Australia's trade in 2000 was still well above that of the early 1990s (Tables 2.3 and 2.4). Europe, including Britain, buys only one-eighth of Australia's merchandise exports now compared with more than twice that share in the early 1970s. But it still supplies nearly one-quarter of Australia's imports of both goods and services, and is a market for one-fifth of Australia's services exports. North America has a similarly large share of Australia's imports and exports of services, and imports of goods, but only half as large a share of our merchandise exports (11 per cent).

The growth in importance of resource-poor Japan to Australia's trade began to reverse in the 1990s; Japan now accounts for just one-fifth of Australia's goods exports, one-eighth of both goods imports and services exports, and just 6 per cent of services imports. Developing East Asia, by contrast, now accounts for one-third of goods trade and more than one-fifth of services trade, both exports and imports – shares that will grow even more as those economies continue to recover from the East Asian financial crisis and as

Table 2.3 Direction of Australia's merchandise (and services) exports, 1951 to 2000 (%)

	1951–55	1968–72	1980–84	1990–92	2000[a]
United Kingdom	36	11	4	4	3(11)
Other Europe	27	16	10	12	8(9)
North America	10	16	13	12	11(19)
Japan	8	26	27	26	20(11)
Developing East Asia	6	12	20	30	37(22)
New Zealand	4	5	5	5	6(7)
Middle East	1	2	8	3	4(na)
Other developing	8	12	13	8	11(na)
Total:	100	100	100	100	100(100)
• of which APEC	28	49	65	73	75(61)
• value AUD billion					111(32)

[a] Regional shares of Australia's services exports is shown in parentheses.

Source: Anderson (1995, Table 1.4), updated from DFAT (2001, Tables 1–4).

Table 2.4 Direction of Australia's merchandise (and services) imports, 1951 to 2000 (%)

	1951–55	1968–72	1980–84	1990–92	2000[a]
United Kingdom	45	21	7	6	6(12)
Other Europe	15	19	17	20	17(12)
North America	15	27	25	26	21(22)
Japan	2	13	21	18	13(6)
Developing East Asia	7	7	14	19	31(21)
New Zealand	1	2	3	5	4(5)
Middle East	4	5	9	3	2(na)
Other developing	11	6	4	3	6(na)
Total:	100	100	100	100	100(100)
• of which APEC	25	40	63	68	70(55)
• Value AUD billion					119(31)]

[a] Regional shares of Australia's services imports is shown in parentheses.
Source: Anderson (1995, Table 1.4), updated from DFAT (2001, Tables 1–4).

China and Taiwan join the World Trade Organization (WTO) in the next year or so, particularly if Japan's economy continues to grow and open up only slowly.

Much of the global economic integration in services comes about through commercial presence abroad; that is, via foreign investment. That, together with foreign direct and portfolio investment in goods production, has boomed for Australia as for other countries since the early 1980s. Again the digital revolution plus opening up through policy reforms in many countries have stimulated that growth.

The direction of Australia's foreign investment is somewhat different from the direction of its trade. The United Kingdom and the United States together account for slightly over half of Australia's inflow and outflow of foreign investment (see Table 2.5), which is more than twice their importance in Australia's trade. Continental Europe's share of Australia's investment, by contrast, is just one-twelfth, the same as its share of Australia's exports and well below its share of imports. The Western Pacific, too, accounts for a much smaller share of Australia's investment than its trade: only one-sixth, compared with about three-fifths of trade.

How large are those trade and investment shares relative to the importance of those trading partners in foreign trade and investment globally? Table 2.6 provides an answer in the form of what are called indexes of intensity of international trade and investment. Those indexes take into account the relative size of the different markets towards which Australia's exports or investment funds are destined. It shows our merchandise exports are traded very intensely into East Asia and New Zealand, but are traded with low intensity into North America and very low intensity into Europe other than the United Kingdom. Australia's services exports, by contrast, are much more evenly traded to the

Table 2.5 Origin and destination of the stock of Australia's foreign investment, as at
30 June 1999 (%)

	Foreign investment in Australia	Australian investment abroad
United Kingdom	26	17
Other Europe	10	11
North America	28	36
Japan	7	6
Developing East Asia	10	8
New Zealand	2	6
Others	17	16
Total	100	100
• of which APEC	44	56
• value AUD billion	613	258

Source: ABS (2000, Table 1).

Table 2.6 Indexes of intensity of Australia's international export trade and
investment abroad, 1999

	Australia's merchandise exports[a]	Australia's services exports[a]	Australia's investment abroad[b]
United Kingdom	0.8	1.8	2.0
Other Europe	0.2	0.2	0.4
North America	0.5	1.1	1.3
Japan	3.6	1.4	7.5
Developing East Asia	3.0	1.7	0.5
New Zealand	31.6	22.1	8.6
Others	1.1	1.3	1.0
Total	1.0	1.0	1.0

[a] Share of Australia's exports to each region as a ratio of each region's share of world imports of
merchandise or services.
[b] Share of the stock of Australia's investment abroad to each region as a ratio of each region's
share of the world stock of inward investment.
Source: As for Tables 2.3 and 2.5 above, with global shares coming from World Bank (2000a)
and UNCTAD (2000).

different regions, again with the exception of continental Europe (intensity
indexes close to unity). As hosts for Australia's investment abroad, the developed countries are targeted twice as intensively as they are for Australia's
exports, and developing East Asia only about one-fifth as much.

How might Australia's trade and investment flows change in terms of composition and direction in the next few years? The composition of Australia's
trade is likely to see the mining export share continue to fluctuate with the
global business cycle around a long-term trend that, like that for rural exports,
is slightly downwards. Conversely, the manufacturing and services export
shares continue to trend slightly upwards. Tourism services in particular have

been boosted by the Sydney 2000 Olympic Games. As for the direction of Australia's trade, assuming recovery from the financial crisis in East Asia returns that region to rapid economic growth and further industrialisation in the next few years, the shares of Australia's exports and (especially) investment funds going to those developing economies will grow further yet. Subdued growth in sales to Japan appears to be set to continue, while trade with South Asia may well keep expanding (from a low base) if that region's reforms continue along with the boom in India's information technology industries.

Despite the dramatic changes in the composition of Australia's trade, the majority of its exports are still natural resource-based, at a time when those products account for barely one-sixth of global trade in goods and services. Not surprisingly, then, Australia's economy is still perceived as being commodity-based and so its currency still follows the international price of primary products (Shields 2001, Figure 5). Unfortunately for Australia, the long-term trend in the relative price of primary commodities has been and is likely to continue to be downwards (Grilli and Yang 1988, Martin and Mitra 2000). That does not mean Australia should abandon exporting primary products; rather, it simply means that fully exploiting our comparative advantages may not yield as much for our type of economy as it would for one whose comparative advantages are in products whose markets are growing faster. This dampening influence will gradually diminish over time, however, as the country's comparative advantages in manufactures and especially services strengthen.

How much are markets abroad opening up to Australian exports?

A further contribution to Australia's economic growth from abroad has been the opening up of overseas markets. That has boosted the demand for Australia's exports both directly and indirectly. The Closer Economic Relations (CER) agreement with New Zealand, the opening of China and other former socialist economies, the broader Asia Pacific Economic Cooperation (APEC) process, and especially the GATT/World Trade Organization (WTO) agreements have all been significant.

Australia was disappointed that earlier multilateral trade negotiations under the GATT (General Agreement on Tariffs and Trade) failed prior to the mid-1980s to address the growth and spread of agricultural protectionism, especially following the loss of markets for farm products when the UK, Denmark and Ireland joined the European Community in 1973.[8] Through forming the Cairns Group of non-subsidising agricultural-exporting countries in 1986, Australia helped to keep agriculture on the agenda of the Uruguay Round of trade negotiations. While the implementation of the Uruguay Round's Agreement on Agriculture itself has not yet lowered agricultural distortions greatly, it has at least placed agriculture in the GATT/WTO mainstream ready for further cuts in farm protection in the next round of multilateral trade negotiations that began in 2000.[9] Meanwhile, Australia is also beginning to benefit from the opening up of services markets abroad, following the Uruguay Round's General Agreement on Trade in Services (although much scope remains for further services trade liberalisation).

The opening up of former socialist economies need not help Australia's economy, since in principle those reforms could turn Australia's terms of trade in either direction. But in practice the process almost certainly has been of benefit to Australia, and will continue to be for the foreseeable future. This is because the process is dominated by rapidly industrialising China, whose economy (which is more than three times that of Russia's) is becoming ever more complementary to Australia's (Anderson and Peng 1998). China (together with the socialist economies of South-East Asia) is thus continuing the process begun by Japan and followed by East Asia's newly industrialised economies of changing its comparative advantage away from primary products and towards (initially unskilled labour-intensive) manufactures, to Australia's benefit (Anderson 1990).

What about non-governmental barriers to internationalisation?

Not only governmental but also other barriers that contribute to the costs of interacting internationally have been dropping. Falls in transport costs and the huge decline in communication and information costs have combined in the late twentieth century to accelerate globalisation to an unprecedented speed that shows no sign of abating. The current digital revolution in transport and communications technology, aided by deregulation of telecom markets in many countries, is lowering enormously long-distance communication costs and especially the cost of rapidly accessing and processing knowledge, information and ideas from anywhere in the world. Science has been among the beneficiaries of the digital revolution, spawning yet another revolution; namely, in biotechnology. A side-effect of the Internet's expansion is the growth in the use of the English language: it has been claimed that there are now more people using English as a second language than there are people for whom it is a first language. This, too, is lowering costs of communicating between countries, as is the ongoing decline in the real cost of international air travel.

This digital revolution benefits Australia in at least two ways: its well-educated, English-speaking population is adopting new digital technologies quickly; and its relatively long distance from key markets is effectively falling. The countries making the most of the digital revolution, however, are those that are becoming not just consumers but also producers of the new information and biotechnologies. That in turn requires large-scale research and development investments by consortia involving private corporations and universities, something that is more common in the United States and to a lesser extent Western Europe than it is in Australia.

Opportunities and challenges ahead for Australia

One of the key challenges for Australia in this new century, if it is to reverse its slip down the per capita income ladder, is to keep on opening up and reforming faster than our trading partners. We have to be faster for at least two reasons: first, former interventions were such that we started well behind others in the 1980s; and second, our comparative advantages are such that we are likely to continue to face a long-term decline in our terms of trade.

Continuing the trade and industry assistance reform process will be more difficult than in the past two decades because the sub-sectors still requiring reform are the most politically sensitive: textiles, clothing and footwear; and motor vehicles and parts in manufacturing (for which the present government in its wisdom has decided tariff reductions can be postponed for five years); plus such things as utilities, telecoms, broadcasting, postal services, higher education, and health. Telecom and associated broadcasting reforms are especially important for Australian business to be able to take full advantage of the ongoing information revolution; and further reforms within universities are needed to slow the brain-drain and give researchers a better chance of contributing to the information and biotechnology revolutions that are ongoing.

An important part of the policy reform challenge is to avoid re-instrumentation from one form of industry protection/assistance to another that may be less overt but more inefficient. Australia has been a relatively active user of anti-dumping provisions, for example (Productivity Commission 2000c), that undermines at least temporarily the tariff reductions on selected items. It has also used excessive regulatory measures as hidden forms of protection, including in agriculture (for example, food standards and import bans ostensibly for quarantine reasons). The Productivity Commission's Office of Regulatory Review and related agencies are beginning to tackle this issue, partly in response to Uruguay Round agreements, but multilateral disciplines on such measures remain relatively weak (Sykes 1999) – so concerted unilateral action is needed.

WTO trade agreements are yet to be all-encompassing in both facilitating market access abroad and encouraging reform at home. Examples of as-yet untouched sectors are education and airlines, both of which still require substantial reform if they are to reach their potential as export-led contributors to economic growth. Australia's discriminatory pricing of education and health services, for example, is inconsistent with the WTO's national treatment principle and may mean that the shares of those services directed to the export market are probably not optimal.

Nor is the WTO truly global in its membership yet. As the former socialist countries join, though, so they will open up more. The most significant non-member is China, whose accession appears imminent. Its ongoing reforms will continue to contribute to China's growth and structural change and thereby to Australia's trade and economic growth, following the earlier examples set by its equally densely populated East Asian neighbours. Europe's socialist economies are less focused on WTO participation than on their accession to the EU that, depending on the Common Agricultural Policy changes that accompany the EU's expansion eastwards, could improve or worsen Australia's trade prospects in that region.

Another key challenge facing Australia as globalisation proceeds is to provide an environment in which producers can more easily develop comparative advantages in industries that are growing. The domestic business environment is certainly much more growth-enhancing now than it was for most of the twentieth century. Australia's wine industry is a shining example of how a concerted effort by leading producers to broaden attitudes within an industry can create, in a small number of years and without government assistance, an export culture that is welfare-generating. But that does not mean there is no room for improvement, particularly in light of the rapidly changing methods of production and distribution.

For example, an important attribute of the current information revolution is that it is increasing the scope to subdivide the processes of production and distribution into parts that can be relocated anywhere in the world according to ever-increasing changes in comparative advantages over time (Jones and Kierzkowski 1997, Feenstra 1998). As well, methods of industrial production are altering dramatically. Specialised, single-purpose equipment for mass production is being supplemented or replaced by flexible machine tools and programmable multi-task production equipment. Because this type of machinery can be quickly and cheaply switched from one task to another, their use permits the firm to produce a variety of products efficiently in small batches (Milgrom and Roberts 1990). These changes to production methods put a premium on flexibility in labour markets, which is an area where Australia still has room for improvement (Wooden 2001).

Productivity growth in industrial and service sectors is altering the key source of wealth of nations away from raw materials and physical capital per worker to human skills and knowledge. In particular, wealth creation in the twenty-first century will depend especially on the ability to access and make productive use of the expanding stocks of knowledge and information, and to build on them through creative research and development to design highly flexible production methods. How well and how quickly people in different countries are able to do that will increasingly determine relative economic growth rates. Premiums are being paid for personnel with those attributes, and such premiums are more likely to rise than fall in the future. While ever Australia's research institutions continue to provide relatively poor salaries and working conditions for such staff, the brain-drain to bigger R&D centres in North America and Western Europe is likely to continue, reducing Australia's prospects for even benefiting from or let alone contributing to the information and biotechnology revolutions.

What roles for government?

For all countries the extent and speed with which economic events abroad are transmitted to domestic markets will increase inexorably. Governments will have less and less capacity to isolate their economies from such trends, as financial markets and electronic commerce have made clear. To prevent a net outflow of financial and human capital, the government needs to ensure that conditions domestically match those abroad for such things as interest rates, income and capital gains tax rates, R&D incentives and the like.

Beyond that, the traditional role of government in prising open markets abroad for our exports of goods, services, and financial and human capital remains. However, it is not only agricultural trade reform that is of interest to Australia's economy. First, rural products make up barely one-fifth of Australia's exports of goods and services these days, compared with two-thirds in the early 1960s. And second, more than 60 per cent of Australia's exports go to East Asia (up from just 20 per cent prior to the mid-1950s), so export growth to those markets depends very much on a return to rapid economic growth in Asia. Hence, Australia has a strong interest in the full implementation of the Uruguay Round's agreement on textiles and clothing: directly because it could expand exports of Australian wool to Asia; and indirectly because freer textile trade means faster economic growth and structural change in densely populated Asia and hence faster growth in their imports of many other products from natural resource-rich economies such as Australia.

Australia, being geographically on the periphery, also has a strong interest in open trade in skill-intensive products whose production location need not matter, such as products related to the digital and biotechnology revolutions and electronic commerce. And being in the East Asian time zone gives Australia a potential comparative advantage in financial services. Thus, keeping trade in services open and liberalising such markets more in the next WTO round will help to further the transformation of the Australian economy into more of a high-tech service provider.

As a small economy, Australia benefits greatly from the reduced uncertainty that a rules-based trading system provides, even if that system took until recently to begin prising open agricultural, textile and services markets. The current WTO round of multilateral trade negotiations offers probably the best prospects ever for agricultural-exporting countries in general – and their rural communities in particular – to secure growth-enhancing reforms abroad. Traditional agricultural market access liberalisation should be a key priority issue in this next WTO round, given the enormous potential for global welfare gains from reducing agricultural protection (Anderson 2001).

Australia is now considered a very responsible WTO member, particularly with the substantial amount of unilateral economic reform it has undertaken in the past 15 or so years. To keep building on that reputation, and the disproportionately large influence that that allows Australia to have in shaping the WTO's future path, the remaining vestiges of our protectionist past need to be removed. The most glaring areas are restrictions on imports of motor vehicles and parts, and of course textiles and clothing, whose reforms the current government has put on hold during 2000–2004. According to Australia's APEC commitments, remaining tariffs on those items should be phased out between 2005 and 2010. Meanwhile, 'nuisance' tariffs of 5 per cent or less are under consideration by the government, and may be phased out soon.

Even in the agriculture area Australia may have to polish its image at the WTO. Its quarantine policies are being perceived by our trading partners as excessively protectionist, and the Wheat Board as a single-desk exporter is also being targeted. Even its food quality standards (for example, for wine) could be subject to challenge, which is why ANZFA (recently renamed Food Standards Australia New Zealand) is in the process of replacing Australia's Food Standards Code and the comparable New Zealand code with a minimalist joint Australia New Zealand Food Standards Code. If Australia wishes to again take a leading role in the next round of WTO agricultural negotiations, accelerating the reforms it has begun in those areas also would be wise.

Critics of reform in Australia (mainly those with a direct vested interest in the remaining market interventions) claim we should not open our economy further until our trading partners reform more, either on 'fairness' grounds or to use our remaining measures as a 'negotiating coin'. That position ignores three facts: first, that Australia is not substantially more open than its main trading partners (it simply had more reforming to do in the late twentieth century); second, to not reform further is to be 'unfair' to the vast majority of Australian producers and consumers who are harmed by our remaining market interventions; and third, Australia is too small to have much bargaining power in the multilateral trade negotiating arena (see Productivity Commission 2000a, chapter 5).

The multilateral route to reform can be supplemented by regional integration initiatives such as via the Asia Pacific Economic Cooperation process, provided APEC members remain committed to WTO-consistent open regionalism. More worrying is the rash of bilateral free-trade agreements under discussion/negotiation among various pairs of APEC members, including Australia, since they are more likely to be stumbling blocks rather than stepping stones to freer trade.

Finally, the government can facilitate international economic integration's contribution to growth via a number of other multilateral institutions. Deliberations at the International Labour Office could address the issue of labour standards in developing countries, one result of which could be to diffuse claims that free trade is not 'fair' trade. Likewise with environmental standards, although recent multilateral environmental initiatives such as the Biosafety Protocol and the Kyoto Convention seem far from optimal from an Australian or global economic growth perspective.

References

ABARE (2000) *Australian Commodities*, Canberra: Australian Bureau of Agricultural and Resource Economics, December quarter.

ABS (2000) *International Investment Position, Australia 1998–99: Supplementary Country Statistics*, Catalogue no. 5352.0, Canberra.

Anderson, K. (1990) *Changing Comparative Advantages in China: Effects of Food, Feed and Fibre Markets*, Paris: OECD.

Anderson, K. (1995) 'Australia's Changing Trade Pattern and Growth Performance', Chapter 1 in *Australia's Trade Policies*, edited by R. Pomfret, London and Melbourne: Oxford University Press.

Anderson, K. (2001) 'Agriculture, Developing Countries, and the WTO Millennium Round', Chapter 1 in *Agriculture and the New Trade Agenda From a Development Perspective*, edited by M.D. Ingco and L.A. Winters, Cambridge: Cambridge University Press (forthcoming).

Anderson, K. and C.Y. Peng (1998) 'Feeding and Fueling China in the 21st Century', *World Development* 26(8): 1413–29, August.

Anderson, K. and R. Garnaut (1986) *Australian Protectionism*, St Leonards: Allen & Unwin.

Arndt, H.W. (1965) 'Australia – Developed, Developing or Midway?' *The Economic Record* 41(95): 418–40, September.

Chapman, B. and G. Withers (2001) 'Human Capital Accumulation: Education and Immigration', in *Reshaping Australia's Economy: Growth with Equity and Sustainability*, edited by P.J. Lloyd, J. Nieuwenhuysen and M. Mead, Cambridge: Cambridge University Press.

DFAT (2001) *Australia's Trade Outcomes and Objectives Statement*, Canberra: Department of Foreign Affairs and Trade.

Dollar, D. (1992) 'Outward-Oriented Developing Economies Really Do Grow More Rapidly: Evidence From 95 LDCs, 1976–85', *Economic Development and Cultural Change* 40: 523–44, April.

Dowrick, S. (1995) 'The Determinants of Long-Run Growth', in *Productivity and Growth*, edited by P. Andersen, J. Dwyer and D. Gruen, Sydney: Reserve Bank of Australia, pp. 7–47.

Dowrick, S. (2001) 'Productivity Boom: Miracle or Mirage', in *Reshaping Australia's Economy: Growth with Equity and Sustainability*, edited by P.J. Lloyd, J. Nieuwenhuysen and M. Mead, Cambridge: Cambridge University Press.

Edwards, S. (1993) 'Openness, Trade Liberalization, and Growth in Developing Countries', *Journal of Economic Literature* 31(3): 1358–93, September.

Feenstra, R.C. (1998) 'Integration of Trade and Disintegration of Production in the Global Economy', *Journal of Economic Perspectives* 12(4): 31–50, Fall.

Forsyth, P. (ed.) (1992) *Microeconomic Reform in Australia*, St Leonards: Allen & Unwin.

Forsyth, P. (2000) 'Microeconomic Policies and Structural Change', in *The Australian Economy in the 1990s*, edited by D. Gruen and S. Shrestha, Sydney: Reserve Bank of Australia, pp. 235–67.

Frankel, J. and D. Romer (1999) 'Does Trade Cause Growth?' *American Economic Review* 89(3): 379–99, June.

Grilli, E.R. and M.C. Yang (1988) 'Primary Commodity Prices, Manufactured Goods Prices, and the Terms of Trade of Developing Countries: What the Long Run Shows', *World Bank Economic Review* 2(1): 1–48, January.

Grossman, G.M. and E. Helpman (1991) *Innovation and Growth in the Global Economy*, Cambridge, Mass.: MIT Press.

Jones, R.W. and H. Kierzkowski (1997) 'Globalization and the Consequences of International Fragmentation', in *Money, Factor Mobility and Trade: Essays in Honor of Robert A. Mundell*, edited by R. Dornbusch, G. Calvo and M. Obstfeld, Cambridge: MIT Press.

Markusen, J.R. (1983) 'Factor Movements and Commodity Trade as Complements', *Journal of International Economics* 13: 341–56.

Markusen, J.R. (1995) 'The Boundaries of Multinational Enterprises and the Theory of International Trade', *Journal of Economic Perspectives* 9(2): 169–89, Spring.

Markusen, J.R., A.J. Venables, D.B. Konan and K. Zhang (1996) 'A Unified Treatment of Horizontal Direct Investment, Vertical Direct Investment, and the Pattern of Trade in Goods and Services', NBER Working Paper 5696, Cambridge, MA.

Martin, W. and D. Mitra (2000) 'Productivity Growth and Convergence in Agriculture and Manufacturing', *Economic Development and Cultural Change* 49(2): 403–23, January.

Milgrom, P. and J. Roberts (1990) 'The Economics of Modern Manufacturing: Technology, Strategy and Organization', *American Economic Review* 80(3): 511–28, June.

Productivity Commission (2000a) *Review of Australia's General Tariff Arrangements*, Canberra, July.

Productivity Commission (2000b) *Regulation and its Review 1999–2000*, Canberra, November (and earlier issues).

Productivity Commission (2000c) *Trade and Assistance Review 1999–2000*, Canberra, December (and earlier issues).

Sachs, J.D. and A. Warner (1995) 'Economic Reform and the Process of Global Integration', *Brookings Papers on Economic Activity* 1: 1–118.

Shields, B. (2001) 'Efficiency in Markets: Capital', in *Reshaping Australia's Economy: Growth with Equity and Sustainability*, edited by P.J. Lloyd, J. Nieuwenhuysen and M. Mead, Cambridge: Cambridge University Press.

Snape, R.H. (1984) 'Australia's Relations with GATT', *The Economic Record* 60(168): 16–27, March.

Sykes, A.O. (1999) 'Regulatory Protectionism and the Law of International Trade', *The University of Chicago Law Review* 66(1): 1–46, Winter.

Taylor, S.M. (1999) 'Trade and Trade Policy in Endogenous Growth Models', Chapter 15 in *International Trade Policy and the Pacific Rim*, edited by J. Piggott and A. Woodland, London: Macmillan for the IEA.

UNCTAD (2000) *World Investment Report 2000*, Geneva: United Nations.

USITC (1997) *The Dynamic Effects of Trade Liberalization: An Empirical Analysis*. Publication 3069, US International Trade Commission, Washington, D.C., October.

Wooden, M. (2001) 'Efficiency in Markets: Labour and Industrial Relations', in *Reshaping Australia's Economy: Growth with Equity and Sustainability*, edited by P.J. Lloyd, J. Nieuwenhuysen and M. Mead, Cambridge: Cambridge University Press.

World Bank (2000a) *World Development Indicators 2000*, Washington, D.C.: World Bank.

World Bank (2000b) *World Development Report 2000/2001*, New York: Oxford University Press.

WTO (1998) *Annual Report 1998*, Geneva: World Trade Organization.

Notes

1 Revision of a paper prepared for a conference on Australia's economic growth, Melbourne, 11 December 2000. Thanks are due to Peter Lloyd and John Nieuwen-huysen for helpful comments.

2 For an investigation into Australia's comparatively rapid productivity growth, see Dowrick (2001).

3 This is still higher than for other OECD countries: New Zealand 3.4 per cent, European Union 3.2 per cent, Canada 2.9 per cent, United States 2.4 per cent and Japan 2.0 per cent (World Bank 2000a, Table 6.6). And WTO-bound tariffs average more than twice the applied rates (Productivity Commission 2000a, Table 2.3). However, Australia uses non-tariff import barriers less frequently than other OECD countries, apart perhaps from anti-dumping duties (Productivity Commission 2000a, Table 5.2 and 2000c, pp. 38–44).

4 Tariffs on motor vehicle imports fell from 40 to 15 per cent over the 1990s and are due to fall to 10 per cent in 2005; for clothing the decline over the 1990s was from 55 to 25 per cent, and for footwear from 45 to 15 per cent (with falls to 17.5 and 10 per cent due by 2005, respectively – Productivity Commission 2000a, Table 4.4).

5 For an early assessment see Forsyth (1992), while an update on the 1990s is in Forsyth (2000). All Productivity Commission reports on the myriad reforms are downloadable at <www.pc.gov.au>. Recent research on barriers to trade in a wide range of services in almost 40 countries found that services markets in Australia, relative to those in the other countries in the study, are now ranked as either very liberal (banking, distribution services, telecoms, engineering professional services) or moderately restrictive (other professional services, maritime services) – see Productivity Commission (2000c, pp. 50–61).

6 The stimulus to growth from openness has been the experience of many countries in recent decades. See, for example, Dollar (1992), Edwards (1993), Sachs and Warner (1995), Frankel and Romer (1999) and, for an extended bibliography, WTO (1998, pp. 62–3). The reasons for faster growth of more open economies have to do with the dynamics of trade liberalisation, something that is not just an abstract idea from new trade and growth theory (Grossman and Helpman 1991, Taylor 1999) but one that is well supported empirically (USITC 1997). Lower barriers to imports of producer goods, for example, can raise the efficiency of capital. On the more general determinants of long-term growth as they relate to Australia, see Dowrick (1995).

7 The area in which Australia – like most countries – has opened up least in recent years is in allowing (particularly poorly skilled) labour to flow in, either on a temporary basis as guest workers or as permanent migrants. Clearly this is as much a social as an economic policy issue. For further discussion see Chapman and Withers (2001).

8 On Australia's half-hearted participation in the GATT prior to the mid-1980s, see Arndt (1965) and Snape (1984).

9 Agriculture still accounts for nearly two-thirds of the cost of all protectionist policies directly affecting global goods trade (Anderson 2001, Table 3).

3

The Regional Distribution of Growth

Kevin O'Connor, Robert J. Stimson and Scott Baum

Introduction

Australia's economic geography plays an important role in shaping the environment for the nation's growth as the modern flexible global economy has become very selective in its choice of location. That selectivity reflects the special advantages that certain places, usually large cities, offer firms by providing a milieu that supports innovation, the utilisation of knowledge in production decisions and linkages to networks or clusters of producers as outlined by Scott (1998). These advantages are complex extensions of the agglomeration advantages associated with physical input–output linkages. They involve the availability of increasing returns identified by Romer (1986), using an institutional–technical infrastructure as described by Lambooy (2000) through what Storper (1997) has called non-traded externalities. The latter includes professional associations, educational and research institutes, and some social and cultural structures that together make it easier for firms to carry out business in some cities rather than others. This major city bias in production has implications for Australian economic growth as we have few cities large enough to offer the range of services that are needed by firms in this modern economy. That means also that parts of the nation will be removed from the core of this major city-based activity; that will generate tensions associated with perceived and real inequality.

The concentrated structure that fits the modern economy has emerged in Australia, as it has shifted from being a protected to a more open trading economy, and from an 'industrial' society to a 'post-industrial' society, in which the services and informational economy activities have become more and more dominant. These changes are expressed in the nation's human geography, that amalgam of income, skill, aspiration and expectation in each and every location in the country. In human geography terms, the transformation of Australia from an 'old economy' to a 'new economy' has seen greater differences in the economic performance of its cities, towns and regions. The divides between the inner city and the outer suburbs, between the 'city' and the 'bush', and between the large and the small rural settlements have widened. In recent elections people living on particular sides of these divides have voted differently than in the past. They have created a new political geography, different from the economic geography that has emerged in jobs, investment and construction. These outcomes have fuelled debate about the implications of the change in Australia, and have consequences for the environment for future growth. This chapter will provide an insight on that broad issue.

The insight is developed from a number of studies that have been carried out on changes in the distribution of population, employment and investment in economic activity (O'Connor and Stimson 1995), regional patterns of employment in major industry sectors (Stimson, Shuaib and O'Connor 1998), the functional characteristics of regional cities and towns (Beer 1999; Beer, Bolam and Maude 1994) and local community outcomes in terms of human capital and overall levels of labour force engagement and disengagement in the new economy (Baum, Stimson, O'Connor, Mullins and Davis 1999). A unifying theme in this research has been the tension between the emerging new economic geography (which is largely inner area, major-city focused) and a human geography (which includes many in outer suburbs, coastal communities, and smaller cities and regions). That tension will be re-expressed later in the chapter in terms of *place prosperity* and *people prosperity*.

Some key aggregate shifts in industry structure and employment

Like those of other industrialised countries, the Australian economy has been changing. This has generated new types of occupations that require different types of skills, discussed by Reich (1992) as a move away from routine occupations associated with the 'old economy' towards *symbolic analyst* occupations associated with the 'new economy'. These changes can be seen in the shifts in the shares of the Australian workforce in the broad industrial categories displayed in Tables 3.1 and 3.2. The resource-based and other manufacturing categories have lost shares of employment, while the producer services and population-related services have recorded increases since 1986. The occupational shifts associated with these changes can be seen in Table 3.2, where the gains are recorded between 1986 and 1996 in the higher level service jobs in management and decision-making (the symbolic analysts), as well as the more day-to-day service activities, while the routine production workers are much less important in the overall workforce. Although not shown here, there have been major changes in the structure of work (with a large rise in the number of part-time jobs) and in the proportion of jobs taken by females. Both shifts are linked to the growth in the service sector.

Table 3.1 The share of the Australian workforce in industrial categories, 1986–1998

Industry categories	Share of national employment by sector				
	1986	1991	1996	1997	1998
Services to business	7.56	8.76	10.51	11.42	11.67
Finance and property	6.85	6.54	5.18	5.01	4.91
Media and publishing	1.92	1.83	1.85	2.04	1.78
Total producer services	**16.33**	**17.13**	**17.54**	**18.47**	**18.36**
Tourism related	3.46	4.39	4.55	4.73	4.71
Transport, storage and wholesaling	10.96	10.81	10.67	10.41	10.50
Total transport and tourism	**14.43**	**15.20**	**15.22**	**15.14**	**15.21**
Food production	7.87	7.21	6.78	6.80	6.47
Forestry and timber industry	1.21	1.05	0.94	0.92	0.93
Mining and mineral-processing	4.51	4.01	3.61	3.28	3.40
Total resource development and related manufacturing	**13.60**	**12.27**	**11.33**	**11.00**	**10.80**
Textiles and footwear	1.88	1.36	1.26	1.24	1.09
Engineering-based manufacturing	4.03	3.41	3.33	3.50	3.27
Electronic and electrical manufacturing	1.30	1.25	1.14	1.20	0.93
Total other manufacturing	**7.21**	**6.02**	**5.72**	**5.94**	**5.29**
Building and construction	7.55	7.01	7.44	7.21	7.84
Population-related services	40.89	42.38	42.74	42.24	42.50
Total population-related activities	**48.44**	**49.39**	**50.18**	**49.45**	**50.34**
Total	100.00	100.00	100.00	100.00	100.00

Sources: ABS *Labour Force Survey*, 1986, 1991, 1996 1998. Unpublished Data, Canberra.

Table 3.2 Australia's changing occupational structure in the new economy

	1986 no.	1986 %	1996 no.	1996 %	Change 1986–96 no.	Change 1986–96 %
Symbolic analysts	1,502,893	23.7	2,019,039	27.2	516,146	34.3
In-person service workers	2,459,778	38.8	3,090,530	41.5	630,752	25.6
Routine production workers	2,371,174	37.5	2,325,114	31.3	46,060	−1.94
Total	6,333,845	100.0	7,434,683	100.0		

Source: ABS *Census of Australia. Characteristics of Population and Dwellings*. Census Years 1986 and 1996, Canberra. Classification of Occupations developed by the authors.

This information shows that there have been steady changes in the character of the Australian economy over the past 20 or more years that have stimulated job opportunities in some places, and led to job losses in others. Over this period, the population expanded steadily, due mainly to international migration. The population geography began to change as people moved to new locations, often in different states at a greater rate than in the past. Problems emerge when those demographic shifts are not matched to the economic changes.

Economic and population change in Australia:
A state perspective

Population changes

The basic human geography of Australia is displayed in Table 3.3, which shows the shares of national population in each state and territory. These reflect the way different shares in each state of international and internal migration and natural increase have reshaped the distribution of Australia's population. The states are organised into three groups, to facilitate discussion and comparison with the distribution of economic activity. The overwhelming aspect of national population geography has been the shift to the sun-belt, lifting its share by eight percentage points over 39 years.

The share of the population living in the south-eastern core has fallen steadily, although the information for 1998 suggests that decline may have slowed. Smaller shares of the national population now live in South Australia and Tasmania. The pattern of population shown in Table 3.3 will now be compared to a number of measures of economic change.

Investment in commercial buildings

The location of new buildings for commercial use provides a good indicator of the way the private sector (by constructing offices and factories) views different parts of Australia. A very general measure is the aggregate patterns of non-residential construction; the shares of this for each Australian state and territory show considerable cyclical variation over time and shifts between the states (O'Connor 1998). In Table 3.4, the details of the location of new production facilities gives a perspective on Australia's economic geography.

Table 3.3 Share of national population in the states and territories, 1961–2000

	1961	1971	1981	1991	2000
South-east core (NSW, Vic, ACT)	65.8	64.6	63.1	61.4	60.3
Rest of the South-east (SA, Tas.)	12.5	12.0	11.7	11.1	10.3
Sun-belt (Qld, WA, NT)	21.7	23.4	25.2	27.5	29.5
Total share	100.0	100.0	100.0	100.0	100.0
Total population (million)	10.508	12.937	14.923	17.284	19.157

Source: ABS *Census of Australia. Characteristics of Population and Dwellings.* Census Years 1961, 1971, 1981, 1991 1996. ABS (1998) *Estimated Residential Population in Statistical Local Areas.*

Table 3.4 The location of new offices and factories in Australia, 1961–1995

	Office construction			Factory construction		
	1961/62– 1965–66	1970/71– 1981–82	1988/89– 1995/96	1961/62– 1965/66	1970/71– 1981/82	1988/89– 1995/96
South-east core (NSW, Vic, ACT)	77	64	74	76	68	72
Rest of the south-east (SA, Tas)	8	10	8	12	8	5
Sun-belt (Qld, WA, NT)	15	26	18	12	24	22
Total share	100	100	100	100	100	100

The numbers refer to the average share of new construction that was located in each part of the country for the years shown.
Sources: 1961/62–1965/66: Linge (1966); 1970/71–1981/82: Edgington (1983); 1988/89–1995/96: ABS *Building Activity Survey*. Unpublished data on the value of construction work done in construction in each year. Adelaide, ABS Building and Construction Statistics Division.

This information illustrates that the change in the distribution of population in favour of the sun-belt did have an impact on the location of commercial building in the 1970s, but that shift has not been maintained. In the 1990s, investment attention has returned to the core states even though the shift in population continued. It is possible that the reorientation in new building construction in favour of the core may lie behind the smaller change in population distribution displayed between 1996 and 2000.

The location of advanced services

One of the features of recent economic growth has been the expansion of employment in what has come to be called advanced services, which includes finance and insurance; computer and information consultancy; legal, accounting and auditing services; management consulting; advertising and market research; architectural and construction services; and technical services to agriculture and mining. The growth of these activities has generated an increase in the number of high-skilled workers, labelled 'knowledge workers' by Lambooy (2000) and 'symbolic analysts' by Reich (1992). The shifts in the location of construction activity displayed in Table 3.4, especially in office construction, may reflect the location of these new activities. The data assembled in Table 3.5 provide a state-level perspective on the location of a range of these workers. It shows the New South Wales and Victorian share of all jobs in occupations within selected specialised industrial activities.

In these activities there is a significant concentration of employment in New South Wales and Victoria. In many of these activities, the two states together account for two-thirds (or more) of the high-level jobs. This is especially so in

Table 3.5 Share of national employment in selected industry and occupation groups located in NSW and Victoria, 1996

Occupational groupings	Industry groups														
	Research and development		Business services		Media		Electronics		Banking and finance		Computing services		Total	
	NSW	Vic.	NSW	Vic.	NSW	Vic.	NSW	Vic.	NSW	Vic.	NSW	Vic.	NSW	Vic.
Managers	31.6	24.4	41.0	27.4	46.9	25.6	37.4	30.4	47.2	24.2	47.5	25.8	42.8	26.2
Science and technology	23.4	25.7	31.2	20.3	32.1	25.0	26.6	20.2	29.1	27.0	43.3	8.5	25.3	24.4
Building and construction	33.9	24.8	37.2	21.3	48.5	22.0	38.3	37.3	36.4	37.4	47.9	26.1	34.6	25.5
Electrical and mechanical engineers	32.1	26.8	30.9	19.1	35.9	19.4	39.7	32.9	45.6	35.9	43.8	25.1	35.4	28.0
Business professionals	36.5	30.9	37.4	27.2	51.7	27.7	42.9	34.8	53.4	26.3	57.3	26.9	40.8	27.3
Finance professionals	30.5	26.9	40.1	25.9	40.9	25.0	52.3	13.6	40.3	26.8	64.9	22.7	40.3	26.7
Computer professionals	29.5	27.9	40.3	28.9	44.5	27.9	38.0	37.7	53.9	31.1	41.4	30.5	43.4	30.6
Other business professionals	30.2	26.7	37.7	28.0	43.4	30.8	40.5	31.7	50.1	27.7	46.5	30.5	39.5	28.1
Property professionals	45.0	11.3	31.9	27.5	53.8	23.1	16.7	33.3	45.9	17.9	50.0	0.0	42.1	19.7
Media professionals	36.4	30.9	40.9	29.6	43.6	25.1	31.0	35.6	45.3	34.2	40.4	33.9	42.4	27.0
Transport professionals	21.7	19.2	25.0	24.3	31.8	40.9	7.7	30.8	64.0	18.0	0.0	0.0	26.5	21.2
Total	31.5	25.5	38.4	27.5	45.2	25.6	38.2	32.4	45.7	26.7	43.3	29.3	40.5	27.3

Source: ABS *Census of Australia 1996.* Customised matrix. Workforce by Industry and Occupation.

banking and finance, media and computing. The table also shows that New South Wales has a strong role in these activities, especially among business professionals, where shares in excess of 50 per cent of national employment are common. That corresponds to the location of head office and other corporate functions in Sydney. The level of concentration within a part of the country displayed above reflects the preference of advanced services for metropolitan areas. That can be seen in their high and rising shares of service-sector jobs in the metropolitan parts of the country, as displayed in Table 3.6.

The differences in the geography of population and the two measures of the economy used here partly reflect the many people who move between states, but are not in the workforce. It is possible that it also means a steadily growing distance between the opportunities of the economy and the distribution of the population. Hence, despite the near doubling of the population since 1961 and the shift to the sun-belt, the substantial role of the south-east core of Australia remains strong, as reflected also in many other indicators, such as airport traffic and telephone traffic, some of which are displayed in O'Connor (1998).

The economy and the population: the metropolitan perspective

Metropolitan dominance and the service sector

The level of concentration within a part of the country displayed above is mirrored in the preference of businesses in the new service and knowledge-based parts of the economy to locate in the metropolitan areas. That can be seen in their high and rising shares of jobs over the past decade as displayed in Table 3.6. The total line indicates that there has been a steady rise in this share and these activities have become more concentrated than employment generally. Often the shares are very high – media, for example, has very high shares displayed in the table while for other activities the levels of concentration have actually increased (for example, for finance, transport, storage and whole-saling). Services to business (a general category of many business services) has also become more concentrated. The steadily growing share of employment in tourism services in the metropolitan areas is an important example of the new concentration of forces. This activity is naturally located in many non-metropolitan areas, but as the industry has expanded (particularly with global demand) since 1986, the share of jobs in the industry in metropolitan areas has increased steadily. This reflects not only the importance of the big cities as tourist destinations in their own right but also the location of the management functions of different parts of this industry.

The concentration of activity detected in metropolitan areas has had an important local outcome. What has happened is that the big metropolitan areas in effect extended beyond their usually recognised borders. McKenzie's (1996) study of the municipalities just outside metropolitan borders showed all

Table 3.6 Metropolitan areas as a location of service industry employment

Industry categories	Share in metropolitan areas				
	1986	1991	1996	1997	1998
Services to business	74.6	75.2	75.5	76.1	76.9
Finance and property	76.7	78.1	79.9	78.9	79.9
Media and publishing	81.3	76.8	79.4	79.8	81.8
Total for producer services	76.2	76.5	77.2	77.2	78.1
Tourism related	55.1	58.2	59.7	57.9	60.9
Transport, storage and wholesaling	68.8	70.1	69.9	71.4	71.5
Total for producer services, transport and tourism	65.5	66.7	66.9	67.2	68.2
Total for all employment	65.2	64.5	64.7	64.9	65.7

Source: O'Connor (1999).

Table 3.7 Metropolitan and non-metropolitan shares of population, 1961–1998

Year	Metropolitan areas[1]	Non-metropolitan areas	Mega-metro regions[2]
1961	56.2	43.8	na
1971	63.3	36.7	na
1981	63.9	36.1	69.5[3]
1991	63.6	36.4	69.5
1996	63.6	36.4	69.9
1998	62.9	37.0	na

Notes:
1 Metropolitan areas are the statistical divisions containing the capital cities, including Canberra but not Darwin.
2 Mega-metro regions include fringe areas as identified in O'Connor and Stimson (1995).
3 Refers to 1986.
Source: ABS *Census of Australia. Characteristics of Population and Dwellings*. Census Years 1961, 1971, 1981, 1991 and 1996; ABS *Estimated Residential Population in Statistical Local Areas*.

had strong commuting links to the rest of the metropolitan area. In particular, there has emerged almost continuous urbanisation in south-east Queensland between Noosa and Coolangatta–Tweed Heads; in New South Wales between Newcastle, Sydney and Wollongong; and in Victoria surrounding Melbourne from Geelong to Cranbourne. In Perth and Adelaide, too, low density suburbanisation and the incorporation of previously free-standing towns into commuter belts also occurred. O'Connor (1993) labelled these places *mega-metropolitan areas*. These hinterland areas accommodated additional population and some jobs, so that counter-urbanisation was actually much weaker than perceived. Many fringe municipalities in these and the other statistical divisions that surround the metropolitan areas are now urbanised to a large degree and are in effect functionally components of the metropolis.

The impact of these new arrangements of population can be seen in the steady share that the mega-metro areas have had of Australia's population since 1986. Between 1986 and 1996 (a period of major change in the distribution of the nation's population between the states, and of population growth) the mega-metropolitan regions have accounted for almost 70 per cent of the nation's population. This outcome has important consequences for planning infrastructure and environmental elements to accommodate future growth in the country.

The outcomes shown for metropolitan areas have not been uniform across the country. Some important differences have emerged as firms in the global and national parts of the economy have sought locations in just one or two places. In the past different city functions were closely linked to variations in population size. Today, however, there are some distinctive features that do not correspond to differences in population size. The location of the advanced services has created a large gap in the roles played by Sydney and Melbourne, as illustrated in Murphy's (1999) research on Sydney and O'Connor's and Edgington's (1984) analysis of the changing roles of the two cities. Stimson's (1993) research on Brisbane exposed a gap between the rates of population and commercial development in that metropolitan area, while O'Connor and Kershaw (1999) showed Perth has a special role as a service centre for the nation's mining industry.

The scale of the differences between the metropolitan areas can be seen in some of the measures of city performance in Table 3.8. In the distribution of national employment shown in the first column the old simple national hierarchy can still be seen, although Perth has now moved ahead of Adelaide. The shares of employment in producer services activities, however, shows that the differences between the cities widens as the level of service specialisation increases. Moving from business services generally to media and publishing in particular, Sydney's share of national employment rises sharply. The smaller

Table 3.8 Measures of metropolitan employment and commercial activity

City	Share of national employment (1998) in:				Share of headquarters of top 100 companies[2]	Estimated nominal office rents 1999 $ per sq. metre[3]
	All jobs [1]	Services to business[1]	Finance and property[1]	Media and publishing[1]		
Sydney	22.1	26.9	33.3	36.1	54	625
Melbourne	19.0	23.8	25.2	19.9	33	300
Brisbane	8.7	9.0	8.2	8.1	3	350
Adelaide	5.6	6.0	4.7	4.3	4	210
Perth	7.6	8.8	6.1	9.2	4	425
Hobart	1.0	0.9	1.2	0.6	2	na

Sources: (1) O'Connor (1998); (2) Newton (1995); (3) The Property Council (1997).

metropolitan cities can only manage around their population share of these activities; Melbourne does a little better in finance, but lags in the media industry. The layering of the cities' role in these services is shaped by the location of the major corporate organisations and reflected in the cost of office space. The distribution of headquarters shows the very powerful role of Sydney in corporate Australia, carried over to the office market where costs in Sydney are on another plane; Melbourne's weaker financial services role, with many of its corporate headquarters outside the CBD, is reflected in its lower office space costs. Perth's role in the mining industry pushes its office space costs beyond those in Brisbane.

In sum, although metropolitan areas remain dominant in the evolving Australian economy, and (in a larger definition) continue to retain a steady share of the population, there are great differences in the vitality of individual places as evidenced also in unemployment rates and house prices (O'Connor 1998). These distinctions show not only that there are important differences between economic and population geography, but that there are very different outcomes across the country.

Non-metropolitan Australia

Non-metropolitan areas continue to be important contributors to Australia's export effort, particularly in the production of gold, the alumina industry, meat and wool-processing, some manufacturing, coal-mining, and tourism. A wide range of both Australian and transnational corporations are involved in new and old activities. New production methods in the agricultural, pastoral and mining industries, as well as new ways of providing services to most local rural communities, have reduced opportunities in some non-metropolitan areas. One change has been the increased proportion of this regional export effort that is managed and coordinated through either Sydney or Melbourne.

Differences in the fortunes of urban areas in non-metropolitan Australia have also been shaped by both public- and private-sector restructuring (Beer et al. 1994). New organisational arrangements and important changes in telecommunications and transport have resulted in a loss of business services (especially in finance) and public-sector employment to the capital cities.

Those changes were shared unevenly, however, as can be seen from Table 3.9. The information is presented in size classes beginning with the large non-metropolitan centres like Newcastle, Wollongong, Geelong and Canberra, and extending to the remote outback where population is sparsely distributed. There are some important differences among the size groups. This shows that (as at the national scale) economic activity tends to favour larger population places. The broad trend in population change has also been towards the larger centres, which have attracted a much greater share of construction activity over the decade. The small population classes, especially the

Table 3.9 Population and non-residential construction in non-metro Australia

Settlement type within	Share of national population		Construction activity, national share	Special family payments 1998, % of local households
	1986	1996		
Large non-metropolitan centres	11.4	12.3	12.7	45.2
Fringe locations			0.9	32.0
Rural regions				
Large towns	5.7	5.7	4.8	52.1
Small towns	5.2	5.1	3.3	55.3
Other rural areas	12.7	12.1	5.0	54.5
Remote areas	1.2	1.1	0.8	47.9
Other remote	1.6	1.5	1.1	

Definition of units: Australia, State of the Environment (1996): An Independent Report presented to the Commonwealth Minister for the Environment by the State of the Environment Advisory Council. Collingwood, Vic. CSIRO Publishing.
Source: Unpublished Centrelink data files and ABS Annual Building Activity survey tabulated by the Centre for Population and Urban Research, Monash University.

'other rural areas' category that accounts for the many small towns and rural areas (where centre populations are less than 5000), have not attracted the level of investment in new buildings that would be expected given their (slowly falling) share of national population.

The difficulties faced by non-metropolitan communities are magnified since large shares of their populations require social security support. This need is greater in non-metropolitan than metropolitan areas, but as communities decline, the share of families receiving support rises rapidly, so that among the small and isolated settlements in the other rural category over half the children live in families receiving additional social security support.

These differences in activity and social and community needs suggest that the emerging economy of the past decade, as reflected in decisions to construct new commercial and community buildings, has turned its back on the smaller and more isolated locations that played such a significant role in supplying farmers when rural Australia was at the heart of the national economy. As the character of the national economy is changing and mobility of goods and people has become easier, a new geography is emerging. This shows substantial preferences for larger cities and for only a few parts of non-metropolitan Australia.

Implications of Australia's new economic geography

This chapter illustrates that the investment in new facilities, the location of management jobs and the pattern of growth of the new and expanding sectors of the national economy are much more spatially focused than population trends would suggest. Sydney, and to a lesser extent Melbourne, account for most of the new activity, while Perth and Brisbane stand out among the other cities; taken together very big cities account for most of the nation's economic activity. Larger service centres in the wheat–sheep belt and intensive agriculture areas are doing very well, and there are a number of vibrant new tourism-based regional cities and towns. In addition, however, many regional cities and towns, and in particular the smaller settlements, are suffering population decline and economic decay.

Hence there is a great divergence between *people prosperity* and *place prosperity*. In earlier eras, the benefits of economic prosperity were distributed among the many towns and cities that were part of the production chains of the mainly rural economies of the time. Today, the success of the new national economy has lifted income levels, reduced unemployment and provided a greater range of jobs and diversity of goods and services for consumption, but fewer places have participated in that outcome. The differences between the clusters of high-income jobs with diverse consumption experiences and those with high unemployment and social security dependence have probably widened over the past decade.

This reflects the differing pace of adjustment between population and economic geographies since the former involves moving house, changing communities and re-skilling for different types of work. The new outcome has some serious consequences for efforts to create an environment for Australia's growth. At one level the trends raise questions about the capacity of our large cities to continue to grow, and the possible strategic assets they may need to sustain the roles they play in national development, as raised by Spiller (2000). The view across that level may need to include some better longer term planning of technical and environmental management to ensure the next round of expansion of investment can be accommodated.

A second consideration is the extent to which we can tolerate differences in the performances of different parts of the nation. Looked at another way, how can policy encourage greater participation in *people prosperity*, given the strong forces of concentration in the modern economy? Australia has little experience in resolving this issue and a recent flurry of activity created by the demands of voters in rural electorates is just a start. The issue will require a long-term perspective and some innovative thinking. It will be necessary to recognise that some regions and cities are strategically more important than others. That approach would produce an outcome very different from the 'all places get something' method used to distribute recent road improvement funding. It would also challenge the efficacy of the Grants Commission formulas. These may have achieved 'more economic equality between the states than in most other Federal systems' (Stilwell 2000: 259), but have clearly been unable to override the powerful underlying geographic forces that have exacerbated differences between parts of the country as shown in this chapter. Perhaps the

Grants Commission needs to adopt a new philosophy, one that recognises the changing population and economic geographies of today.

References

Baum, S., Stimson, R., O'Connor, K., Mullins, P. and Davis, R. (1999) *Community Opportunity and Vulnerability in Australia's Cities and Towns: Characteristics, Patterns and Implications*, Brisbane, University of Queensland Press for the Australian Housing and Urban Research Institute.

Beer, A. (1999) 'Regional Cities Within Australia's Evolving Urban System, 1991–96', *Australasian Journal of Regional Studies*, vol. 5, pp. 329–48.

Beer, A., Bolam, A. & Maude, A. (1994) *Beyond the Capitals: Urban Growth in Regional Australia*, Australian Government Publishing Service, Canberra.

Edgington, D. (1983) Central Melbourne in its National Context. Background Working Paper. Central Area Task Force, Ministry for Planning and Environment, Melbourne.

Lambooy, J.G. (2000) 'Learning and Agglomeration Economies: Adapting to Differentiating Economic Structures', in F. Boekema, K. Morgan, S. Bakkers, and R. Rutten (eds), *Knowledge, Innovation and Economic Growth, The Theory and Practice of Learning Regions*, Cheltenham. Edward Elgar, pp. 17–37.

Linge, G.J.R. (1966) 'Building Activity in Australian Metropolitan Areas: A Statistical Background', in P. Troy, (ed.) *Urban Development in Australia*, Research School of Social Sciences, ANU Canberra, pp. 403–41.

McKenzie, F. (1996) *Beyond the Suburbs: Population Change in the Major Exurban Regions of Australia*, Australian Government Publishing Service, Canberra.

Murphy, P. (1999) 'Sydney Now: Going Global in the Space of Flows', in K. O'Connor (ed.) *Houses and Jobs in Cities and Region: Research in Honour of Chris Maher*, University of Queensland Press for the Australian Housing and Urban Research Institute, Brisbane, pp. 167–78.

Newton, P.W. (1995) 'Changing Places? Households, Firms and Urban Hierarchies in the Information Age', in, J. Brotchie, M. Batty, E. Blakely, P. Hall & P. Newton (eds) *Cities in Competition. Productive and Sustainable Cities for the 21st Century*, Longman Australia, Sydney, pp. 161–90.

O'Connor, K. (1993) *The Australian Capital City Report, 1993*, Centre for Population and Urban Research and Department of Geography and Environmental Science, Monash University, Clayton.

O'Connor, K. (1998) *The Australian Capital City Report, 1998*, Centre for Population and Urban Research and School of Geography and Environmental Science, Monash University, Clayton.

O'Connor, K. (1999) 'Economic and Social Change and the Futures of Australian Metropolitan Areas', in *Benchmarking 99: Future Cities Research Conference*. Conference papers. Melbourne. Melbourne City Council, pp. 59–66.

O'Connor, K. and Edgington, D. (1984) 'Tertiary Industry and Urban Development: Competition Between Melbourne and Sydney', in C. Adrian (ed.) *Urban Impacts of Foreign and Local Investment in Australia*, Australian Institute of Urban Studies, Canberra.

O'Connor, K. and Kershaw, L. (1999) 'Outsourcing, Producer Services and Shifts in the Geography of the Australian Mining Industry', *Australasian Journal of Regional Studies*, vol. 5, no. 1, pp. 73–86.

O'Connor, K. and Stimson, B. (1995) *The Economic Role of Cities: Economic Change and City Development, Australia 1971–1991*, Australian Government Publishing Service, Canberra.

Property Council (1997) The Office Space Report. Sydney.

Reich, R. (1992) *The Work of Nations: Preparing Ourselves for 21st Century Capitalism*, Vintage Books, New York.

Romer, P. (1986) 'Increasing Returns and Long Run Growth', *Journal of Political Economy* 94, 1002–37.

Scott, A. (1998) *Regions and the World Economy. The Coming Shape of Global Production, Competition and Political Order*. Oxford. Oxford University Press.

Spiller, M. (2000) *The Capital Cities and Australia's Future*, The Property Council of Australia and the Council of Capital City Lord Mayors.

Stillwell, F. (2000) Review of R. Mathews and B. Grewal (1997) *The Public Sector in Jeopardy: Australian Fiscal Federalism from Whitlam to Keating*, in *Australasian Journal of Regional Studies*, 6, pp. 259–60.

Stimson, R.J. (1993) *Issues and Options for Economic Development in Brisbane and the Southeast Queensland Region: Global, National and Local Perspectives*, Faculty of Built Environment and Engineering, Queensland University of Technology, Brisbane.

Stimson, R.J., Shuaib, F.A. and O'Connor, K.B. (1998) *Population and Employment in Australia. Regional Hot Spots and Cold Spots, 1986 to 1996*, University of Queensland Press for the Australian Housing and Urban Research Institute, Brisbane.

Storper, M. (1997) *The Regional World. Territorial Development in the Global Economy*, New York. Guildford Press.

PART 2

Growth and Equity

4

Liberalism and Economic Policy

Fred Argy

Liberal ideas have had a major influence on economic policy over the last quarter of a century. Some of these ideas have been essentially value-free while others have been more ideological in character. This chapter outlines the role both kinds of liberalism have played in shaping public policy in Australia.

The non-ideological strand of liberalism we call 'economic liberalism'. It has considerable support from the economics profession and has had a great influence on Australian economic policy, especially in the 1980s.

By contrast, ideological liberalism seeks to change fundamental national priorities; it is value-based rather than firmly grounded in economic consensus. Ideology can be of the 'dry' (hard) or 'wet' (progressive) variety. The chapter focuses mainly on hard liberalism (which favours a more individualistic, less egalitarian society), because in the last decade it has been the more potent force at work in policy reform in Australia.

The chapter then asks: does hard liberalism only offer a new set of values or does it also have a strong economic rationale, as many of its advocates claim?

The conclusion draws the threads together.

Economic liberalism

There is one strand of liberalism that has the overwhelming support of virtually all kinds of liberals – whether progressive or hard – because it can be mostly applied in a *value-neutral* way. We call this strand 'economic liberalism'. It is 'liberal' in the traditional sense that it tends to increase the scope for individual freedom of choice: its basic tenet is that, unless there is clear market failure which governments can sensibly correct, competitive markets are better than politicians and bureaucrats at allocating and efficiently utilising productive resources.

Economic liberalism is largely 'value-free' in two senses. First, its belief in
the efficiency benefits of competitive markets has a strong scientific basis and
has the overwhelming support of professional economists.[1] Second, its reform
agenda seeks only to change the *methods* of policy intervention used by
governments – not their policy *goals* or priorities. It is concerned with means
(how best to achieve given goals most effectively and efficiently) – not ends
(the intrinsic merit of the goals). Economic liberals therefore do not need to get
involved in a philosophical debate about the appropriate size of government,
level of economic freedom or level of inequality.

Many of the economic reforms of the 1970s, 1980s and 1990s in Australia
fall into the category of economic liberalism. This is true of:

- the opening up of pubic-sector service delivery to more competition from
  the private sector
- the transfer of some ownership risks from the public to the private sector
  where the latter was considered better able to manage those risks
- the exposure of private markets to greater competition through reductions
  in trade barriers, the removal of state-based trade barriers, deregulation,
  and so on
- deregulation of the banking and financial system (although with tighter
  prudential safeguards) where this improved economic management and
  produced a more efficient range and quality of financial services
- the roll-back of some award regulations that encouraged inefficient workplace practices and hindered human resource mobility and managerial
  flexibility
- shifts to more market-based methods of policy intervention with less use of
  regulations, controls, protective barriers or cross-subsidisation of public
  services, and more use of market incentives such as subsidies or tax concessions, or at least more market-neutral devices such as direct budgetary
  payments (see Argy 2000b).

The intention of these reforms was:

- to achieve economic outcomes more consistent with the preferences of consumers
- improve economic performance by making markets more competitive
- reduce unnecessary interference with the price mechanism (subject to the
  usual economist qualifications about public goods, externalities, information asymmetries, learning curves)
- help achieve desired national policy goals more effectively and efficiently.

The reforms did not seek to change Australian norms and values. That is
why they had the support of both governments of the Right and Centre-Left
parties such as the ALP. Thus:

- the public-sector reforms did not require or seek any change in the range and quality of government services: they only sought to deliver given services more cost effectively
- increased competition in private markets did not require governments to abandon their social and regional goals: it sought only to achieve a better allocation and more productive use of existing resources
- workplace reform did not require a decline in the living standards of low-paid workers: it sought only to improve flexibility and productivity
- the shift to more market-based methods of macroeconomic intervention did not mean giving less priority to policy goals such as full employment, stability or industry development; its aim was to achieve these goals more effectively, as the old methods of intervention were losing most of their relevance and effectiveness (Argy 1995: 12).

It was known that some of the liberalisation reforms had the potential to have undesirable social, environmental or quality-of-life effects. But it was assumed that these effects would be offset by other measures such as structural adjustment assistance, active labour market and regional programs, new forms of employment creation, earned income tax credits, new environment measures, and so on.[2]

In these ways, the cost of implementing non-economic goals would be met equitably, efficiently and transparently by taxpayers as a whole instead of being met arbitrarily by a few consumers, small depositors and the unemployed. In short, the theory underlying the economic liberal reform program of the 1980s and 1990s was that it would expand the national cake but its distribution would remain a matter for political choice.

And in the main this is what seems to have happened in practice. After a lag, the reforms led to marked improvements in productivity and living standards. The performance of the Australian economy in the 1990s was quite outstanding relative to the two previous decades and to other countries. And Australian governments took deliberate countervailing action to ensure that the social outcomes were acceptable – Hawke's improved family benefits, Keating's Working Nation reforms and Howard's GST compensation (Argy 1998: chapter 2). They tried to 'manage' the reform process.

That said, the results were not always consistent with government expectations or community desires. Some reforms were not successful even in economic terms. We know for example that:

- it was unwise to privatise public services where there was uncertainty about the ability to reliably deliver essential services and meet community obligations (as in prisons, water filtration, refugee detention centres and ambulances)
- some of the ownership risks associated with new infrastructure, for example, urban roads, were non-commercial in character and should not have been transferred to the private sector

- some government assets such as Telstra 1 and the Commonwealth Serum Laboratories were sold too cheaply
- some of the out-sourcing (for example, of information technology) was ill-judged
- blunt monetary instruments were used when other measures might have been more appropriate; and so on (see Quiggin 1996, Walker 2000 and Argy 2000b).

And there were unexpected social effects. Despite the apparent long-term stability in many broad measures of income inequality, some Australians fell unintentionally between the cracks during the 1980s and 1990s. Thus, low-paid workers did not benefit substantially from the Hawke Government welfare improvements but were adversely affected by both the wage Accord and the new enterprise-bargaining arrangements. In fact, the full social impact of the reforms on low-paid workers was not fully anticipated or understood. Skill-specific or region-specific dimensions of adjustment assistance were not given enough weight. And it is arguable that at times the pace of change was too rapid – some reforms such as competition policy could have been phased in more gradually.

Many middle-class families got 'squeezed' as 'user pays' became an increasing practice in education, health and childcare, and parents were asked to support their teenage unemployed children. And full employment proved elusive.

These all represent serious policy failures but they were failures in political implementation – not in the concept or intent of economic liberalism.

Ideological strands of liberalism

A government reform program initially based on value-neutral notions of economic liberalism can become 'ideological' if:

- some of the reforms seek not only to improve efficiency but also to deliberately reorder social priorities, either through positive action (for example, to restructure the tax system) or through inaction (for example, failing to compensate a large group of already disadvantaged losers)
- those reforms rely heavily on value judgements rather than objective economic analysis.

This chapter will argue that some of the economic reforms of the past decade or so have been ideological in that sense. This is hardly surprising, as liberalism is concerned with ends as well as means; it is basically a kind of ideology, albeit very imprecise. The range of ideologies encompassed under liberalism and the effects of liberal ideology on policy are discussed below.

The nature of liberalism

Liberalism is not a clear system of ideas. It 'worms around a central thread whose only definition is the indefinable idea of freedom' (White 1978: 117). Its primary concern is to safeguard freedom of conscience, speech, association, and so on, and to leave wide room for individual choice, as it believes that, in an increasingly diverse society, this offers the best way to reconcile conflicting interests and aspirations.

Given the ambiguity in the concept of freedom, it is not surprising that liberalism encompasses a broad range of ideologies – from 'hard' (dry) to 'progressive' (wet).

'Hard' liberals – sometimes called 'economic rationalists' in Australia[3] – assign a dominant role to freedom of choice. They believe that, as a general principle, the state should not intrude upon personal freedom except to protect others from harm (safeguarding life and property). Their ideal is a society built on competitive markets, consumer sovereignty and the sturdy values of individual responsibility and self-reliance. The early views of J.S. Mill (later modified) and those of F.A. Hayek and J.M. Buchanan typify this social philosophy. One exponent in Australia is Wolfgang Kasper (2000).

They see freedom as something that belongs to the individual and is diminished if he or she is *prevented* by the state from attaining his or her goals. However, 'mere *incapacity* to attain a goal is not a lack of freedom' (Berlin 1969: 131–3).

Hard liberals are suspicious of redistribution policies. They claim that it is impossible to compare the marginal utility of different persons (as this involves arbitrary ethical judgements), and in any case it is not 'equitable' for individuals to be denied the fruits of their effort and enterprise. So the state should simply ensure there are fair rules and processes in place (for example, adequate competition laws to prevent abuse of monopoly power) and largely stand aside from distribution issues (apart from establishing a basic subsistence safety net).

Hard liberals are also suspicious of governments. They argue that while in theory governments have a role to play in correcting market failure, in practice they have neither the competence, knowledge nor the integrity to intervene effectively in economic or social affairs. (This is an extreme version of so-called public choice theory.)

At the other end of the spectrum are the *'progressive' liberals* (also called 'small l' liberals, 'positive' liberals and 'wets').[4] They depart from the hard view in several ways.

First, they argue that unless people have a *capacity for choice* – a set of meaningful options – freedom is a sham. For example, without government support, teenagers from poor families will have less education, less access to the new IT and communications technology (Lloyd and Hellwig (2001)) and more limited employment choice than those from better off homes.

Second, they want to ensure that more freedom for one group (for example, employers and skilled, and knowledge-rich employees) does not mean less freedom for another group (for example, vulnerable unskilled employees) as is the case when one frees up labour markets too zealously (Bauman 1999).

For these reasons progressive liberals believe governments need to intervene to ensure reasonable equality of opportunity. By doing so they can enhance economic and political freedom, promote the self-development of citizens, remove obstacles to the good life and create a genuine level playing field in the marketplace.

Third, progressive liberals are more concerned about distribution outcomes than their 'hard' counterparts. They are prepared to give special weight to poorer people (for example, when deciding whether to compensate losers from the adverse effects of economic reform), even if it means making the ethical judgement that their marginal utility is generally higher than the rest of the community. Vertical equity (avoidance of wide social inequality) is, they say, as important as horizontal equity (fair rules and processes). They warn that the legitimacy of policy and the cohesion and stability of society require that the fruits of government reforms are shared fairly widely across the community. Policies and societal institutions should not confer long-term advantages on one group over another.

Finally, they are less cynical about the competence and integrity of governments. While acknowledging that competitive markets are better at allocating resources than governments, they believe governments generally have a comparative advantage over markets in macroeconomic management and distribution and can often play a meaningful role in offsetting market failure in resource allocation (where social and private costs and benefits diverge markedly).

Ironically, when it comes to 'moral' issues the roles are reversed. Progressives have less faith than hard liberals in the moral judgement of government (or at least its ability to read the electorate's predominant moral beliefs). For example, they are less willing to interfere with individual freedom on such issues as censorship, IVF, the response to drug abusers, euthanasia, sexual preferences and abortion. And they are more reluctant to inject moral judgements when providing welfare; for example, by seeking to limit it to 'deserving' poor.

Given these different perspectives, the practical process of translating liberal principles into economic policy inevitably produces deep differences of opinion among liberals. (Today's Australian Liberal Party is very different from the old party of Deakin, Menzies, Gorton and Fraser.) These differences essentially arise because of a clash of values.

The dominance of hard liberalism

Over much of the last decade it is hard, not progressive, liberalism that has been in the ascendancy (although this may now be changing); that is, governments have sought to change policy goals to bring them more into line with radical liberal or market values. The current Howard government in particular has enthusiastically embraced such values as low public debt, further large-scale privatisation, minimal protection of vulnerable workers and tax cuts in preference to spending increases – in short small government.[5] It has also shown a leaning towards more conservative social values.[6]

The influence of hard liberalism is evident in the growing acceptance of new policy paradigms that were once anathema to Australians.

First, reflecting the higher priority given to low inflation and small government, *we seem to have turned our back on full employment as we once knew it*. We appear resigned to historically high levels of unemployment and underemployment. This manifests itself in a degree of policy apathy towards:

- long periods of slow growth relative to productive capacity
- high levels of long-term unemployment
- a growing skill and regional mismatch in the labour market (Argy 1998: 154, Walsh 1999: 209–12).

These developments were not principally caused by liberal reform, being mainly a product of rapid structural and technological change, but the lack of adequate response to them is a product of 'small government' ideology. Apart from a brief experiment with Working Nation in the mid-1990s and a brief period in 1997–2000 when monetary policy was highly accommodating, governments have tended to give these problems low priority.

Second, reflecting the increasing bias in favour of commercial infrastructure with high cash flow, *government spending on social infrastructure is used much less extensively as an instrument of redistribution* (Argy et al. 1999: 13–15).

This is reflected in a long-term trend decline in public infrastructure investment relative to GDP, and partly explains why we are seeing:

- a decline in low-cost tenanted accommodation
- falling Year 12 education participation rates in many Australian states (mainly affecting low-income families)
- growing community concerns about our public schools and hospitals
- a widening gap in health and death rates between poor and wealthy
- a trend to self-provision and user pays rather than universality.[7]

Third, *the old commitment to unconditional, need-based welfare is being redefined*. The present government is making assistance subject to increasingly onerous tests and conditional on prescribed forms of participation. The rhetoric suggests a desire to limit assistance only to 'deserving' poor (like the old Poor Laws and with the same potential for abuse). There also seems to be an attempt to gradually transfer responsibility for (and associated costs of) welfare from governments to corporations, charities and family.

Fourth, although this may now be changing, *governments have shown little concern about the growing imbalance in regional services and incomes* (Argy 1998: 154ff).

Finally, and most importantly, *we seem to be less caring and protective towards the more vulnerable Australian workers* (those with no individual bargaining power in the market). This is evident in a widening dispersion of earnings and quality of life within the workforce. A new class of working poor is emerging: it has lagging incomes (relative to the community average), it is more dependent on welfare, and it holds more stressful jobs with increased work pace and intensity, more unpredictable hours of work and more unpaid overtime.[8]

Rising *market* inequalities in workers' incomes and quality of life would not matter if action were taken to neutralise these effects through taxes, transfers and infrastructure spending. And to a significant extent this has been happening but has it been enough? Two tests are often applied: trends in (a) social spending and (b) inequality.

Social spending in Australia, although tending to fall a little relative to GDP in recent years,[9] has remained at high levels (Keating 2000, Warby 2000). However, the high level of social spending must be viewed against other developments. One is a shrinking in government assistance previously available to low-income working families through the 'social wage',[10] through public ownership (cross-subsidisation) or through industrial and human rights regulation.[11] Another development is that *non-government* sources of support (the nuclear family, the local community, public-spirited volunteers, trade unions, churches and benign employers) have been contracting.[12] Further, rapid structural change and globalisation are impacting very strongly on market inequalities, thus requiring a bigger response from government. There is also a steady ageing of the population and unemployment has been higher on average in the 1990s than the 1970s.

Viewed against these developments, it is not clear that levels of social spending are 'high'. Also, current levels of spending are under constant pressure from business groups seeking lower taxes and less government borrowing.

The other common test of the adequacy of government response is to look at trends in levels of inequality since the 1970s. These are hard to read. On some measures there has been no trend increase, at least until the mid-1990s (Johnson et al. 1995, Argy 1998 and Wooden in this volume). But other measures suggest otherwise. Saunders (2001) examines the data comprehensively for the ABS, drawing on the Luxembourg Income Study, and concludes that the increase in market inequality since the mid-1980s 'has been moderated but not eliminated by the social security and tax systems' (p. 289). He also points out that the increase in inequality since the mid-1980s, although less than in the United Kingdom and United States, has been much greater than in many other countries (291ff). (Saunders, however, unlike Johnson et al. did not take account of trends in the social wage.) In any case, standard measures of inequality do not capture fine nuances like the impact on low-paid working families noted above.

On that basis, it is far from clear that governments have been doing enough to offset growing *market* inequalities. We are seeing a perceptible change in our egalitarian ethos, especially in regard to low-paid working families. And the process of structural change has not yet run its full span.

The reasons for this shift away from egalitarianism are complex. Apart from the fact that a government with conservative values has been in power since 1996, the key factors are three-fold (all related to globalisation and structural change):

- a shift in the structure of interest groups, with an increase in the power base of the business sector (especially large mobile corporations) relative to competing interest groups with more socially progressive ideas, such as trade unions and consumer, conservation and community groups
- the surge in importance of global financial markets: these markets want ever smaller government and have the potential to create a great deal of economic and political instability if they don't like government policies
- an apparent drift in the mood of Australians towards social conservatism on some issues.[13]

Does hard liberalism have an economic rationale?

The fact that radical liberals are challenging existing egalitarian ethos and traditions is not *per se* a cause for concern. Indeed it is a symptom of a healthy democracy at work. If hard liberals eventually convince the broad community that their way makes for a 'better' (freer) society and if they rely on broad philosophical and moral arguments to win their case, who can complain about the processes?

The problem is, however, that ideological liberals often clothe their ideas in economic garb. They contend that a shift to their preferred values would produce a stronger, more prosperous economy. They use a range of economic arguments to beef up their policy paradigms. These arguments are set out below. The alternative, more mainstream, view of economists on these paradigms is outlined in the section on counter-arguments.

The economic arguments for hard liberalism

Employment

(i)   Most unemployment these days is supply-driven, being caused by wage rigidities and work-shirking.
(ii) Expansionary government policies directed at demand would mostly make matters worse by fanning inflation.
(iii) The only effective long-term solution is to force 'job snobs' out of welfare, deregulate wages and step up workplace reform to enhance economic flexibility.

(iv) The goal of genuine 'full employment' (enough full-time jobs for everyone able and willing to work) is incompatible with the present egalitarian culture in Australia. Australians must choose between one or the other.

Redistribution and welfare

(i) Poverty is principally a moral problem.
(ii) Welfare assistance is wasted: it does nothing for poverty in the longer term.
(iii) Worse still, it creates a mentality of dependence.
(iv) Redistribution policies (beyond a basic safety net) are incompatible with economic liberalism.
(v) Redistribution policies are also counter-productive: the economic damage they cause can nullify the benefits of reform.

Small government and economic performance

(i) Smaller government generally leads to improved economic performance.
(ii) In today's globalised economy, taxes and regulations need to be kept low to prevent a major flight of key productive factors, which would sap the vitality of the economy.
(iii) Net public borrowing over the economic cycle (that is, running structural budget cash deficits) is economically irresponsible because it tends to raise interest rates and/or generate higher inflation and external account deficits.
(iv) Private borrowing (and investment) is superior in efficiency terms because it is subject to market disciplines (responsive to the preferences of consumers).[14]
(v) Australians will not tolerate a further increase in their existing tax burden. They prefer to spend their money as they wish.

The counter-arguments

It is fair to say that there is far from consensus in the economics profession on these propositions. Indeed surveys suggest there would be more economists opposed to them than for them. The kinds of response that mainstream economists would make are summarised below.[15]

Employment

(i) The reasons why Australia still has around 7 per cent unemployment, after nearly a decade of strong growth, are complex, with both supply-side and demand factors at work.

If one analysed a sample of unemployed persons at any one time one would find a great diversity of reasons why they were out of work (apart from being in between jobs). Some of them could be low-productivity workers who find employment difficult at current wage levels; the problem here is an *inflexible wage structure*. Some may lack the skills and experience to fill available vacancies; the problem here is a *skill mismatch*. Some may be living in an economically recessed region: *regional mismatch and labour immobility*. Some again may have personal characteristics unattractive to employers such as too old, too long out of work, possessing inadequate knowledge of English, and so on. The problem here is *negative employer attitudes*. For some unemployed the problem may be that there are simply not enough jobs across Australia relative to the number of job-seekers: they could only get a job by denying a job to other people: *insufficient aggregate demand; that is, inadequate economic growth*. And there may be a few who lack adequate motivation and job-search effectiveness – what has been called *voluntary unemployment*.

(ii) It is arguable that too much priority has been given to low inflation and small government relative to unemployment. There is increasing evidence that over-cautious demand policies have not only made recessions longer, but also slowed the trend growth in employment and widened the incidence of long-term unemployment (see Dungey and Pitchford 1998, Nevile 2000 and Chapman et al. 2000). Most economists accept that Keynesian expansionist remedies still work when total job-seekers greatly exceed job vacancies (as is the case at the time of writing) and that, because of over-conservative economic policies, economic growth has consistently fallen short of its sustainable productive capacity.

(iii) Hard liberals exaggerate the quantitative significance of wage-induced and voluntary unemployment.

Wages are not currently a major hurdle to employment in Australia and are unlikely to become a problem in the future, given our new decentralised wage-setting arrangements, intensely competitive product markets and strong underlying productivity trend. Moreover, the wage structure is now already quite flexible. That said, increased flexibility would be helpful if it could be done humanely.

Again, the overall numbers of deliberate job-shirkers are small in Australia. The range over which welfare recipients experience high effective marginal tax rates is not wide, work tests are very severe, and there is a 'strong enthusiasm for work' among young welfare recipients (Saunders 2000). Nonetheless, there is a *perceived* problem and it requires attention.

(iv) Given the range of causes of unemployment, there is no simple 'one fits all' remedy. A range of government responses is needed,[16] including:

- the trading off of some safety-net wage increases against earned income tax credits or the exemption of low-paid workers from payroll tax[17]

- more extensive investment in training, retraining and education, including early intervention to assist school-leavers at-risk
- the allocation of more resources to regional development
- increased incentives for the unemployed to move geographically
- individual case management of, and employer support for, long-term unemployed
- government-financed wage subsidies for low-productivity workers
- a more growth-oriented macroeconomic policy
- some job-creation programs targeted at less-skilled workers
- effective action to deal with work disincentives, welfare dependence and poverty traps (see below).

With such a mix of policies (and with the costs financed through progressive taxes), structural, long-term unemployment could be reduced without any increase in inequality: the cost would be equitably borne by the winners from globalisation and economic reform – not the losers. In short, full employment and Australian-style egalitarianism are not intrinsically incompatible.

It is worth noting that the supply of labour, which was growing fast in the 1980s, began to slow down in the 1990s and will slow down further in the future as the cohort of school-leavers dwindles. This will make unemployment easier to handle.

Redistribution and welfare

(i)   Poverty is more a result of socioeconomic and structural factors than of individual moral failings. If a person's parents are economically disadvantaged, he or she will tend to leave school early, lack technology skills, experience longer periods of unemployment and become welfare dependent (Pech and McCoull 2000, Lloyd and Hellwig 2001).

(ii) Welfare is not 'wasted'. Improvements in welfare benefits in Australia in the late 1980s (coupled with a bigger investment in the social wage) did significantly help to reduce poverty and inequality. Without these interventions social inequality would have greatly increased (Johnson et al. 1995, Harding and Szukalaska 1999, Saunders 2001).

(iii) As noted earlier, work-shirking is not a serious problem in Australia. More generally, there is no evidence of a permanent welfare class or a higher incidence of welfare dependency in social democratic (high welfare) countries relative to the United States (Goodwin et al. 1999).

That said, there is community concern that 'passive' forms of assistance may create an extreme entitlement mentality and an insufficient sense of obligation. A risk of long-term dependency arises when there are so-called 'poverty traps' or work disincentives. These need addressing. Effective responses can include:

- earned income tax credits
- a rationalisation of welfare income tests, which need not involve huge additional outlays (Keating and Lambert 1998)
- a softening of the policy of clawing back middle-class benefits
- a Work for the Dole scheme that provides generous reciprocal government assistance.

(iv) Economists see no analytical inconsistency in supporting both social activism and economic liberalism – provided non-distorting instruments of redistribution are used. While economists overwhelmingly support liberal economic policies, a majority of them, when asked, indicate they also want to reduce existing levels of inequality or at least stop further increases in inequality (see surveys of economists in Argy 2001a).

(v) The international experience suggests that egalitarian policies and strong economic growth can all co-exist very well.[18]

Small government

(i) Within a wide spectrum (that is, excluding extremes such as centralist third-world countries and very small economies like Hong Kong), there is no systematic correlation between size of government and economic performance. And economic theory alone tells us very little about the 'optimal' size of the state.

(ii) The international evidence suggests that governments still have considerable discretion on levels of taxation and government spending and borrowing. Capital markets have not greatly penalised countries with high taxes and public debt, nor have they imposed high-risk premiums on countries like Australia with high foreign debt levels.[19] So governments can still determine their own social priorities – provided they choose their instruments carefully so as to minimise the impact on business costs. Most types of skilled and professional labour are immobile, capital markets are not perfectly integrated and tax factors are only one of many factors determining investment location.

(iii) In macroeconomic terms, net government borrowing over the economic cycle is no more or less economically irresponsible than net private borrowing: the effects on inflation and external debt, for example, are much the same in both cases.

(iv) At the micro-level, most people seem prepared to trade off some private for public goods (see Withers and Edwards 2001). Collective consumption can often yield more community wellbeing than individual consumer choice (a view that now has support in the literature).[20] While the private sector can play a major role in delivering public goods and sharing the investment risks, governments should not be excluded from financing new infrastructure investment. They are often better able to manage the ownership risks involved and can better provide for non-market benefits (see Argy et al 1999).

This assumes new infrastructure investments are subjected to fairly rigorous cost-benefit evaluation. Those that are not so evaluated are less defensible.

(v) Australia is a low-tax country and this may be partly why surveys find most Australians willing to pay higher taxes if the funds are used in specific ways they approve of; for example, to improve community services (Withers et al. 1994, Withers and Edwards 2001).

In short, the shift in community values sought by hard liberals is not firmly grounded in mainstream economics. Radical liberals are perfectly entitled to promote their values on moral or philosophical grounds, but (unlike economic liberals) they are not entitled to claim economic legitimacy.

Conclusions

Liberal ideas have fundamentally changed the mix of policy instruments used in Australia. Increasingly they are also seeking to change the basic policy parameters and goals.

Liberal reforms have come under sustained attack from critics of so-called 'economic rationalism'. But the attack is very undiscriminating. It does not distinguish those liberal reforms that simply seek more efficiency and effectiveness from those that seek also to *trade off* some societal goals such as egalitarianism against more market-oriented values such as small government and individualism. The first we have called economic liberalism and the second hard liberalism.

Economic liberal reforms are generally value-neutral in intent and have wide support in the economics profession. Hard liberal reforms are value-based and, I have argued, are economically controversial. Both groups of reform are 'liberal' in that they widen individual choice but their long-term policy implications are very different.

Hard liberalism has strong support in business circles and impersonal financial markets. These two power blocs are putting pressure on governments to further deregulate, privatise, cut back spending and taxes, and continue to repay public debt. They have a capacity to cause economic disruption and to create an unstable political climate. This risk is often exaggerated but the preferences and sensitivities of the two power blocs cannot be ignored.

However, governments are also under pressure from the broad community to protect existing Australian industries, provide better public services and (despite signs of social conservatism in some areas) to intervene more actively to 'look after the losers'.

It may seem that governments are caught between 'a rock and a hard place'. In fact, the dilemma is not as acute as it seems. The concerns of the community can be mostly met by:

- pursuing a more measured pace of reform
- discarding unnecessary and unpopular ideology; for example, making more extensive use of government borrowing to improve public services
- giving full employment higher priority in the scale of policy values
- addressing social impacts at the design stage of reform (Argy 1999 and Savage 1999)[21]
- addressing potential poverty traps.

At the same time, the concerns of business and markets can be largely met by:

- maintaining a commitment to economic liberalism; that is, continuing to search for more efficient and effective means of fulfilling government responsibilities
- choosing redistribution instruments carefully to minimise the impact on mobile capital and business (see Argy 2001b for a policy agenda that could counter these conditions).

The challenge, as always, is to find the right balance.

References

Argy, F. (1995) *Financial Deregulation: Past promise – Future Realities*, CEDA Research Study, p. 42.

Argy, F. (1998) *Australia at the Crossroads: Radical Free Market or Progressive Liberalism?* St Leonards, Allen & Unwin.

Argy, F. (1999) *Distributional Effects of Structural Change: Some Policy Implications*, Conference Proceedings, Productivity Commission.

Argy, F., Lindfield, M., Stimson, B. and Hollingsworth, P. (1999) *Infrastructure and Economic Development*, CEDA Information Paper no. 60, April.

Argy, F. (2000a) 'Arm's Length Policy-Making: The Privatization of Economic Policy', in Keating, M., Wanna, J. and Waller P. (eds) *Institutions on the Edge*, St Leonards, Allen & Unwin.

Argy, F. (2000b) Towards a Better Balance Between Governments and Markets, paper presented to IPAAA conference, Perth, to be published in Journal of Institute.

Argy, F. (2001a) 'Attitudes of Economists', *Economic Papers*, March 2001.

Argy, F. (2001b) 'The Changing Face of Social Democracy', in collection of papers ed. Race Mathews, to be published.

Argy, F. (2001c) 'Economic Governance and National Institutional Dynamics', in anthology of papers coordinated by Stephen Bell of Queensland University.

Atkinson, A.B. (1999) The Economic Consequences of Rolling Back the Welfare State, Massachussets Institute of Technology, USA.

Australian Centre for Industrial Relations Research & Training (ACIRRT) (1998) *Australia at Work*, Prentice Hall, Sydney.

Australian Financial System Inquiry (AFSI) (1981) *Final Report*, AGPS, Canberra.

Barnes, A. and Fields, D. (2001) Study of hospitality industry, University of NSW, reported by Nina Field in *AFR*, 25–28 January.

Bauman, Z. (1999) *Globalization: The Human Consequences*, Policy Press, Cambridge.

Bell, S. (2000) 'The Unemployment Crisis and Economic Policy', in Bell, S. (ed.) *The Unemployment Crisis in Australia*, Cambridge University Press, Cambridge.

Berlin, I. (1969) Four Essays on Liberty, OUP, London.

Chapman, B. and Kapuscinski, C. (2000) Avoiding Recessions and Australian Long Term Unemployment, Australia Institute, DP 29.

Dawkins, P. (1999) A Plan to Cut Unemployment – an Elaboration of the Five Economists' Open Letter to Prime Minister – Talk to Economic Society in Canberra.

Dawkins, P. (2000) The Australian Labour Market in the 1990s, in The Australian Economy in the 1990s, proceedings of a conference, 24–25 July, RBA, Sydney.

Dixon, H.D. (1997) 'Economics and Happiness', *Economic Journal*, November.

Dungey, M. and Pitchford, J. (1998) 'Prospects for Output and Employment Growth with Steady Inflation', in G. Debelle and J. Borland (eds) *Unemployment and the Labour Market*, RBA Conference Proceedings.

Frank, R.H. (1997) 'The Frame of Reference of a Public Good', *Economic Journal*, November.

Goodwin, R. et al. (1999) *The Real Worlds of Welfare Capitalism*, Cambridge University Press, Cambridge.

Harding, A. (1997) The Suffering Middle, NATSEM Discussion Paper 21, June.

Harding, A. and Szukalaska, A. (1999) Trends in Child Poverty 1982–1995–96, NATSEM Discussion Paper no. 42, April.

Henderson, D. (1999) *The Changing Fortunes of Economic Liberalism*, Institute of Public Affairs, Melbourne.

Johnson, D., Manning, I. and Hellwig, O. (1995) Trends in the Distribution of Cash Income and non-Cash Benefits, Department of PM & C, December.

Kasper, W. (2000) *Building Prosperity: Australia's Future in the Global Economy*, CIS, St Leonards.

Keating, M. (2000) 'Realizing People's Potential: Labour Market Policies', in G. Davis and M. Keating (eds) *Future of Governance*, St Leonards, Allen & Unwin.

Keating, M. and Lambert, S. (1998) 'Improving Incentives', *Australian Economic Review*, 31 (3).

Keating, M. and Mitchell, D. (2000) 'Security and Equity in a Changing Society', in G. Davis and M. Keating (eds) *Future of Governance*, St Leonards, Allen & Unwin.

Kelly, P. (2000) 'The Politics of Economic Change, in 'Australia's Economy in the 1980s and 1990s', RBA, Sydney.

✳Little, I.M.D (1950) *A Critique of Welfare Economics*, London.

Lloyd, R. and O. Hellwig (2001) Barriers to the Take Up of New Technology, NATSEM DP no. 53.

Neutze, M. (2000) 'Economics, Values and Urban Australia', in Pat Troy (ed.) *Equity, Environment Efficiency*, MUP, Melbourne.

Murtough, G. and Waite, M. (2000) The Diversity of Casual Contract Employment, Productivity Commission Staff Research Paper, December.

Oswald, A.J. (1997) 'Happiness and Economic Performance', *Economic Journal*, November.

Parham, D. et al. (2000) Distribution of Economic Gains of the 1990s, Productivity Commission Staff Research paper, November.

Pech, J. and McCoull F., (2000) 'Transgenerational Welfare Dependence: Myths and Realities', *Australian Social Policy*.

Putterman, Louis, Roemer, John & Silvestre, Joaquim (1998) 'Does Egalitarianism have a future?' *Journal of Economic Literature*, vol. xxxvi, June.

Quiggin, J. (1996) *Great Expectations*, St Leonards, Allen & Unwin.

Quiggin, J. (2001) Economic Governance and Microeconomic Reform, Paper to Q'ld University Symposium, February 2001.

✱ Rawls, J. (1971), *A Theory of Justice*, Harvard University Press, Cambridge, MA.

Richardson, S. and Harding, A. (1998) Low Wages and the Distribution of Family Income in Australia, NATSEM Discussion Paper 33, September.

Saunders, P. (ed.) (2000) *Reforming the Australian Welfare State*, Australian Institute of Family Studies, Melbourne, Victoria.

Saunders, P. (2001) Household Income and its Distribution, *ABS Year Book*, 2001.

Savage, E. (1999) Issues in Structural Reform, Productivity Commission Workshop Proceedings, 21 May.

✱ Self, P. (1993) *Government by the Market?* Macmillan, London.

Walker, A. (2000) Measuring the Health Gap, NATSEM Discussion Paper 50, August.

Walker, B. and B. (2000) *Privatisation: Sell Off or Sell Out?* ABC Books, Sydney.

Walsh, C. (1999) *Structural Adjustment: A Mainly Regional Development Perspective*, Productivity Commission Workshop Proceedings, Canberra, 12 May.

Warby, M. (2000) 'Writing About Somewhere Else', *Agenda*, vol. 7 no. 4.

White, D.M. (1978) *The Philosophy of the Australian Liberal Party*, Hutchinson, Melbourne.

Withers, G. et al. (1994) 'Public Expenditure in Australia', *EPAC*, October 1994.

Withers, G. and Edwards, L. (2001) Spending Priorities of Voters, GPPP Discussion Paper, ANU forthcoming.

Wooden, M. (1999) Job Insecurity and Job Instability: Getting the Facts Straight, BCA papers, vol.1, No.1, May.

Notes

1 Surveys consistently find that more than three-quarters of economists accept the need to promote competitive free markets, lower tariffs, further deregulate product markets, and so on. Also more than three-quarters oppose the use of market-distorting instruments such as wage regulation to pursue equity goals, preferring other instruments such as cash benefits, the tax system and equal opportunity programs (Argy 2001c).

2 For example, this was clearly the intent of the Campbell Inquiry into the financial system in 1981 when it recommended large-scale deregulation of the financial system (see AFSI 1981: 1.88 and Argy 1995: 33). Sometimes compensation of losers is not practical; if so there are other options available to smooth the social effects (Argy 1999).

3 In this chapter, as in my other writings, the term 'hard liberalism' is deliberately preferred to 'economic rationalism' because the latter term has been used in a number of different senses in the public debate. Sometimes it is equated with what we call hard liberalism but sometimes with what we elsewhere call economic liberalism, and sometimes with both. Furthermore, 'economic rationalism' implies a rational, scientific view of the world – a notion that is alien to any ideology or set of values, including hard liberalism.

4   T.H. Green, L.T. Hobhouse, John Rawls, T.H. Marshall, I.M.D. Little and John
     Maynard Keynes were the pioneers of such thinking (although none of these
     people can be described as egalitarian). See *Biography of Keynes* by Robert Skidelsky,
     Macmillan (2000); Little (1950); John Rawls (1971); and Peter Self (1993: 252).

5   A stark illustration of the 'small government for its own sake' mentality is the fre-
     quently raised suggestion that the public sector should be limited to one-quarter of
     GDP by legislation or even by constitutional amendment. The latest such sugges-
     tion comes from Kasper (2000).

6   That said, it is premature to call the current Howard government policy platform
     'hard liberal'. The Government has taken several cautious steps in the direction of
     hard liberalism and would be moving farther and faster if it controlled the Senate,
     but it is pragmatic and does not want to get too far ahead of public opinion.

7   Sources of information include Budget Papers, Productivity Commission Reports
     on Government Services: 1999 to 2001, Australian Housing & Urban Research
     Institute, the writings of Professor Richard Teese, Agnes Walker (2000: p. 15),
     Social Health Atlas, and various opinion surveys.

8   Sources: Parham et al. (2000: xxix), Harding and Szukalaska (1999: 22), Harding
     (1997), ACIRRT (1998), Quiggin (2001), and Barnes and Fields (2001). There is no
     conclusive evidence of rising job insecurity (Wooden 1999 and chapter in this
     volume) and casuals are a diverse group (Murtough and Waite 2000). However, the
     strong relative increase in casual contract employees suggests that an increasing pro-
     portion of workers are without regulatory protection on benefits, lay-off notices,
     working hours and working conditions, and are more exposed to income variability.

9   (See Warby 2000: 373; and Department of Family and Community Services,
     Income Support statistics 1998–1999: 110) – while last year's figures for social
     spending may kick up one should ideally remove the one-off distorting effects of
     GST compensation.

10   These are non-cash benefits for low- to middle-income families, for example, from
     subsidised education and health care. These benefits are dwindling because of
     government reluctance to borrow and the middle-class squeeze.

11   At the federal level, protection of workers through awards and human rights laws
     and human rights has shrunk (see Argy 2000a). However, at the state level, Labor
     governments are trying to strengthen existing laws to protect low-paid workers but
     the opposition is so strong (both from the Upper Houses and from industry and
     the media) that there is no certainty how these will proceed.

12   A new book by Robert Pultnam (*Bowling Alone*) has attempted to show quantita-
     tively the 'disappearing togetherness' of modern societies. Some argue that this
     phenomenon is in good part caused by excessive involvement of the state and that
     a lesser involvement would help rebuild social capital (*Economist* 31/3/2001: 54).
     But it would be a high-risk option to test out such a hypothesis in practice because
     of the inevitable short-term social disruption it would cause. In any case what is
     'fair' about leaving the task of social responsibility for the poor to just a few kind
     souls (some of whom could require recipients to embrace particular moral or reli-
     gious positions) and giving other citizens a free ride?

13   See Withers and Edwards (2001). The evidence of growing social conservatism is
     still inconclusive and is discussed in other papers by the author, including Argy
     (2001b and 2001c).

14   Even Greenspan (the US Federal Reserve Chairman) believes that if you want to
     reduce the budget surplus lower taxes are preferable to higher spending. Why?
     Because he trusts individuals more than politicians.

15   The counter points here are developed in Argy (1998 and 1999). The results of
     surveys of economists are in Argy (2001a).

16 As discussed in Argy 1998; Borland (this volume); Dawkins 2000; Keating 2000; CEDA's Pathways to Work (CEDA Bulletin March 2001) and various chapters in Bell (2000).

17 Borland in this volume is sceptical of the employment merits of a freeze on safety net wages, even with compensatory payments, as proposed by Dawkins and his four fellow economists and on a lesser scale by Argy (1998: 97–8). Borland suggests a better option might be to exempt some low-wage employees from payroll taxes. Argy (1998) also focused on payroll tax as an element in tax reform (p. 141).

18 This is the conclusion drawn from international evidence, see Argy (1998); (Goodwin et al. 1999); Putterman et al. (1998); and Atkinson (1999).

19 Using updated figures, two RBA economists question the Vince Fitzgerald view that Australia has paid a sizeable risk premium as a result of its external debt build-up (David Gruen and Glenn Stevens, *RBA Conference Proceedings* 2000: 60)

20 There is extensive survey-based economic literature on the determinants of happiness. It shows that, while aggregate economic outcomes such as economic growth and unemployment are important sources of happiness, a person's happiness also depends critically on how he or she compares with and relates to others, so communal services shared by all yield more satisfaction than private consumption, especially if the latter is unevenly shared. See, for example, Dixon (1997), Oswald (1997) and Frank (1997).

21 As compensation is not always practical and there are few policies without losers, Savage (1999) argues that phasing in reforms over a long period and even abandoning some reforms altogether may be more welfare-enhancing than using compensatory redistribution policies. Ian Manning (in this volume) warns that the approach of letting markets rip and then attending to equity concerns solely through redistribution is inadequate. Argy (1999) explores alternatives to targeted compensation such as log rolling (introducing alternative reforms in tandem) and reform dilution (for example, postponing a reform or modifying it to make it more socially acceptable).

5

Equity and Growth

Ian Manning

An important result of Keynes' emphasis on active macroeconomic management was that economic growth came to be quantified. Growth in GDP has
become the standard definition, though various alternatives are available from
the National Accounts. For those interested in standards of living, National
Income is more relevant than GDP, and indeed one might narrow this to
Household Income or to Aggregate Consumption. Despite this range of
choice, the convention remains that economic growth can be quantified as
growth in a flow of goods and services at market value. By contrast, there is no
conventional quantification for equity.

There is a sense in which equity stands for those values that are not incorporated into GDP; that is, for off-market values. Substitution of prior non-market
values for market values can substantially revalue GDP and can also change the
trend. By revaluing GDP to create a Genuine Progress Indicator, the Australia
Institute has claimed that there has been very little genuine economic growth in
Australia since the mid-1970s (Hamilton and Denniss 2000). However, the widespread acceptance of GDP as the conventional growth indicator makes it
difficult to propose the substitution of prior values for market values. In any case,
the hard liberalism that currently dominates politics holds that market prices are
valid measures of the social value of different goods and services produced.
(Hard liberalism is a convenient synonym for 'market dogma', defined by Self as
the 'cut-down, simplified and action-oriented' version of neo-liberal economics,
which holds that 'free markets are the principal source of wealth'; that 'large
incentives are necessary to market efficiency' and that 'market-led growth
trickles down to the benefit of all' (Self 2000, chapter 1; Argy, this volume).

Market valuation has also been indirectly supported by postmodern intel-
lectuals. It is not that they approve of market values, but that the nihilism
which prevents their endorsement of market values also prevents endorsement
of systems of prior values by which market values may be judged and found

wanting. However, nihilism has not been accepted as the final end of the European intellectual tradition (Küng 1980), and is certainly not accepted in less individualistic traditions. Discarding both nihilism and hard liberalism opens up a wide field of ethical criticisms of market valuation, and hence of economic growth as conventionally measured.

The prior values that may lead to reassessment of the quality and direction of economic growth are bewildering in their variety. They include both secular and religious systems of ethics, and may be egalitarian or hierarchical; of recent provenance or deeply traditional. In Australian discussions, equity has frequently been glossed as fairness, justice and the absence of exploitation, all of which are capable of both process and outcome interpretations. The difference between process and outcome is typified by the frequently analysed divergence between equality of opportunity and equality of income and wealth. Equity is about how economic activity is carried out, and also about the distribution of results. The compromise between these interpretations that underlay Australian government policy in the postwar era was that there should be equality of opportunity in education and in employer recruitment, but that the inequality of market rewards should be accepted, tempered by a social security system providing a minimum income to people who were not able to earn for themselves.

An uncomfortable aspect of ethics is the question of individual dessert. Hard liberalism holds that those who profit from markets deserve their riches, and conversely that those who do not so profit deserve their poverty. This is denied by all other systems of ethics, some of which disagree mildly (as does neo-liberal economics when it denies that monopolists deserve their profits), but most of which disagree strongly. From nearly all ethical points of view, market systems often reward the undeserving and punish the deserving. Even to the extent that they reward deserving recipients, the range of reward – from filthy rich to abject poverty – is far greater than can be justified. There is an interesting echo here of the New Testament, which is happy to enjoy the ordinary material life of working, eating, drinking and feasting, but is deeply suspicious of riches – they are likely to be ill-gotten, and are the mark of an individual with the wrong priorities – and adopts a non-judgemental approach to poverty.

From these equitable points of view, growth in GDP is not necessarily desirable. Growth is inequitable if it rewards the undeserving rich rather than the poor; it is also inequitable if it imposes undeserved environmental costs on future generations. Insofar as GDP reflects price patterns determined by the market (and marketing) power of the rich, the very measure itself is faulted.

In the rest of this chapter, we will consider three approaches to the relationship between equity and growth. The first is the hard liberalism claim that equitable rules inherited from the past are an impediment to growth. The second is that growth should be the primary end of economic policy, but with supplementary redistribution to satisfy equitable concerns. The third is that equitable constraints to the range of market outcomes are not only justifiable in themselves, but actually enhance growth.

Equity as an impediment to growth

Hard liberalism holds that the pursuit of equity often restricts the growth of GDP. Apart from taxation, the most frequently vilified set of moralistic restrictions limit the flexibility of the labour market, generally in the employees' favour. However, for an example of equitable curbs to economic growth we turn to the restrictions on gambling that persisted up to the early 1990s.

The removal of restrictions on gambling indeed led to a burst of economic growth (NIEIR 1997, Costello and Millar 2000). Investors rushed to finance the construction of casinos, clubs and pubs, and employment was generated servicing a previously latent demand. Yet there are several reasons to re-evaluate this growth. The first is that the net contribution to growth depends on how much disbenefit is deducted for the despair of a new generation of problem gamblers. This negative adjustment is likely to rise with time (Productivity Commission 1999). Even were this not so, traditional ethics holds that gambling generates undeserved incomes for those who control the odds. Finally, economic analysis has found that the surge in gambling was financed from savings, which is not a good idea in a country that under-saves (NIEIR 2000).

This final problem is merely a symptom of the Federal Treasurer's dilemma, which first arose during the 1980s. The dilemma was this: the level of investment in production of tradable goods and services has not been sufficient to create enough aggregate demand to generate full employment and economic growth. Treasurers have accordingly condoned easy money policies, which in the 1990s were directed mainly towards increasing consumer demand. This fed a boom, but unfortunately reduced household savings. The result is that consumers are now heavily indebted to financial intermediaries, to a point that is not merely of domestic significance: the poor performance of the Australian tradables sector has resulted in a balance-of-payments deficit, and the consumer boom has been financed by the banks becoming heavily indebted to overseas lenders. The casino economy was but a facet of the consumption economy (Beder 2000).

This brings us to a further example of the removal of equitable impediments to the working of markets. Many if not all of the regulations that were imposed on the banks after the depressions of the 1890s and 1930s were equitable in purpose, particularly those that controlled interest rates and limited the creation and directed the flow of credit. By the 1970s financial innovation had found its way round many of these regulations, which accordingly were not serving their intended purpose. Rather than update the regulations, it was decided to remove them as impediments to market-led growth.

The deregulated financial sector prides itself on its ability to identify investment opportunities that will contribute to economic growth, and to package risk and uncertainty so that they are carried by willing risk-takers. Judged by technical indicators, the Australian financial sector may indeed claim to be efficient (Shields, this volume). However, there are at least two problems with this claim. A first, serious, problem is that it lets governments, other industry and the financial institutions themselves (with some honourable exceptions) off the hook. In a country where investment opportunities in the tradable sector are deficient, there is a need to work together to create and sustain such opportunities and so resolve the Treasurer's dilemma (Marceau, Cutler, this volume). The second problem is that the financial sector, left to itself, has a propensity to generate market values for financial instruments that are out of kilter with the values in underlying product and service markets. In the course of absorbing risk and uncertainty, speculative activity randomly walks into booms and slumps (Shiller 2000). We are back with Keynes' 1930s description of the stock exchange and its related institutions as a casino.

A major difference between the financial casino in inter-war London and current Australian financial markets derives from the Commonwealth's attempt to reconcile hard liberalism with equity through its National Super-annuation policy (Disney and Krever 1996). The rich punters of Keynes' day have been replaced by fund managers, the insecure agents of the trustees of superannuation funds, who in turn are under legal obligation to seek high and stable returns. Not a casino so much as a theatre, with the fund managers anonymous in the darkened auditorium, and the CEOs of major corporations performing on the other side of the lights. Performers have the impossible task of delivering both capital gains and a high flow of dividends, and receive celebrity rewards. The acknowledged weakness of this system is its concentration on short-term returns, from which may be traced other more general economic weaknesses: excessive dividend payouts and CEO salaries; insufficient exploration of investment opportunities in small, medium and regional business; and insufficient supply of venture capital. Net corporate savings, which used to contribute substantially to capital accumulation, have, like household savings, substantially disappeared.

The imperative to maximise both dividends and capital gains directs attention towards short-term cost control, including economising on technological development and minimising wage and tax costs. Strict wage control undermines demand, but heavy expenditure on marketing has prolonged the boom, underpinned by a flow of consumer loans that, individually, seem low-risk but that, in the event of a recession, will land many households in deep financial trouble. As with gambling, there is a suspicion that excess rewards have accrued within parts of the financial system (though flows of funds are so complex that the pattern is hard to determine), that some of the borrowers will fall into undeserved poverty, and that some of the lenders will undeservedly lose their assets.

This account does not deny the potential contribution that the financial sector can make to economic growth. However, on the evidence of the pattern of growth over the past two decades, there is a strong case that Australia's financial deregulation interacted with other institutional weaknesses and so failed to create a system that meets equitable tests; not only the distributional tests already discussed, but the test of equity between generations. At present this is a provisional judgement, but it is all too likely that the high level of indebtedness, particularly overseas indebtedness, coupled with the low level of real capital accumulation in industries producing tradable goods and services, will place an undeserved burden on future generations.

The deregulation of the banks in the 1980s, like the subsequent deregulation of gambling, removed ethically based impediments to the play of market forces. Judging by the growth of value added in the financial services and gambling sectors, both deregulations were successful in accelerating short-run growth. However, there are good reasons to doubt the long-run contribution to growth of the deregulation of gambling, and to ponder the contribution of deregulated banking to the present consumer/casino economy.

Supplementary equity

The view that equity is an impediment to growth is not the only approach to the relationship. A second view is conceptually sequential. Growth is maximised by the unfettered play of market forces, which, in conjunction with the initial distribution of wealth, results in a market distribution of income and a market distribution of goods and services produced. The state then redistributes to counter the inequitable aspects of these market distributions. This approach is compatible with the removal of impediments to market forces other than taxation, on which it relies for funding. It can be made to fit with the view that there should be minimal interference with markets, but it is also compatible with the imposition of equitable restrictions on markets. Where it is combined with a hands-off attitude to markets, it may be termed the 'equity-fix' approach; where it is combined with management of markets on equitable grounds it leads to welfare states.

Redistribution by governments supplements the redistribution that takes place within families, including the pooling of income between spouses, the transfer of income from parents to meet children's needs, and the sharing of income within extended families. The primary task of intra-family redistribution is to meet the needs of dependants within the family. The government system concentrates more on provision of income for people who, for acceptable reason, have no or little market income and are not in a position to receive intra-family transfers. However, the systems overlap: the government system pays more to claimants with dependants than to single people, and the family system often provides additional help to extended family members whose primary source of income is government cash benefits.

Those whose archetype for government-sponsored redistribution is intra-family sharing are regularly challenged by those who see government redistribution as an extension of market activities such as insurance. The advantage of the analogy with insurance in countries infected with hard liberalism is that schemes can be more generous; they are also inevitably more complicated. There can also be attempts to substitute financial markets institutions for redistribution, as in the National Superannuation scheme. By their nature, however, such schemes cannot effect any real redistribution (Shiller 2000: 220–2).

In all wealthy and middle-income countries, redistribution of income is considerably supplemented by redistribution through tax-financed services, particularly education and health services. Redistribution of wealth (the stock rather than the flow) is also a possibility, but with the abolition of death duties Australian governments have ceased to tax stocks of wealth as distinct from flows of income and expenditure. Finally, redistribution in Australia includes an elaborate system of fiscal equalisation that determines Commonwealth grants to the states and territories, coupled with a complete lack of attention to the distribution of income, wealth and productive capacity between regions within states.

According to the equity-fix approach, the primary task of taxes, social security and redistributive services such as health and education is to convert the pattern of market incomes (and to a much lesser extent the pattern of inherited wealth) to a pattern that is equitably tolerable, and that in particular prevents destitution. Market rewards are taken as given, so there is no attempt to penalise undeserved riches. In Australia this forbearance has, over the past few decades, been balanced by a quite Biblical willingness to forgo the distinction between deserved and undeserved poverty.

The Australian redistributive system as it developed in the postwar period was founded on the full employment of men, in full-time jobs. Consolidated revenue financed pensions, subject to means test, for the elderly, for widows and the disabled; and provided benefits, subject to a strict means test, for temporarily sick people and the unemployed. Unemployment benefit was also subject to a work test, and, with full employment, it was unusual for claimants to remain on benefit for more than a month. Other major elements in the system were the provision of free, secular and compulsory education and public hospitals by the states.

The Australian system contrasted with contemporary systems in Europe. These systems were financed from social insurance contributions, and were on the whole more generous, and certainly less targeted, than the Australian system. During the 1970s, at the end of full employment, tentative steps were being taken to reform Australian social security on European lines; for example, by abolition of the means test for age pensions. More significantly, government funding for tertiary and private education was increased, and government subsidies for private health insurance were replaced by direct finance of health services.

The end of full employment considerably increased the stresses on the system. With the fall in the rate of economic growth, the number of eligible claimants rose, increasing expenditure requirements, but at the same time tax resistance became popular (Manning 1998). Following hard liberalism, governments attempted to off-load responsibilities on to private provision, but found that off-loading had to be sweetened with government subsidies, and accordingly yielded little in tax cuts. It also generated opposition on equitable grounds. The main emphasis was therefore to target social security on the relief of poverty. Two main difficulties arose. First, under conditions of high unemployment it was difficult to apply the work test as a means of targeting those who should not be expected to earn their own living. Second, tighter targeting stressed the means test. Steep means tests had not been much of a practical problem in the days of full-time jobs and a minimum wage set above social security levels, but have created marked adverse incentives and poverty traps in a world where many jobs, particularly unskilled jobs, are part-time, casual or both. The hard liberalism of tax minimisation confronted the hard liberalism of incentive maximisation.

Despite these problems, if the Australian redistributive system is judged as a means of converting the distribution of private income into something a little more egalitarian, it responded magnificently to the end of full employment. At the individual level, the private market trends were for increased inequality of earnings, reflecting increased dispersion both in hours worked and in wage and salary rates. At the household level, increased job-holding by married women tended to align household incomes with household size and hence had an egalitarian effect, but this was counterbalanced by an increase in the number of no-earner households. In the early 1990s there was a strong trend for the middle to fall out of the individual income distribution: between 1991 and 1996 the proportion of individuals with incomes under $(1991) 25 000 increased, as did the proportion with incomes over $(1991) 50 000, balanced by a fall in the proportion receiving middle incomes. Several investigators have independently assessed trends in Australian income distribution in the decades from the first ABS income survey in 1975 to the most recent in the mid-1990s, and concluded that the distribution of private income was becoming less egalitarian, but that this trend was countered by redistribution both within households and by governments (Johnson et al. 1995). Unfortunately there are not yet any data on trends since 1996, but at least till then the redistribution system earned high marks for its contribution to non-judgemental, egalitarian equity.

This is not to argue that the Australian redistributive system is above reproach. Recently, Goodin et al. compared the social security systems of The Netherlands, Germany and the United States. They concluded that The Netherlands system, which combines high social insurance contribution rates with relatively generous payouts and relatively few means tests, is superior to the American in prevention of destitution, yet does not appear to be a practical impediment to economic growth (Goodin et al. 1999). Due to lack of a longitudinal data set, the Australian system could not be incorporated into this comparison, but in its low payment rates and pervasive means tests it comes closer to the American than to The Netherlands' system.

A more fundamental criticism is that unemployment benefit is no substitute for employment. Not only does widespread reliance on social security in lieu of employment incomes threaten the economics of the social security system; unemployment generates social costs in its own right. These costs give rise to the hard liberals' dilemma: how is it possible that an increasingly market-based, competitive economy does not yield full employment? Hard liberalism provides an answer: there cannot be sufficient competition in labour markets. This answer leads to an attack on trade unions, but the social security system may also be partly to blame; it may be too generous and so be undermining the needed competition.

If insufficient competition is the problem, how is it that unemployment is concentrated among the young, the unskilled and the deskilled? This must be because these groups of workers are not in demand; accordingly governments should sponsor training schemes, and should ease means tests so that people can combine social security and whatever part-time and casual work is available. This approach has had its successes, but also its failures: people who go through all the hoops but still somehow do not find work. In the 'mutual obligation' expression of this approach put forward in the McClure (2000) report, social security recipients of workforce age are to be subject to social worker attention, and if they don't find work after a reasonable amount of assistance has been provided, they may be denied further benefits. The report does not contemplate what they are expected to do if they still cannot find work.

The McClure report reflects the recent revival, in the United States, of faith in social work intervention (Meade 2000). It disregards the experience of the US War on Poverty of the 1960s, when social worker intervention on a mass scale was tried and found wanting. The report has no appreciation of the scale required; it is notable for a complete lack of quantification. It is notable also for giving very little weight to a shortcoming of the market economy that is at once politically embarrassing, important for social security policy, and revealing of the deficiencies of economic policy: the very wide divergence in economic performance between Australian regions over the past decade or two. This is all the more surprising in that, *de facto*, the social security system has long distinguished between regions of high and low unemployment. Long periods of unemployment tend to make people unemployable, and often depress their spirit, and there comes a point where the administration transfers them to disability payments and so out of the statistical workforce. Not surprisingly, the flow on to disability pensions is strongest in regions of high unemployment. Mutual obligation policies that work in areas of full employment are likely to be rapidly discredited in areas of high structural unemployment. This provides the theme for our last section, on equity as the *sine qua non* of growth.

The complementarity of equity and growth

The equity-fix approach of letting the market rip and attending to equity concerns solely through redistribution is inadequate on several grounds. From the point of view of equality of opportunity, the current Australian economy is providing serious inequalities of educational opportunity, and is failing to provide paid work opportunities for all who want them. From an egalitarian point of view, it is generating too wide a spread of income and wealth. Too many of the high incomes, and too much wealth, is undeserved.

The limits of the equity-fix approach can be seen in the strain that is currently being imposed on redistribution by high unemployment exacerbated by regional inequalities. The Australian redistribution system was designed for full employment, and despite its sterling performance since the end of full employment, benefits are no substitute for jobs. The deficiencies of hard liberalism were also implicit in the criticism, in the first part of this chapter, of changes made to remove perceived equitable barriers to growth. The various deregulations may have yielded short-term growth, but growth in the longer term requires taking the hype out of casinos (which will help rebuild household savings) and calming the financial theatre (which will help rebuild corporate savings). It also requires the generation of a surge of long-term investment, to utilise the increased savings and replace casinos and debt-financed consumption as the demand foundation of growth.

This sounds like a conservative recommendation for a return to the foundations of growth as they applied in the postwar period. However, the other chapters in this book show that there can be no such return. In the postwar economy, maintenance of aggregate demand was sufficient to prevent unemployment. That is no longer the case. The boom now ending was notable both for its lack of job generation and for its geographic patchiness. After allowance for government window-dressing by transfer of the unemployed to Disability Support Payments, the national unemployment rate fell by less than a percentage point from 1996 to 2000, while over the same four years unemployment in Sydney east of Olympic Park decreased to full-employment levels even on postwar definitions; and in other areas such as north-west Tasmania it increased to (officially) 10 per cent and (after adjustment) to over 20 per cent. (For further analysis see O'Connor, Stimson and Baum, this volume.)

Regional disparity is yet another example of an inequitable market result. It blights the opportunities of people in the disfavoured regions, and punishes them further with undeserved capital losses; it rewards people in the favoured regions with undeserved capital gains. It also constrains economic growth, since aggregate demand has to be managed so as not to be excessive in the favoured regions at the same time as resources are under-utilised in the disfavoured regions. This is a novel situation in Australia, though not in the United States or Europe. Why do such regional disparities arise?

One explanation for the increase in regional disparity interprets the recent boom along the lines put forward in the first part of this chapter: the boom was essentially a consumption/casino bubble; and the benefits went mainly to the people who organised the bubble – the financiers, the ad-personnel, media people and the like, all of them heavily concentrated in the major cities. The second explanation senses something more fundamental: a change in world best practice in the organisation of production, relying on information technology, on networking and the development of industry clusters, and leading to profound changes in labour markets (Brain 1999, Marceau, Cutler this volume). Demand for the services of unskilled and traditionally skilled workers is falling away, but demand for symbolic analysts is rising while demand for workers with interpersonal skills is being maintained. According to this explanation, the concentration of growth in the major cities reflects the formation of mutually supportive brain-work networks in these cities. The next recession will correct the consumption/casino excesses, but the underlying changes in industry organisation will not go away so easily, and so far have strongly favoured the metropolitan regions. Some would argue that this is necessarily the case, given the nature of the knowledge economy, but it is also arguable that the non-metropolitan regions are falling behind due to an educational and infrastructure lag.

If this is the case, not only does the 1990s pattern of growth, with its heavy bias towards the major cities, create problems for redistribution; it limits growth. Aggregate demand cannot be allowed to exceed levels sustainable in Global Sydney. This level of aggregate demand leaves resources unemployed in the high-unemployment regions, and includes suppression of investment opportunities in these regions. The obvious remedy is region-specific assistance through direction of financial flows and by infrastructure investments and education. This remedy is contra to hard liberalism, and provides an example of how this dogma limits growth. Enhancing the flow of investment to non-metropolitan areas will challenge the combined skills of regional business, local, state and national government, and the financial sector. An important first step will be to stop the superannuation funds from harvesting regional savings and investing the proceeds in metropolitan property and overseas.

The lack of regional policy in Australia provides an example of hard liberalism that both limits growth and makes it difficult to maintain equity. Another example is the failure to provide education in the skills demanded by the knowledge economy, including educational opportunity for all without regard to parental income or region. Despite the current fashion for business courses, the skills required by the knowledge economy are highly disparate, and include an emphasis on cultural skills: the 'arts' skills so denigrated by hard liberalism (Soete 2000). When people are equipped with such skills, the content of production (and the values on which GDP is based) can shift away from mass goods to a more varied and sophisticated mixture that takes advantage of the opportunities opened up by developments in information technology. Improving skills must be matched with the capacity to employ the skills (the alternative is a brain-drain); hence, a requirement for a much more sophisticated pattern of investment, with regional policy as a key aspect.

Conclusion

We have considered two cases where legal restrictions, based on equity, have been perceived as impediments to growth. In both cases (gambling and financial deregulation) deregulation has been favourable to growth in the short run, but dubious in the long. More generally, rising unemployment and regional divergence in unemployment rates have greatly increased the difficulty of redistribution, to the point where the system faces breakdown. Both redistribution, and markets themselves, work best within legal frameworks that express equitable requirements much more strongly than the laws envisaged by hard liberalism.

Such a system would also accord with values that are increasingly being recognised: that we, the participants in economic life, should work to satisfy our needs (as distinct from wants); that we should not rob future generations; that we should share the fruits around, and that we should take time to enjoy them. And that we should develop sufficient self-confidence to ridicule the undeserving rich and the patterns of economic growth that derive from their values.

References

Beder, S. (2000) *Selling the Work Ethic*, Melbourne, Scribe.
Brain, P. (1999) *Beyond Meltdown*, Melbourne, Scribe.
Costello, T. and Millar, R. (2000) *Wanna Bet?* St Leonards, Allen & Unwin.
Disney, J. and Krever, R. (eds) (1996) *Superannuation, Savings and Taxation*, Canberra, Centre for International and Public Law, Australian National University.
Goodin, R. et al. (1999) *The Real Worlds of Welfare Capitalism*, Cambridge, Cambridge University Press.
Gregory, B. (1996) 'Wage Deregulation, Low Paid Workers and Full Employment', in Sheehan, P., Grewal, B. and Kumnick, M. (eds) *Dialogues on Australia's Future*, Melbourne, Centre for Strategic Economic Studies, Victoria University.
Hamilton, C. (1998) 'Measuring Changes in Economic Welfare: The Genuine Progress Indicator for Australia', in Eckersley, R. (ed.) *Measuring Progress, is Life Getting Better?* Melbourne, CSIRO.
Hamilton, C. and Denniss, R. (2000) 'Tracking well-being in Australia: The Genuine Progress Indicator', Canberra, Australia Institute Discussion Paper no. 35.
Johnson, D., Manning, I. and Hellwig, O. (1995) *Trends in the Distribution of Cash Income and Non-Cash Benefits*, Canberra, Dept of Prime Minister and Cabinet.

Küng, H. (1980) *Does God Exist?* London, Collins.

Lloyd, R., Harding, A. and Hellwig, O. (2000) *Regional Divide? A Study of Incomes in Regional Australia*, Canberra, NATSEM Discussion Paper no. 51.

Manning, I. (1998) 'Policies: Past and Present', in Fincher, R. and Nieuwenhuysen, J. (eds) *Australian Poverty Then and Now*, Melbourne, Melbourne University Press.

McClure, P. (Reference Group on Welfare Reform) (2000) *Participation Support for a More Equitable Society*, Canberra, Minister for Family and Community Services.

Meade, L. (2000) 'Welfare Reform and the Family: Lessons from America', in Saunders, P. (ed.) *Reforming the Australian Welfare State*, Melbourne, Institute for Family Studies.

National Institute of Economic and Industry Research (1997) *The Impact of Gambling on Victorian Employment*, Melbourne, Victorian Casino and Gaming Authority.

National Institute of Economic and Industry Research (2000) *The Economic Impact of Gambling*, Melbourne, Victorian Casino and Gaming Authority.

Productivity Commission (1999) *Australian Gambling*, Canberra.

Self, P. (2000) *Rolling Back the Market*, London, Macmillan.

Shiller, R.J. (2000) *Irrational Exuberance*, Melbourne, Scribe.

Soete, L. (2000) 'Technology, Globalisation and Employment: Analytical and Policy Challenges', in Heijke, H. and Muyksen, J. (eds) *Education and Training in a Knowledge-Based Economy*, London, Macmillan.

6

Economic Growth and the Ethical State: Refashioning an Australian Settlement

Brian Howe

Political debate over the past two decades has been dominated by macroeconomics. Latest balance-of-trade figures head the nightly news bulletins and, along with the weather report, the exchange rate of the dollar and the Dow Jones close them. It is indicative of how much politics in Australia has collapsed almost entirely into a discourse of economic management. Reflecting on the 1980s, cultural commentator Meaghan Morris recalls:

> I saw men on television (trade union stars, Cabinet Ministers, left-wing think-tank advisers) visibly hystericized by talking economics: eyes would glaze, shoulders hunch, lips tremble in a sensual paroxysm of 'letting the market decide', 'making the hard decisions', 'levelling the playing field', 'reforming management practices', 'improving productivity' and 'changing the workplace culture' (1992: 51–2).

Of course, economics has always figured in a major way in Australian public policy debates. Economic arguments were central to the debates about why the Australian colonies should federate, and disjunct political struggles have coalesced around the right to a living wage, guaranteed by the state (Morris 1992: 78). However, the rise of neo-liberal economics over the past two decades is a major challenge to the way in which economics has been mobilised in Australian public debate. As Morris points out, neo-liberalism's belief that markets allocate resources better than planners might appear on the surface a simple proposition, except for the fact that for much of its modern history Australia has been governed by the opposite assumption (Morris 1992: 52).

This chapter traces some of that earlier history in an attempt to uncover a notion of economic policy used in pursuit of certain social and ethical ends. This involves moving beyond a simple dichotomy of 'free marketeers' versus 'planners'. It involves a recognition that, in earlier periods, economic exchange operated in a cultural context that presumed there were limits to the reach of the market.

For example, economists have long recognised that aspects of growth – the production and reproduction of labour, on a daily and generational basis – depend vitally on the non-market functioning of households, but have tended to take this for granted (Elson 1998). The nature of the gender 'contract' that governs household work has changed over time, but in most economic discourse it remains as overshadowed as it was for nineteenth-century economists. We might not wish to simply resurrect those earlier cultural forms of non-market activity. However, any new imagining of an Australian policy settlement can no longer afford to ignore the important flows of material, emotional and cultural resources generated in the non-market sphere of caring labour, nor attempt to simply subsume such flows into the logic of the 'free' market (see Cass 1994: 5).

Marian Sawer's recent work on the nineteenth-century liberal conception of the ethical role of the state is useful here. That conception saw the state as a vehicle of social justice and a countervailing power to the market (Sawer 2000). By way of example, this chapter focuses on the interconnection between workplace arrangements and the burden of paid and unpaid work. By raising the importance of the so-called 'private' or non-market sphere, and the failure of public-policy responses to recognise this importance, the discussion around the state's capacity for social investment is widened.

Economic policy as social policy: the rise and rise of the Australian settlement

In his account of Labor in government in the 1980s and 1990s, Paul Kelly used the term 'the Australian settlement' to refer to a combination of five policy elements that were consolidated or 'settled' in the first years of Federation: White Australia, Industry Protection, Wage Arbitration, State Paternalism and Imperial Benevolence (Kelly 1994). Kelly's aim was to give an account of fairly recent political events, and his brief historical analysis is clearly subordinated to this purpose. The old policy 'settlement' – characterised as eight decades of policy inertia – is mobilised as a counterpoint to the more vibrant, forward-looking, internationally open and multicultural contemporary era inaugurated by Hawke and Keating (Maddox 1998: 64).

Kelly's account is important, for it helped recast political debate as a simple dichotomy between those 'international rationalists . . . who know the Australian Settlement is unsustainable' and the 'sentimental traditionalists . . . who fight to retain it' (1994: 2). However, the idea of an Australian settlement has a richer lineage and a more complex trajectory than Kelly's account allows, and one that cannot be reduced to a simple economic debate between neoliberalism and a discredited protectionism. Kelly bowdlerises a far more nuanced account by Frank Castles who identified an interlocking set of policies brokered around the time of Federation, whereby capital was guaranteed favourable conditions for investment (through protective tariffs) and labour was offered the protection of minimum wages and conditions through conciliation and arbitration, and protection from putatively cheap non-white immigrant workers.

Castles and others point to H.B. Higgins' 1907 Harvester judgment as a key moment of the Australian settlement. In that case, Higgins determined the basic wage by reference to what would constitute a fair living standard for a male worker and his family rather than by what the market would bear (*Ex parte McKay* (1907) 2 CAR 1). However, it would be wrong to see the Harvester judgment as both the beginning and end point of the Australian settlement. Although the fixing of a minimum wage was initially explicitly linked with tariff protection, the legal basis for this link was struck down by the High Court soon after Harvester (*R v Barger* (1908) 6 CLR 41). The generalisation of the Harvester judgment as a genuine minimum standard to the mass of white male workers then became a fairly long and slow process. It entailed extending the Arbitration Court's jurisdiction to include controls over the supply of cheap labour such as non-union workers, subcontractors, outworkers, piece workers and apprentices. The emergence of a 'standard employment relationship', underpinned by substantial award coverage, did not really occur until the postwar period. It was the result not only of arbitral decisions that attempted to 'de-casualise' certain industries, but also trade union struggles to standardise employment around full-time contracts of indefinite duration, and employer strategies in major industries to vertically integrate their profit-making activities and retain workers in a time of increased labour scarcity and labour turnover.

Furthermore, while the Federation settlement identified by Castles depended for its success on the generalisation of the wage-earner model, it also depended, at the level of the household, on the male breadwinner/female carer model of the nuclear family. Whereas for adult men it was vital that they could find a job, for other family members it was vital that they could secure themselves a breadwinner (see O'Donnell and Hancock 2000). This was because the earliest arbitral decisions set a 'family wage' for male workers but not female workers, assuming that men would normally be the providers while women would normally perform maternal roles. Thus Australian settlement was extended and consolidated through the rapid rise in marriage during the postwar period. For the three decades from the early 1940s to the early 1970s, the age of first marriage for men and women dropped steadily and the marriage rate rose steadily (Murphy 2000: 19). In effect, an increasing number of women, not entitled to the 'family wage' on their own account, gained access to male wages through marrying a 'breadwinner'.

In short, the postwar model was based on quite specific assumptions about working life and social relations, especially the desirability of uninterrupted full-time paid employment for men and married women's full-time unpaid work in the home. In terms of the generalisation of the wage-earner model and a full-employment economy, the postwar settlement represented quite a different beast from the structures set up in the first decade of Federation and identified by Kelly.

Social liberalism and the ethical state

The ideas that informed Federation policy debates have recently been revisited by Marian Sawer. Her work and that of other historians is useful for reminding us that the ideas behind the policy settlement were those of radical liberalism and were, to some extent, quite separate from their institutional legacy (see Macintyre 1989). Sawer identifies the influence of British liberals such as T.H. Green in developing an idea of positive liberty that signalled a move beyond the nightwatchman state:

> Individuals only developed their full potential in relationship with the community, and required the means, education and access to culture to participate fully in community life . . . The state had the capacity and the duty to remove social and economic restrictions [on human development] and to promote the positive liberty of the individual; this had priority over rights of property or sanctity of contract . . . The state was no longer seen simply in terms of its role as law enforcer and upholder of contracts, but rather in terms of its ethical mission in nurturing the development of its citizens (Sawer 2000: 69–70).

The social liberals criticised so-called 'free contracts' that became 'an instrument of disguised oppression' due to inequality between the parties. This critique took on a particular saliency in the Australian colonies in the 1890s. During the major industrial disputes of that period, employers had reasserted the principle of 'freedom of contract'; that is, the freedom to settle the terms and conditions of employment by direct negotiation with their workers free from intervention by third parties such as trade unions (Creighton, Ford and Mitchell 1993: 859; Shanahan 1999). In contrast, as Sawer (2000: 80) points out, the social liberal belief was that there should be third-party intervention in market contracts, in particular labour contracts, in the interests of a 'fair go' and, in the wake of the violent confrontations of the 1890s, in the interests of social peace. The rationale behind compulsory conciliation and arbitration was to force employers to negotiate with unions by providing the mechanism whereby parties could apply to an independent tribunal to obtain an arbitrated settlement irrespective of whether employers recognised that a trade union had any legitimate interest in the dispute (Creighton, Ford and Mitchell 1993). Seen in this light, Higgins' minimum wage underpinned workplace bargaining 'as a check on the despotic power' that masqueraded as 'freedom of contract'.

The continuing relevance of social liberalism also explains some of the modifications of the Australian settlement. As already noted, the arbitration system initially enforced a clear gender division of labour by setting differential wage rates for men and women's paid work. As Sawer points out, however, when the notion of gender equality and pay equity gained ground in the late 1960s, 'the social liberal idea of third party intervention in wage contracts, institutionalised in the arbitration system, enabled significant closing of the gender wage gap . . . A wage-fixing system enshrining non-market considerations such as fairness meant that, in terms of equal pay, Australia was able to move well ahead of countries relying on market forces' (Sawer 2000: 88).[1]

Goodbye to all that?

Kelly and others are right to suggest that the past two decades have seen major challenges to many of the policy paradigms established in Australia. What has changed in the past quarter of a century, however, is not just the 'big picture' of macroeconomic policy, but also the nature of daily life. In the workplace, there has been a major growth in non-standard employment arrangements, in particular casual employment, fixed-term employment and contractor- or agency-based employment. Recent studies show that only just over one-third of the labour force now work standard hours, with another third working longer than standard hours, nearly a quarter working only part-time and around 8 per cent not working at all. A fundamental shift in gender relations has also occurred. The shift is clearly seen in the increasing labour force participation of women, especially middle-class married women, a trend that has been consistent regardless of the underlying business cycle or changes in women's wage relativities.[2]

The increasing labour force participation of women, especially middle-class married women, results from an amalgam of factors: changing aspirations and cultural attitudes; new patterns of labour demand in a changing economy; increased participation of women in education, as well as changing patterns of child-bearing and child-rearing. Women are becoming more available for employment and are spending less of their lives with responsibility for children: first births are occurring later, completed families are smaller, the use of child-care has increased, and more women are remaining childless. The presence of children still represents a major divide in women's labour force participation, although recent cohorts of women are returning to paid work more quickly after the birth of a child than women before them.

Taken together, the shifts in gender relations and employment arrangements have radically altered the typical interface between home and work, and have made households' income trajectories increasingly diverse. Paid work at the household level has intensified among people of workforce age; that is, the average number of paid workers per family has increased and the average family is working longer hours to maintain its standard of living. Household needs during these working years have increased, as people make superannuation contributions, pay off HECS debts, meet childcare costs or support children in higher education at home and meet mortgage repayments in a time of declining housing affordability. Under these conditions of work intensification, less work-intensive families are increasingly marginalised. Australia appears to be faced with a growing gulf between 'employment-rich' and 'employment-poor' households, a gulf that now has regional and spatial aspects as well as social. Recent experience shows that jobs growth alone cannot resolve the marginalisation of large numbers of people of workforce age, nor bring down welfare caseloads (Gregory 1999a).

But what we now understand by 'workforce age' has also changed as people stay in education longer and retire earlier. The extent of full-time paid work over the life course has shrunk and full-time work for men – and hence high incomes – is now concentrated in a relatively short period between the ages 35 and 55 (Gregory 1999b). The concentration of working life in a compressed period exacerbates many of the problems of reconciling paid work and family responsibilities.

While the positive effects of women's increasing labour force participation should not be under-estimated, the trend also reveals some stark continuities with the traditional division of labour. First, there is little evidence that women's increased labour force participation has led to men accepting any significantly greater responsibility for the practical or emotional work of householding than they took on under the single breadwinner model (Bittman and Pixley 1997). Rather than representing a choice between *either* paid work *or* domestic labour, many women's increased labour force participation is predicated on the 'double-burden', where, in trying to adapt paid employment to traditional domestic obligations, they become both overworked and under-waged. For a more privileged group, it is predicated on out-sourcing domestic work. In this second case, what has not changed 'is the pattern of paid work of their male partners – a pattern of work they now share' (Probert and Macdonald 1996: 63).

A nation-building state loses its mind[3]

People's wellbeing is sustained by a mixture of non-paid work within households and paid work in the labour market. Non-market work involves many components, and its gendered division and relation to labour market circumstance has been extensively studied (see Ironmonger 1989). This gendered division has at least one clear effect: whereas the presence of children – or other dependent family members – makes little significant difference to men's paid employment patterns, it remains an important determinant of women's labour force participation. There is, then, a clear tension between a market liberalism that encourages women to develop their human capital and sell their labour, and a social conservatism that maintains a gendered division of work in the household.

The issue of fairness in the division of work between men and women, and the capacity for society to guarantee the important flows of material, emotional and cultural resources generated by families that ensure a society's reproduction clearly demand a policy response (Cass 1994). However, during the 1980s, many governments, including Australia's, gave up many of their traditional powers of control over market activity. This does not mean that the state has retreated from economic management; rather a strong and interventionist state has been required to secure the conditions for the operation of market norms, especially in those areas where such norms used not to operate (such as in education, for example, or employment services). In short, social relations and cultural forms previously seen as 'out there', beyond the realm of the market, are increasingly being reconfigured as market relations. Market relations, those of 'free contract', are now seen as the only desirable relations in a society where the aim is to maximise individual autonomy (Bainbridge 1997: 25).

Work, time, family and community

One key area here is the field of the employment relationship, central to earlier imaginings of the Australian settlement. The Coalition government has legislated to encourage individualisation and to marginalise the role of third parties in workplace bargaining, such as trade unions and the Industrial Relations Commission (Deery and Mitchell 1999). Whereas the postwar settlement sustained an increasing homogenisation and external regulation of working life, we are now witnessing an increasing diversification of employment relationships along a number of axes, as regards tenure, hours and location. To some extent, this has provided enhanced possibilities for workers and potential workers. However, the diversity of earnings is one clear example of how these employment arrangements are increasingly mediated through the market. In the postwar period, collective bargaining and internal labour markets meant many workers' tenure and remuneration were dependent on seniority and meeting some minimal performance standard but were buffered from market pressures, such as downturns in product markets or peaks and troughs in demand (see Cappelli et al. 1997: chapter 1). In contrast, the new forms of employment (subcontracting arrangements, short-term contracts, casual labour, variable hours contracts, and so on) are less predictable in terms of tenure and pay and often contingent on market outcomes. On the one hand, they provide managers with tighter control over how labour is employed on the job to ensure all hours worked are productive (Buchanan and Watson 2000). On the other, they shift the burden of market risk on to individual workers and their households.

It is clear that there has been a rapid expansion in part-time, casual and marginal employment in recent times, and also that there are new mechanisms to extend workers' hours, with the current emphasis on greater flexibility affecting the working arrangements of 'standard' and 'non-standard' employees alike. Further, the individualisation of contracts and the move towards performance-related pay can break down the notion of employment being related to time. Task-related pay, as opposed to time-related pay, can require evidence of work commitment; that is, willingness to work extra hours where necessary (Rubery 1997, McCallum 2000). According to Kathryn Heiler, this is cause for some concern. She suggests that: '[T]he progressive assumptions and ideology which often surround the push for greater flexibility in working time arrangements gloss over the variability in outcomes for many workers, and the social and community downside of this so-called flexibility' (Heiler 1998: 76). As suggested above, a key aspect of this trend is the increasing deregulation of the industrial relations environment in which bargaining takes place, but it is also what Heiler (1998: 77) describes as a current policy 'vacuum' around the direction of working time policy in Australia.

There has been an historical trend towards a shortening of the standard working day and week, but this may now have been arrested. Indeed, we are heading towards an average of 42–43 hours for average weekly hours worked for full-timers. Furthermore, a significant proportion of full-timers (33 per cent of men and 15 per cent of women) now work over 49 hours per week with large proportions of this overtime being worked for free. This trend is particularly evident in the increasingly popular model of employment in Australia; that is, white-collar, service sector, 'salaried', and less likely to be unionised (Heiler 1998: 84–5).

Such a move has important implications not only for working conditions in specific industries and workplaces, but also for the establishment and maintenance of community standards in relation to work time and the balance between work and non-work time, including leisure, family and community responsibilities. Heiler argues that the notion of a 'standard' day and week, encapsulated in the awards system, has served as some kind of community standard, implicitly incorporating some distinction between workdays and community and social time (Heiler 1998: 86). As such, the move towards enterprise bargaining, with associated reduction in dependence on awards, potentially weakens the principle of industry and community standards in relation to the use of time, now relegated to discussion at the workplace level.

While it is becoming increasingly clear that home and work can no longer be easily compartmentalised, the capacity of workers to successfully negotiate for working arrangements that will enable them to meet their family responsibilities is still open to question. According to the second Australian Workplace Industrial Relations Survey (undertaken in 1995), 27 per cent of workers surveyed in workplaces with 20 or more employees reported a decline in their satisfaction with the balance between work and family life the year prior to the survey (ACIRRT 1998: 30). Further research by the Australian Centre for Industrial

Relations Research and Training (ACIRRT) points to some rather disappointing outcomes from enterprise agreements negotiated to date in relation to the provision of family-friendly measures. Furthermore, evidence suggests that the inclusion of family-friendly measures in enterprise agreements is limited. According to the *Agreements Database and Monitoring Service*, only 10 per cent of currently operative agreements contain a provision covering at least one such measure. Unpaid personal leave is the most widespread family-friendly measure (9.4 per cent). Paid personal leave, in addition to that offered under sick leave entitlements, is the next most frequent entitlement (3.8 per cent). Job sharing and paid parental leave both appear with equal frequency (3.2 per cent). Other forms of family-friendly provision, including childcare, telecommuting, referral and career break schemes, appear in only 1 per cent of agreements or less (ACIRRT 1998: 30). Given that this report does not include flexibility in hours of work arrangements or parental leave granted as part of sick leave or bereavement leave entitlements, it has been suggested that the ACIRRT report may understate the extent of family-friendly provisions in agreements (see Ross 2000).

The increase in non-standard work, including casual and part-time work, remains an important issue in relation to the integration of work and family responsibilities. While such flexible working hours provisions may enhance the ability of workers to allocate their time effectively between different activities, there is concern as to the potential diminution in conditions such provisions can allow. As casuals do not have access to arbitral and statutory family-friendly initiatives such as carer's leave and parental leave, they are already at a serious disadvantage. While part-time work may enable some to retain security of employment and other benefits while undertaking a caring role, the risk of marginalisation within a system that favours the full-time employee in relation to benefits, training and promotion opportunities remains high. What is clear, however, is that the working hours of many employees do not match their preferences, with the number of part-time employees who would prefer longer hours having grown substantially in Australia. In September 1998, 23 per cent of all people in part-time jobs indicated that they would like to work longer hours. Sixty per cent of these were women (ABS *Australian Social Trends 1999*, Cat. 4102.0, cited in Ross 2000).

Combining 'flexibility' with a deregulated environment may not, therefore, lead to the desired outcomes in relation to work/life balance. Certainly, the ability of the state to take part in the establishment and maintenance of community standards through intervention in the labour contract process is severely limited.

Conclusion

It is in the balance of work, family and community responsibilities that we see a critical convergence of issues related to changes in the labour market and in households. Framed by a diminishing role for the state in the negotiation of workplace contracts and conditions, the key question centres on how to integrate new patterns of household participation in paid and unpaid work with a labour market stripped of much of the external, protective regulation that characterised most of the twentieth century. In particular, the capacity of the state to play a role in the reformulation of community standards on the balance of time spent on various activities is now unclear, despite the importance of such a task in the light of rapid changes taking place both at work and at home.

The rise in the labour force participation of women, an increasingly differentiated array of household types, and a growing range of attitudes and expectations about the roles of men and women require new interactions between work, family and community life. When combined with the ageing of the population and a recognition that family responsibilities extend to caring for elderly, disabled or chronically ill family members as well as children, the importance of such a shift is reinforced. Indeed, according to the Australian Institute of Family Studies, '[t]he reconciliation or harmonisation of workplace demands with domestic and caring tasks may be among the most critical undertakings of this generation' (Wolcott and Glazer 1995: 1).

Historically, a key focus of regulatory concern in the workplace has been on hours of work, signalling the interest of the state not only in workplace conditions but also in ensuring adequate time away from work for those activities and interactions that take place outside the market framework. As Patricia Hewitt puts it: '[f]or as long as there have been employers and employees, there have been disputes over working hours' (1993: 1). These campaigns have been centred on the shorter working day and week for standard workers and, more recently, on the need to recognise changing patterns of work, including in particular the increase in non-standard work, and the desire for a better integration of work and family life. Such changes are fundamentally reordering the ways in which working time is organised in and of itself, as well as changing the relationship between the public and private realms of paid and unpaid labour. The key challenge is how to simultaneously increase flexibility in working time, as well as levels of employment security (see Buchanan and Bearfield 1997: vii) in order to better balance work, family and community commitments.

Marian Sawer concludes her survey of social liberalism with the following observation:

> We seem to have unlearned many of the things which social liberalism taught us, such that 'freedom of choice' is meaningless if we don't have the material and cultural means for self-development. A hundred years ago social liberals knew that it was the duty of the state to intervene, whether in the labour market, the housing market or in other ways, such as through the provision of free schools, libraries, museums and galleries, to ensure such equality of opportunity . . . Today our expectations of what our

governments can or should do have been dramatically reduced. Most worrying is the unlearning of what the social liberals taught us about the oppressive nature of contract where there are inequalities of economic and social power. If government does not intervene in such contracts we have indeed given up on the 'ethical state' in which so much faith was placed a hundred years ago (2000: 90).

This chapter has drawn attention to the issue of both workplace and domestic contracts, and their interconnections, in the context of unequal social and economic power.

There are hopeful signs that, increasingly, economists are turning their attention to those cultural and community contexts in which markets operate. Questions of altruism, reciprocity, trust and social capital are now important topics of research. In pointing to this new research focus, Nancy Folbre and Thomas Weisskopf ask, 'Why this rather surprising loss of confidence in rational economic man? Perhaps he is running into problems because his rational economic wife is no longer taking such good care of him' (1998: 171).

I have identified a tension between a market liberalism that encourages women to develop their human capital and sell their labour in a 'flexible' labour market, and those values, norms and preferences that continue to assign women more responsibility for caring than men. Making it difficult for couples to combine earning with the bearing and care of children will not mean women will rush back to the 'home-and-hearth' model of family life; rather, couples will struggle with alternating periods in and out of employment or simply choose not to have children. One way forward, argue Folbre and Weisskopf, is to develop a new social contract that generates a sense of responsibility for caring labour in both men and women. In doing so it could equitably balance the goals of individual self-realisation and social responsibility. They suggest that policies designed to foster a greater supply of caring labour, through a redistribution between men and women of unpaid care and paid employment, will appear unproductive only to those who define economic efficiency in terms of mis-leadingly narrow measures such as contribution to gross domestic product.

As Sawer's argument makes clear, we in Australia are perhaps well placed because we have the historical resources to aid us in an imaginative rethinking of public policy. Any brief history of the Australian settlement gives us a more complex tale than the simplistic dichotomies that the past two decades allow. If we concentrate solely on the institutional legacy of social liberalism at a given point in time, or presume that that legacy did not change over time, then we lose sight of the wider implications of social liberalism. As Peter Beilharz has suggested, Kelly's account 'presumes that there are only two choices, that there is nothing left to be salvaged from a way of life which many people would still take to be salutary. It claims that this is now our chance to make a history, but it shows only contempt for the history that has gone before' (1994: 10). Redis-covering the history of the ethical state, rather than the economic state, is vital if we wish to begin a constructive political dialogue around the issue of growth.

References

ACIRRT (1998) *Agreements Database and Monitor*, no. 16, March.

Bainbridge, B. (1997) 'A Nation-building State Loses Its Mind', *Arena Magazine*, no. 31, Oct.–Nov., pp. 21–7.

Beilharz, P. (1994) *Transforming Labor: Labour Tradition and the Labor Decade in Australia*, Cambridge University Press, Melbourne.

Bittman, M. and Pixley, J. (1997) *The Double Life of the Family*, Allen & Unwin, St Leonards.

Buchanan, J. and Bearfield, S. (1997) *Reforming Work Time: Alternatives to Unemployment, Casualisation and Excessive Hours*, Brotherhood of St Laurence Future of Work Project, Melbourne.

Buchanan, J. and Watson, I. (2000) 'Beyond the Wage Earner Model', in *Reshaping Australian Social Policy: Changes in Work, Welfare and Families*, L. Hancock et al. (eds), CEDA, Melbourne.

Cappelli, P. et al. (1997) *Change at Work*, Oxford University Press, New York.

Cass, B. (1994) 'Connecting the Public and the Private: Social Justice and Family Policies', in *Social Security Journal*, December, p. 5.

Creighton, W.B., Ford, W. and Mitchell, R.J. (1993) *Labour Law*, Law Book Company, Sydney.

Deery, S. and Mitchell, R. (eds) (1999) *Employment Relations: Individualisation and Union Exclusion: An International Study*, Federation Press, Sydney.

Elson, D. (1998) 'The Economic, the Political and the Domestic: Businesses, States and Households in the Organisation of Production', *New Political Economy*, vol. 3, no. 2, pp. 189–208.

Folbre, N. and Weisskopf, T. (1998) 'Did Father Know Best? Families, Markets and the Supply of Caring Labour', in *Economics, Values, and Organization*, A. Ben-Ner and L. Putterman (eds), Cambridge University Press, Cambridge.

Gregory, R.G. (1999a) *Children and the Changing Labour Market: Joblessness in Families With Dependent Children*, Discussion Paper no. 406, Centre for Economic Policy Research, Australian National University, Canberra.

Gregory, R.G. (1999b) 'Competing With Dad: Changes in the Intergenerational Distribution of Male Labour Market Income', *Australian Social Policy*, vol. 1, no. 1, 1999, pp. 115–32.

Heiler, K. (1998) 'What has Happened to Standard Hours of Work in Australia', in *Divided Work: Divided Society: Employment, Unemployment and Income Distribution in 1990s Australia*, B. Cass and R. Couch (eds), RIHSS, University of Sydney, Sydney.

Hewitt, P. (1993) *About Time: The Revolution in Work and Family Life*, Polity Press, Cambridge.

Ironmonger, D. (ed.) (1989) *Households Work: Productive Activities, Women and Income in the Household Economy*, Allen & Unwin, St Leonards.

Kelly, P. (1994) *The End of Certainty: Power, Politics and Business in Australia*, Allen & Unwin, St Leonards, pp. 1–2.

Macintyre, S. (1989) 'Neither capital or labour', in *Foundations of Arbitration: The Origins and Effects of State Compulsory Arbitration, 1890–1914*, S. Macintyre and R. Mitchell (eds), Oxford University Press, South Melbourne.

Maddox, G. (1998) 'The Australian Settlement and Australian Political Thought', in *Contesting the Australian Way: States, Markets and Civil Society*, Paul Smyth and Bettina Cass (eds), Cambridge University Press, Melbourne.

McCallum, R. (2000) *Employer Controls Over Private Life*, UNSW Press, Sydney.

Morris, M. (1992) *Ecstasy and Economics*, EmPress, Sydney.

Murphy, J. (2000) *Imagining the Fifties: Private Sentiment and Political Culture in Menzies' Australia*, Pluto Press, Sydney.

O'Donnell, A. and Hancock, L. (2000) 'The Challenge of Reshaping the Social Settlement', in *Reshaping Australian Social Policy*, Growth no. 48, L. Hancock, B. Howe and A. O'Donnell (eds), CEDA, Melbourne.

Probert, B. and Macdonald, F. (1996) *The Work Generation: Work and Identity in the Nineties*, Brotherhood of St Laurence, Melbourne.

Ross, I. (2000) 'Balancing Work and Family Responsibilities – An Australian Perspective', paper presented at *Search for Flexibility, Fairness and Prosperity: Alternative Employment Policies in the Twenty-First Century*, International Industrial Relations Association, 12th World Congress, Tokyo, 2000, 29 May–2 June.

Rubery, R. (2000) 'What Do Women Want From Full Employment?', in *Working For Full Employment*, J. Philpott (ed.), Routledge, London.

Sawer, M. (2000) 'The Ethical State: Social Liberalism and the Critique of Contract', *Australian Historical Studies*, vol. 31, no. 114, pp. 67–90.

Shanahan, R. (1999) 'Making Work Agreements Contractual: Then and Now', in *Australian Labour History Reconsidered*, D. Palmer et al. (eds), Australian Humanities Press, Adelaide.

Wolcott, I. and Glazer, H. (1995) *Work and Family Life: Achieving Integration*, Australian Institute of Family Studies, Melbourne.

Notes

1 On the closing of the wage gap, see R.G. Gregory and R. Duncan (1981) 'Segmented Labour Market Theories and the Australian Experience of Equal Pay for Women', *Journal of Post-Keynesian Economics*, vol. 3, pp. 403–28. Despite their prior linking with racist immigration controls, Australian labour market institutions arguably also led to a more equitable incorporation of immigrant workers in the postwar period than in many countries that relied on immigrant labour for postwar nation-building. See C. Lever-Tracy and M. Quinlan (1988) *A Divided Working Class: Ethnic Segmentation and Industrial Conflict in Australia*, Routledge & Kegan Paul, London, p. 308.

2 See, for example, Economic Planning and Advisory Commission (1996) *Future Labour Market Issues for Australia*, Commission Paper No. 12, AGPS, Canberra; M. Wooden (1998) *The Changing Nature of Employment Arrangements*, National Institute of Labour Studies, Flinders University, Adelaide; Y. Dunlop and P. Sheehan (1998) 'Technology, Skills and Changing Nature of Work', in P. Sheehan and G. Taggart (eds), *Working for the Future*, Victoria University of Technology, Melbourne; P. Barnes et al. (1999) *Productivity and the Structure of Employment*, Productivity Commission Staff Research Paper, AusInfo, Canberra.

3 Michael Pusey's 1991 study, *Economic Rationalism in Canberra*, was subtitled 'A Nation-Building State Changes Its Mind'. The phrase I use here comes from a critique of Pusey's approach by Bill Bainbridge, published in *Arena Magazine*, no. 31, Oct.–Nov. 1997, pp. 21–7.

7

The Environment, Sustainable Development and the Australian Economy[1]

David Throsby

Introduction

The industries that have traditionally contributed most strongly to Australian economic growth – including agriculture, mining and, more recently, tourism – have significant interactions with the environment. At one level the beneficence of nature, reflected in the abundant supply of Australia's natural resources, has been a major source of growth; at another level, however, the need for care in the utilisation of those resources has acted as a constraint on the rates of economic growth that, at least in the short term, might have been achieved. Thus the relationships between Australia's actual and potential growth – both past and future – and the natural environment are of considerable importance, not only economically but also socially and culturally.

This chapter examines these relationships in the context of sustainability, a concept that has economic, ecological, social and cultural ramifications, and hence provides an integrating framework for analysis. The initial questions relate to the state of play – what are the principal areas of environmental concern associated with the growth of the Australian economy, and what do the indicators tell us about Australian performance in these areas? The emergence of the concept of sustainable development during the 1980s as a guiding principle for considering environment/economy interactions is then discussed, and the impact of this notion on thinking and on policy formation in Australia over the last decade is traced, using the issue of climate change as a particular illustration. Finally, the focus is widened to embrace questions currently being raised about the nature of the development process itself in the light of changing perceptions of the economic, social and cultural aspirations of society. Does sustainability provide a valid means for bringing these disparate aspects together?

Australia's environmental performance

In the 10 years to 1997–98, Australia's real GDP grew by 38 per cent in total and by 21 per cent in per capita terms. The pressures that these rates of growth have imposed on the environment can be considered under various headings, corresponding to the principal impacts or problem areas involved. However, assessment of environmental impacts is limited by the lack of adequate data. Whereas economic growth is easy to measure, environmental performance is multifaceted and often difficult to quantify. Progress towards a set of standardised environmental indicators has been slow, and even when reliable measures are found, they cannot be readily combined into a single performance index. Evaluation must therefore rely on qualitative reporting, supported by whatever fragmentary data that can be assembled. The most recent comprehensive report on environmental problems produced by or on behalf of the Australian government was that of the State of the Environment Advisory Council in 1996 (a new edition is due in 2001). Subsequently, a tabulation of a range of environmental indicators for OECD member countries was published in 1998 (OECD 1998a); in the same year the OECD also produced its first Environmental Performance Review for Australia (OECD 1998b). These OECD publications provide one benchmark against which the Australian situation can be measured; namely, average performance levels for the major industrialised economies. However, it must be remembered that this is a relative and not an absolute standard, and that the comparison may be misleading if the environmental performance of OECD countries collectively is poor in any particular respect when judged against objective or independent criteria. Moreover, the coverage of the published indicators is sparse, and many aspects of environmental performance relevant to the Australian case are not represented in these data.

The main areas of environmental concern that have implications for Australian economic growth, and the principal industries that are affected, are: land and water use (agriculture); other natural resource use (mining, forestry and fisheries); atmospheric pollution (energy production, energy use and transport); waste management (manufacturing and the household sector); and nature conservation (tourism). The problems arising in each area are considered in turn. Some relevant comparative data are provided in Table 7.1.

Land and inland water resource use

The growth rates in agricultural output recorded in Australia since the early days of settlement have been achieved at increasing environmental cost. Land degradation is apparent in the structural decline of soils, loss of fertility, soil acidification, salinity, and water and wind erosion. On irrigated land, problems of waterlogging, salinisation and pesticide residues are becoming

Table 7.1 Selected environmental indicators: Australia and all OECD countries: mid-1990s

	Australia	OECD average
1 Land and water		
Annual rate of land clearance (km^2 per year)	3000	n.a.
Proportion of all land considered highly erosion prone (%)	20	n.a.
Proportion of arable land potentially liable to erosion and salinisation (%)	87	n.a.
2 Other natural resources		
Forest area (% of land area)	19.4	33.5
Proportion of state and crown-land forest area available for logging (%)	60	n.a.
Proportion of wooded area held in reserves (%)	11.3	n.a.
Fish catches per capita (kg per cap.)	10.8	26.4
Change in fish catch per cap. since 1980 (%)	+20	−19
3 Atmospheric pollution		
Emissions per unit GDP:		
Carbon dioxide (tonnes per $US'000)	0.89	0.65
Oxides of sulphur (kg per $US'000)	6.7	2.5
Oxides of nitrogen (kg per $US'000)	6.7	2.4
Emissions per capita		
Carbon dioxide (tonnes per cap.)	15.8	10.9
Oxides of sulphur (kg per cap.)	119.1	40.6
Oxides of nitrogen (kg per cap.)	120.4	39.9
Ozone depleting gases (kg per cap.)	0.15	0.11
4 Waste management		
Municipal waste per capita (kg per cap.)	690	530
Industrial waste per unit GDP (kg per $US'000)	130	90
Pollution abatement and control expenditure (% of GDP)	0.8	1.4
5 Nature conservation		
Threatened species		
Mammals (% of species known)	13.8	n.a.
Birds (% of species known)	5.9	n.a.
Fish (% of species known)	0.4	n.a.
Endangered or vulnerable plants (% of taxa)	20.1	n.a.
Protected areas (% of territory)	8	12
per capita (km^2 per '000 inh)	33	4
Strict nature reserves, wilderness areas, national parks (% of territory)	6	4
per capita (km^2 per '000 inh)	26	1.4

Sources: Adapted from data contained in OECD 1998a; OECD 1998b; Yencken and Wilkinson 2000; Young 2000.

more acute. A particular source of these problems has been what is now seen as an excessive – and in some areas accelerating – rate of land-clearing, a process that also has implications for biodiversity and greenhouse gas emissions. Of the 77 million hectares suitable for cropping and improved pastures, it has been estimated that only 10 million hectares are not liable to erodability or potential salinisation of soils (Young 2000: 34; McTainsh and Boughton 1993). About 2.5 million hectares is now affected by dry land salinisation, much of it in Western Australia, and about 160 000 hectares is threatened by salinisation due to rising groundwater tables resulting from irrigation (OECD 1998b: 77; Young 2000: chapter 3; Yencken and Wilkinson 2000: chapter 9). The various problems of land degradation across the agricultural sector have been exacerbated over the years by the effects of uncontrollable climatic events such as drought and flood.

Other natural resource use

The principal environmental issues concerning *non-renewable* resources relate to divergences between socially and privately optimal extraction rates and to the immediate land-use impacts of mining. The first of these questions is linked to wider global concerns surrounding the potential exhaustion of non-renewable resource stocks, a matter that Australia cannot ignore given its pre-eminence as a supplier of minerals to world markets; in the mid-1990s Australia ranked first in the world in the volume of production of bauxite and lead, second in zinc and uranium, third in gold and fourth in iron ore (Crowson 1996). In the case of uranium, a further environmental concern that has directly affected growth in production has been the nuclear safety policies of successive Australian governments, policies that continue to proscribe nuclear power generation for domestic use and to impose quotas on uranium exports.

As for the exploitation of *renewable* resources – forestry and fisheries – the problems of management of what are essentially common property resources are well known. The over-harvesting of old-growth forest areas and the development of plantation-based agro-forestry, both motivated to an important extent by a drive towards short-run returns, have raised a number of environmental issues ranging from loss of biodiversity and wildlife habitat to both positive and negative effects on greenhouse gas emissions. As for fisheries, stocks have been threatened not just by overfishing but also by destruction of habitat, nutrient run-off and other problems caused by coastal development (Young 2000: 121–3).

Atmospheric pollution

Atmospheric problems fall into three categories. First, the possibility of climate change resulting from the enhanced greenhouse effect has focused attention especially on the energy sector (OECD 1998a, UN 1998). On the energy production side, Australia is unusually dependent on carbon-dioxide-producing energy sources for its primary energy supply, with 45 per cent of its supply coming from solid fuels, compared with 24 per cent for all OECD countries. Further, in terms of per capita energy use, Australia ranks third in the world among major economies (not including the Middle East). As a result, Australia's energy-related CO_2 emissions per head are about 50 per cent higher than the OECD average, and, alongside Canada, are second only to those of the United States among the major OECD countries. The second atmospheric problem is that of ozone depletion. During the 1980s the hole in the ozone layer increased in depth and extent, but the conclusion of the Montreal Protocol in 1987 has substantially curtailed the continued emission of the offending gases, allowing the problem of ozone depletion to be controlled if not yet eliminated. The third issue relates to urban air quality. Australian per capita emissions of the oxides of sulphur and nitrogen are considerably greater than OECD averages, and particulate emissions and photochemical reactions have noticeable effects on air quality in major cities; nevertheless, ambient air quality guidelines as laid down in 1985 by the NH&MRC are generally satisfied, although periodic high concentrations are a cause for concern.

Waste management

The management of solid wastes presents a series of problems confronting manufacturing industry; waste disposal is also of particular importance to the household sector. Land-filling is the main method of dealing with solid wastes in Australia, given the relatively plentiful supply of suitable sites. However, recycling is gradually increasing as a proportion of total waste disposal; in 1995 the recycling of paper and glass accounted for 50 and 42 per cent respectively of total apparent consumption of these items, placing Australia around the mid-range of OECD countries in terms of recycling practices (OECD 1998b: 95). Nevertheless, the levels of waste generation per capita in Australia remain relatively high and waste management performance continues to lag behind international best practice (OECD 1998b: 91–106).

Nature conservation

The protection of natural assets such as wilderness areas and outstanding environmental features has significant implications for the tourism industry, insofar as the enjoyment of Australia's unique natural and cultural heritage is one of the principal drivers of the tourist market. More broadly, the issue of biodiversity protection is a particularly important one for Australia, given this country's position as habitat for a large proportion of the world's species. The economic importance of these biological resources remains unclear, though current international interest in the commercial potential for exploiting genetic material suggests that the prospects could be substantial. Thus in regard to nature conservation, whether for tourism or for scientific purposes, there are continuing possibilities for synergy rather than conflict between environmental values and economic performance (see further in State of the Environment Advisory Council 1996, *Executive Summary*: 22–5, 43–5).

If the overall picture of Australia's environmental performance presented in this section is drawn together, a somewhat mixed assessment emerges. Although the potential impact of environmental problems in Australia over the years has been mitigated by factors such as the abundance of natural resources, low population densities (note, however, that low overall population densities are misleading in the Australian case because of the high degree of urbanisation), and so on, the findings of the environmental performance assessments referred to above, supported by the rudimentary data assembled in Table 7.1, suggest that Australian economic growth has been achieved at considerable environmental cost. In particular, land management practices in the agricultural sector have led to environmental deterioration that threatens present and future viability; expansion of the mining and forestry industries has raised serious public concern about resource depletion and loss of environmental amenity; and, to the extent that increasing energy production and use has underpinned growth in almost all sectors of the economy, the adverse environmental impacts of the energy and transport sectors have ramifications across the board. The environmental outcomes discussed are important for their own sake, and they have significant economic implications through their past, present and future effects on achievable economic performance. The following section of this chapter looks at how these problems have been addressed in Australia over the last decade or so.

Sustainable development

Although the possibility of conflict between economic growth and environmental values had been brought to public attention during the 1960s and 1970s by books such as Rachel Carson's *Silent Spring* and by agencies such as the Club of Rome (Carson 1963, Meadows et al. 1972), it was not until the 1980s that these concerns found a serious place on the international agenda. The UN World Commission on Environment and Development produced a report in 1987 (the 'Brundtland Report') that had a profound effect on the conceptualisation of environmental problems in both the developing and the industrialised world. The report linked problems of poverty in the Third World with profligate consumption patterns in developed countries, and showed how the capacity of the planet to support human life in the future was being threatened by degradation and misuse of the world's air, land and sea resources. The Brundtland Commission put forward the notion of *sustainable development*, defined as 'development that meets the needs of the present without compromising the ability of future generations to meet their own needs' (World Commission on Environment and Development 1987: 43), as a key element in integrating economic and ecological aspects of the development process.

The identification of sustainability in this context by the Brundtland Report paralleled a transformation in thinking that had been occurring within environmental economics. Problems associated with the environment had been originally introduced into economic analysis as examples of externalities – air and water pollution were interpreted as external costs, environmental amenity and other positive aspects were portrayed as external benefits, indicating intervention by means of Pigovian taxes and subsidies to correct the market distortion, or via identification and enforcement of property rights through reform of market institutions.[2] The formalisation of the economic concept of natural capital during the 1980s allowed principles of sustainability, especially the key phenomenon of inter-generational equity, to be enunciated as fundamental elements in reconfiguring an economic approach to the environment. In the emerging sub-discipline of ecological economics, environmental problems were no longer seen as peripheral but as integral to any consideration of economic activity. Once the operations of natural ecosystems were recognised as essential in supporting the workings of the real economy, it became no longer tenable to consider questions of economic growth and development in isolation from the ecological processes upon which they relied (see, for example, Costanza 1991, 1997).

The Brundtland Report laid down a serious challenge to national governments and the international community to do something about reconciling the relentless drive for economic growth in all corners of the globe with what was presented as a burgeoning environmental crisis. In Australia this challenge was felt all the more immediately because of the growing hostility between conservation groups and industry over a number of specific development projects that had captured a great deal of public attention throughout the decades of the 1970s and 1980s – for example, disputes over Lake Pedder and the Franklin River in Tasmania, the wet tropics in north Queensland, Coronation Hill in the Northern Territory and old-growth forests almost everywhere (see further in Doyle 2000). Hence, the idea of sustainable development, if indeed it did hold out a prospect of uniting disparate opinions, was a very appealing one to both federal and state governments at that time.

The first response to the Brundtland Report in Australia was an 'Agenda for the Environment', released in 1989, entitled *Our Country, Our Future* (Hawke 1989). This was followed by a Discussion Paper dealing more directly with the concept of ecologically sustainable development (ESD) and how it could be applied in Australia (Commonwealth of Australia 1990). The positive public reaction to this paper was sufficient to persuade the government to set up a formal process for detailed consideration of how sustainability might be achieved in the principal industrial sectors of the Australian economy. This process, to be known as the Ecologically Sustainable Development (ESD) process (for further details of the operations of the ESD process itself, see Harris and Throsby 1998), was built around nine Working Groups, covering Agriculture, Fisheries, Forestry, Manufacturing, Mining, Energy Production, Energy Use, Transport and Tourism. It brought together industry representatives, environmental advocates, federal and state bureaucrats, scientific advisers and others to work out what constituted an ecologically sustainable development path for each industry and to make recommendations as to how that path could be attained. The Final Reports of the ESD process were released at the end of 1991 and the beginning of 1992.[3] Subsequently, the recommendations of the ESD process were drawn together by the Australian government and an assignment of responsibilities to lead agencies was made (Commonwealth of Australia 1992a). This led in 1993 to agreement by the Council of Australian Governments on a National Strategy for ESD (Commonwealth of Australia 1993) that set out both a broad framework for ESD and enunciated specific policies for implementation at all levels of government. This strategy has remained in the intervening years as a blueprint for Australia's overall achievement of ESD.

Has the National Strategy for ESD proved effective in integrating economic and environmental concerns in Australia? There have been several assessments of progress in implementing ESD principles and policies in Australia, all of which have come up with a mixed report card. The Intergovernmental Committee for ESD in 1996 surveyed progress to date and concluded that clear progress had been made (Commonwealth of Australia 1996), especially in agriculture through land care programs and in some areas of mining and manufacturing; for example, in the adoption of sustainable practices and cleaner production methods in industry. Although some economic instruments had been used to enhance the achievement of ESD, for example in allocating water use and controlling water pollution, the report found that the use of pricing and taxation measures had not gone as far as would be necessary to have a significant effect. Two years later the OECD Environment Performance Review mentioned earlier was released. It broadly supported the findings of the Intergovernmental Committee report, and added its voice to the criticism that insufficient use had been made of economic instruments in the policy measures applied (OECD 1998b: 18–19).

The most recent assessment of the implementation of ESD in Australia has been made by the Productivity Commission (1999). Its inquiry, conducted during 1998–1999, was limited to how Commonwealth departments and agencies have applied ESD principles and objectives in policy-making, and how they have monitored, evaluated and reported on the implementation of ESD. The inquiry was effectively a review of the success of the National

Strategy for ESD at the Commonwealth level. The inquiry found that progress in implementing ESD had varied widely, with good results in areas such as natural resource management, but with lesser achievement in other areas such as transport, industry and health, where sustainability objectives were seen as having been too broad to impinge directly on the policy process, and where opportunities for stakeholder partnerships and participation have not been pursued. The Commission found that policy analysis was often not undertaken, and hence that significant potential short- and longer term costs and benefits were not properly evaluated. The Productivity Commission recommended that:

> Guidelines of existing policy development and evaluation mechanisms (such as . . . environmental impact assessment guidelines) should include specific reference to assessing the likely social, economic and environmental costs and benefits of proposals, in both the short term and long term (1999: 89).

The Productivity Commission's report also pointed to the difficulties in monitoring ESD outcomes caused by the lack of appropriate data and environmental performance indicators.

Notwithstanding the many specific reservations that observers, especially conservationists, have expressed about progress towards ecological sustainability in Australia, most evaluations have at least pointed to the way in which the concept of ESD has come to be accepted by politicians, bureaucrats, many industry leaders and the community at large as an appropriate means of reconciling the desire for economic growth with the need for environmental responsibility. More particularly, there appears to have been a diffuse but significant shift in the ethos within which decisions are made in many parts of the federal and state bureaucracies whereby the need for ESD as a guiding principle is recognised, even if this recognition is only rarely translated fully into practice. (For further consideration of what sustainability means in the Australian context, see Krockenberger et al. 2000.)

Climate change

One of the most conspicuous areas where economic growth and environmental values come face to face is in the debate about climate change. We provide a brief account of this issue here as an illustration of the problems involved.

The first concerted effort in Australia to confront the problem of global warming caused by excessive levels of carbon dioxide and other trace gases in the atmosphere occurred in October 1990, when the Commonwealth government agreed to interim targets for emissions reductions (the 'Toronto targets'), which were aimed at stabilising emissions at their 1988 levels by the year 2000 and reducing them by 20 per cent by the year 2005. At that time Australia was, after the United States and Canada, the third-largest per capita emitter of greenhouse gases in the world. A number of factors had contributed to this situation, including Australia's relatively low energy prices and relatively high per capita energy demand, its dispersed population creating strong demand for long-distance transport, its heavy reliance on fossil fuels for power generation, its high concentration of energy-intensive industries, and other factors. Conservative projections suggested that under a business-as-usual scenario, emissions would increase by 23 per cent over 1988 levels by 2005 (ESD Chairs 1992b: 26), indicating that significant intervention would be required to reduce the growth in greenhouse gas output if the Toronto targets were to be met. Because of the potential for dislocation to industry from such intervention, the government added the proviso that no unilateral action would be taken if it had adverse impacts on the Australian economy or on Australia's trade competitiveness.

Within a short space of time a number of studies appeared[4] that purported to show that almost any action designed to limit emissions would have catastrophic effects on the Australian economy whether undertaken unilaterally or not, with one report predicting eventual losses in domestic production as high as 20 per cent of the then current level of GDP if the Toronto targets were to be met (Moran and Chisholm 1991: 4). More sober assessments such as that of the Industry Commission put the reduction in real disposable income in Australia from participation in a feasible international strategy to cut emissions at just over 1 per cent (Industry Commission 1991: 75), an estimate within the range projected for other countries at that time (as surveyed by Winters 1992: 98–99). Many of the analyses carried out in the early 1990s relied on various macro-models of the Australian economy, such as ORANI, to estimate intersectoral impacts on output and employment (see Brooker and O'Meagher 1991). They generally assumed that the emissions reductions would be brought about by the imposition of a carbon tax of a sufficiently large magnitude to induce the level of reductions sought. The studies were therefore criticised as unrealistic because they neglected other policy measures that might achieve reductions at less cost, and because they failed to account for the sorts of beneficial structural readjustments that might occur as part of an abatement strategy, but that were not captured in 'top-down' models. Further, they were attacked as being unduly pessimistic, especially because, with few exceptions, they paid no attention to the potential benefits of avoiding the adverse effects of climate change. (One exception was the Industry Commission's Report (1991), which attempted to weigh up benefits as well as costs.)

The ESD process referred to above produced a report on the greenhouse issue (ESD Working Group Chairs 1992b) that pointed to the importance of climate change in the overall array of environmental problems facing the Australian economy, and made some relatively cautious recommendations for action. Particular emphasis was placed on so-called 'no-regrets' measures that could be expected to have benefits irrespective of their effects on emissions, and might therefore be adopted even if global warming were not regarded as a threat; such measures included fuel-switching in power generation, more efficient energy use in the commercial and household sectors, and improved mass transit systems in urban areas. However, the recommendations stopped short of proposing the imposition of a carbon tax, even of only modest size, because of the fears expressed by industry groups concerning the economic impacts of such a measure.

In December 1992 the Commonwealth government, having ratified the UN Framework Convention on Climate Change, adopted a National Greenhouse Response Strategy (NGRS) (Commonwealth of Australia 1992b), which was derived from the ESD recommendations, and which contained a range of actions to be taken at all levels of government as part of Australia's obligations under the Convention. The strategy included implementation of microeconomic reform in the electricity and gas sectors, the promotion of increased energy efficiency within the residential and commercial sectors, and moves to improve fuel consumption in the national vehicle fleet. However, these measures fell a long way short of a full commitment to achieving the target reductions in emissions, again because of apprehension about the possible adverse economic consequences of more drastic action; for example, the NGRS was specifically orientated towards 'causing minimal disruption to the wider community, any single industry sector, or any geographical region' (Commonwealth of Australia 1992b: 12–13 – this proviso was seen as especially significant in protecting the coal industry).

In December 1997 proposed emissions reductions targets were revised as a result of the Kyoto Protocol. The new Australian target of an 8 per cent *increase* in net emissions over 1990 levels by the years 2008–2012 was considerably softer than the average target of a 5 per cent *reduction* across all participating countries, a concession won on the basis of Australian insistence on its particular economic vulnerability to more stringent reductions. Nevertheless, it was apparent that significant action to curb growth in emissions would still be required to meet even these weakened targets. Accordingly, the NGRS was reformulated as a new National Greenhouse Strategy (NGS) in 1998, designed 'to provide a fresh impetus for action by governments, stakeholder groups and the broader community and set directions for that action into the next century' (Commonwealth of Australia 1998: 2). As with its predecessor, the NGS contains a variety of measures covering power generation, energy efficiency, urban planning and land use, with increased focus on the development of carbon sinks in the agriculture and forestry sectors.

The effectiveness of Australia's efforts to combat the problem of climate change can be assessed for the decade of the 1990s by reference to trends in the major indicators. Table 7.2 shows the trends in emissions compared with trends over the same period in real GDP and population. It is apparent that

Table 7.2 Greenhouse gas emissions:[a] Australia, 1990–98

	1990	1991	1992	1993	1994	1995	1996	1997	1998
Aggregate emissions (*megatonnes carbon dioxide equivalent*)									
Energy sector	299.6	301.0	305.1	307.8	310.9	325.2	335.8	343.3	362.9
Other sectors	90.3	91.0	88.1	88.2	87.8	87.2	87.9	89.9	93.0
TOTAL	389.8	392.1	393.2	396.0	398.7	412.4	423.7	433.2	455.9
Per capita emissions (*tonnes carbon dioxide equivalent per head*)									
	22.8	22.7	22.5	22.4	22.3	22.8	23.1	23.4	24.3
Per unit GDP[b] emissions (*kg carbon dioxide equivalent per $GDP*)									
	0.893	0.902	0.902	0.875	0.847	0.837	0.824	0.816	0.820
Year-on-year growth (*per cent per annum*)									
Total emissions	–	0.6	0.3	0.7	0.7	3.4	2.7	2.2	5.3
Real GDP[b]	–	–0.3	0.2	3.8	4.1	4.6	4.4	3.2	4.6
Population	–	1.3	1.2	1.0	1.1	1.2	1.3	1.2	1.1

Notes: [a]Excluding forest and grassland conversion.
[b]Product, chain volume measures, reference year 1996–97.

Sources: Commonwealth of Australia (2000), p. 23 and ABS data.

total emissions have risen significantly over the period since emissions reduction strategies were first introduced. Emissions per capita have fluctuated but have trended upwards, while emissions per unit of real GDP have declined somewhat, thanks to vigorous GDP growth over the period. The Australian Greenhouse Office's most recent assessment concludes that 'it is difficult to detect any effects of the . . . (NGRS) or the . . . (NGS) or of programs such as the Greenhouse Challenge from these indicators alone' but expresses the hope that these and other programs should have increasing impacts over time (Commonwealth of Australia 2000: 59–60). Despite this cautious optimism, however, the fact remains that sectional concerns about adverse economic impacts of measures to reduce greenhouse gas emissions that surfaced in the early 1990s have persisted until the present day, and have greatly constrained policy action to bring about emissions reductions. While these concerns are understandable in immediate self-interest terms, they can scarcely be justified in the wider context of a world facing serious threats from climate change. Yet government policy has so far failed to capitalise on the opportunities for beneficial resource reallocation that are there for the taking. In particular, the political sensitivity assumed to surround any move to increase Australia's relatively low energy prices as a means of curbing energy demand has ruled out the use of potentially the most powerful weapon – a carbon tax – to encourage a restructuring of Australian energy production and use. Fear of the economic costs of response measures and scepticism about the benefits from avoiding the likely future effects of global warming persist in Australia, notwithstanding the consolidation of scientific evidence on the apparent inevitability of climate change and the inexorable pressure on the international community to do something about it.[5]

Thus, although as noted earlier the idea of sustainability has been broadly accepted in Australia as a framework within which to approach the question of economic growth, the area of climate change is a sharp illustration of the fact that rhetoric is still considerably stronger than action.

Conclusions: sustainability in a broader context

This chapter has discussed the concept of sustainability as providing a wider context within which economic growth, narrowly defined as increases in real per capita GDP, can be situated. To conclude, it is appropriate to draw attention to recent thinking that is extending the interpretation of sustainable development even further, raising some fundamental questions about the nature of economic growth and what it delivers when set against what is known about the goals and aspirations of society. These trends in thinking can be seen to spring from two sources.

First, it is usually taken as axiomatic that more growth is better. Even when this assumption is tempered by a concern for the distributional consequences of

growth, there is nevertheless still an underlying acceptance that a direct relationship exists between improvements in material circumstances and human
happiness. Yet criticism of such a view dates back at least 40 years; in the 1950s,
for example, Moses Abramovitz was questioning the welfare interpretation of
secular increases in national income (see Abramovitz 1959, Easterlin 1974),
while Arthur Lewis was arguing that wealth and happiness were very hard to
correlate (Lewis 1955: 420).[6] Since then these concerns have re-surfaced from
time to time in an emerging literature about the economics of human happiness
(see Scitovsky 1976, 1992; Oswald 1997), which among other things has
examined the importance of wealth and income relative to other arguments in
standard utility functions. Empirical evidence is now accumulating to support
the proposition that improvements in material economic circumstances do not
necessarily lead to increases in individuals' fundamental senses of wellbeing,
particularly because other values that are independent of economic success, or
even negatively related to it, are seen as more important in many people's lives
(see, for example, Eckersley 1998). In these circumstances a set of policy objectives in a country such as Australia which allowed growth to dominate over all
else, might be somewhat out of keeping with the basic aspirations of society.

The second source of revisionist thinking about these issues derives from a
questioning of the nature of the development process itself. Although this
aspect of the debate has been more concerned with developing rather than
developed economies, much of it is relevant to a consideration of growth in
high-income countries as well. It is well known that during the 1970s and
1980s the theory of economic development continued to widen its focus, rein-
terpreting progress in the economy as a process where indicators of educational levels, nutrition and health status, access to public services, and other
aspects of quality of life were seen as just as important as real incomes per head
when it came to measuring development achievement. Then at the end of the
1980s the notion of *economic* development began to be refocused on to a people-
centred strategy of *human* development (reflected, for example, in the United
Nations Development Strategy for the 1990s and the UNDP *Human Development Reports*, the first of which appeared in 1991; see further in Sen 1990),
described by Keith Griffin as one that:

> (enhances) the ability of people to lead a long life, to enjoy good health, to have
> access to the world's stock of knowledge and information, to participate in the
> cultural life of their community, to have sufficient income to buy food, clothing and
> shelter, to participate in the decisions that directly affect their lives and their com-
> munity, and so on. These are the things that matter – increasing the capabilities of
> people – and the enhancement of capabilities, not the enlargement of domestic (or
> material) product, should be the objective of development policy (1996: 233).

This paradigm was further extended during the 1990s to give a sharper
focus to the cultural underpinnings of the development process, especially

through the work of the UN World Commission on Culture and Development, a successor to the Brundtland Commission referred to earlier (World Commission on Culture and Development 1995; see also UNESCO's *World Culture Reports* 1998 and 2000).

This emerging paradigm has implications for developed countries such as Australia because it extends the concept of sustainable development from a concern with the relations simply between economic growth and the natural environment to one involving the social and cultural circumstances of society as well. In doing so, it suggests parallels between ways in which natural and cultural systems underpin economic activity. Just as it has been demonstrated that natural capital and the ecosystem balance have a two-way relationship with the economy, so also can it be proposed that cultural capital and what can be termed cultural ecosystems have significant connections with achievement in the economic sphere.[7] Thus the principles of sustainability can be argued to be as applicable to phenomena such as cultural traditions, beliefs, values, networks, and so on, as they are to characteristics of the natural world (see further in Throsby 1997, 2001). In particular, the principle of inter-generational equity, which is fundamental to sustainable development, can be suggested to have as much relevance to the preservation of cultural capital, both tangible and intangible, as it has to natural capital.

These considerations are essentially arguments for a holistic treatment of the processes of growth and change in society. The admission of ecological concerns into the arena of debate about economic progress has been a major step forward, if only because it has indicated that high rates of economic growth cannot be maintained in the long term if the interconnections between environment and economy are disregarded, and if those who cause environmental damage continue to escape bearing the full social costs of their actions. A strong case is now emerging that there are further dimensions to this picture that relate directly to the nature of society and to the needs of human beings within it and that, if accepted, would indicate a further shift in thinking about policy priorities in the years ahead.

References

Abramovitz, M. (1959) 'The Welfare Interpretation of Secular Trends in National Income and Product', in Moses Abramovitz et al., *The Allocation of Economic Resources: Essays in Honor of Bernard Frances Haley*, Stanford: Stanford University Press, pp. 1–22.
Brooker, R. and O'Meagher, B. (1991) 'Economic Modelling, Ecologically Sustainable Development and the Greenhouse Effect', in ESD Working Groups, *Economic Modelling*, Canberra: *mimeo*.
Carson, R. (1963) *Silent Spring*, London: Hamish Hamilton.

Commonwealth of Australia (1990) *Ecologically Sustainable Development: A Commonwealth Government Discussion Paper*, Canberra: AGPS.

Commonwealth of Australia (1992a) *Compendium of the Recommendations of the ESD Working Groups*, Canberra: AGPS.

Commonwealth of Australia (1992b) *National Greenhouse Response Strategy*, Canberra: AGPS.

Commonwealth of Australia (1993) *A National Strategy for Ecologically Sustainable Development*, Canberra: AGPS.

Commonwealth of Australia (1996) *Report on the Implementation of the National Strategy for Ecologically Sustainable Development, 1993–1995*, Canberra: Intergovernmental Committee for ESD.

Commonwealth of Australia (1998) *The National Greenhouse Strategy: Strategic Framework for Advancing Australia's Greenhouse Response*, Canberra: Australian Greenhouse Office.

Commonwealth of Australia (2000) *National Greenhouse Gas Inventory: Analysis of Trends and Greenhouse Indicators 1990 to 1998*, Canberra: Australian Greenhouse Office.

Costanza, R. (ed.) (1991) *Ecological Economics: the Science and Management of Sustainability*, New York: Columbia University Press.

Costanza, R. (ed.) (1997) *Frontiers in Ecological Economics*, Cheltenham: Edward Elgar.

Crowson, P. (1996) *Minerals Handbook 1996–97*, London: Macmillan.

Dasgupta, P. and Serageldin, I. (2000) *Social Capital: A Multifaceted Perspective*, Washington DC: World Bank.

Diesendorf, M. (1998) 'The Fate of the ESD Recommendations on Greenhouse Response in the Energy Sector', in Clive Hamilton and David Throsby (eds), pp. 41–52.

Diesendorf, M. and Hamilton, C. (1997) 'The Ecologically Sustainable Development Process in Australia', in Mark Diesendorf and Clive Hamilton (eds), *Human Ecology, Human Economy, Ideas for an Ecologically Sustainable Future*, St Leonards: Allen & Unwin, pp. 285–301.

Dorfman, R. and Dorfman, N.S. (1972) *Economics of the Environment: Selected Readings*, New York: W.W. Norton & Company.

Doyle, T. (2000) *Green Power: The Environment Movement in Australia*, Sydney: University of New South Wales Press.

Easterlin, R.A. (1974) 'Does Economic Growth Improve the Human Lot? Some Empirical Evidence', in Paul A. David and Melvin W. Reder (eds), *Nations and Households in Economic Growth: Essays in Honor of Moses Abramovitz*, New York: Academic Press, pp. 89–125.

Eckersley, R. (ed.) (1998) *Measuring Progress: Is Life Getting Better?*, Collingwood: CSIRO Publishing.

Ecologically Sustainable Development Working Group Chairs (1992a) *Intersectoral Issues Report*, Canberra: AGPS.

Ecologically Sustainable Development Working Group Chairs (1992b) *Greenhouse Report*, Canberra: AGPS.

Ecologically Sustainable Development Working Groups (1991) *Final Reports*, Canberra: AGPS.

Edwards, G. (1992) 'Economics and Sustainability: A Critique of the ESD Working Group Reports', paper presented to 21st Conference of Economists, Melbourne, July.

Griffin, K. (1996) *Studies in Globalization and Economic Transitions*, London: Macmillan.

Hamilton, C. and Throsby, D. (eds) (1998) *The ESD Process: Evaluating a Policy Experiment*, Canberra: Academy of the Social Sciences in Australia, and Graduate Program in Public Policy, ANU.

Harris, S. (1996), 'Economics of the Environment: A Survey', *Economic Record*, vol. 72, no. 217 (June), pp. 154–71.

Harris, S. and Throsby, D. (1998) 'The ESD Process: Background, Implementation and Aftermath', in Clive Hamilton and David Throsby (eds), *The ESD Process: Evaluating a Policy Experiment*, pp. 1–19.

Hawke, R.J.L. (1989), *Our Country, Our Future*, Canberra: AGPS.

Industry Commission (1991) *Costs and Benefits of Reducing Greenhouse Gas Emissions*, Canberra: AGPS.

Johnson, H.G. (1964) 'Towards a Generalised Capital Accumulation Approach to Economic Development', in Study Group in the Economics of Education, *The Residual Factor and Economic Growth*, Paris: OECD, pp. 219–27.

Kellow, A. and Moon, J. (1993) 'Governing the Environment: Problems and Possibilities', in Ian Marsh (ed.), *Governing in the 1990s: An Agenda for the Decade*, Melbourne: Longman Cheshire, pp. 226–55.

Krockenberger, M., Kinrade, P. and Thorman, R. (2000) *Natural Advantage: A Blueprint for a Sustainable Australia*, Melbourne: Australian Conservation Foundation.

Lewis, W.A. (1955) *The Theory of Economic Growth*, London: Allen & Unwin.

London Economics (1992) *The Impact of Global Warming Control Policies on Australian Industry*, London: London Economics.

Lothian, J.A. (1994) 'An Evaluation of the Ecologically Sustainable Development Process in Australia: A View from the Inside', in D. Hawke (ed.), *Proceedings of the Inaugural Joint Conference of the NZ Geographical Society and the Institute of Australian Geographers*, Auckland, NZ Geographical Conference Series No. 16.

Lowe, I. (1992) *Costs and Benefits of Meeting Emission Targets: A Comparative Analysis*. A report prepared for the Department of the Arts, Sport, the Environment and Territories, Canberra: *mimeo*.

McEachern, D. (1993) 'Environmental Policy in Australia 1981–91: A Form of Corporatism?' *Australian Journal of Public Administration*, vol. 52, no. 2, pp. 173–86.

McTainsh, G. and Boughton, W.C. (eds) (1993) *Land Degradation Processes in Australia*, Melbourne: Addison Wesley Longman.

Meadows, D.H. et al. (1972) *The Limits to Growth: A Report for the Club of Rome's Project on the Predicament of Mankind*, New York: Universe Books.

Moran, A. and Chisholm, A. (1991) *Greenhouse Gas Abatement: Its Costs and Practicalities*, Melbourne: the Tasman Institute, Occasional Paper No. B9.

National Academies Forum (1997) *The Challenge for Australia on Global Climate Change*, proceedings of a workshop held in Canberra, 29–30 April, Canberra: Academy of the Social Sciences in Australia.

Organisation for Economic Cooperation and Development (1998a) *Towards Sustainable Development: Environmental Indicators*, Paris: OECD.

Organisation for Economic Cooperation and Development (1998b) *Environmental Performance Reviews: Australia*, Paris: OECD.

Oswald, A.J. (1997) 'Happiness and Economic Performance', *Economic Journal*, vol. 107, pp. 1815–31.

Owen, A.D. (1992) *The Use of a Carbon Tax for Controlling Carbon Dioxide Emissions: A Review*, a report prepared for the Department of the Arts, Sport, the Environment and Territories, Canberra: *mimeo*.

Papadakis, E. and Young, L. (2000) 'Mediating Clashing Values: Environmental Policy', in Glyn Davis and Michael Keating (eds), *The Future of Governance: Policy Choices*, St Leonards: Allen & Unwin, pp. 153–76.

Parliament of the Commonwealth of Australia (2000) *The Heat is On: Australia's Greenhouse Future*, report of the Senate Environment, Communications, Information

Technology and the Arts Reference Committee, Canberra: Australian Parliament.

Productivity Commission (1999) *Implementation of Ecologically Sustainable Development by Commonwealth Departments and Agencies*, Report No. 5, Canberra: AusInfo.

Productivity Commission (2000) *Microeconomic Reform and the Environment*, proceedings of a workshop held in Melbourne on 8 September, Canberra: AusInfo.

Scitovsky, T. (1976) *The Joyless Economy: An Inquiry into Human Satisfaction and Consumer Dissatisfaction*, New York: Oxford University Press; revised edition (1992) published under the title *The Joyless Economy: the Psychology of Human Satisfaction*, New York: Oxford University Press.

Sen, A. (1990) 'Development as Capability Expansion', in Keith Griffin and John Knight (eds) *Human Development and the International Development Strategy for the 1990s*, London: Macmillan, pp. 41–58.

State of the Environment Advisory Council (1996) *Australia: State of the Environment 1996*, Collingwood: CSIRO Publishing.

Tasman Institute (1991) *Carbon Taxes: Effects on Prices and Incomes*, Melbourne: Tasman Institute.

Throsby, D. (1997) 'Sustainability and Culture: Some Theoretical Issues', *International Journal of Cultural Policy*, vol. 4, pp. 7–20.

Throsby, D. (1999) 'Cultural Capital', *Journal of Cultural Economics*, vol. 23, nos 1–2, pp. 3–12.

Throsby, D. (2001) *Economics and Culture*, Cambridge: Cambridge University Press.

UN Department of Economic and Social Affairs (1998) *Energy Statistics Yearbook 1996*, New York: United Nations.

UNESCO (1998 and 2000) *World Culture Reports*, Paris: UNESCO.

Wills, I. (1992) 'The Ecologically Sustainable Development Process: An Interim Assessment', *Policy*, vol. 8, no. 3, Spring, pp. 8–12.

Winters, L.A. (1992) 'The Trade and Welfare Effects of Greenhouse Gas Abatement: A Survey of Empirical Estimates', in Kym Anderson and Richard Blackhurst (eds) *The Greening of World Trade Issues*, Hemel Hempstead: Harvester Wheatsheaf, pp. 95–114.

World Commission on Culture and Development (1995) *Our Creative Diversity*, Paris: UNESCO.

World Commission on Environment and Development (1987), *Our Common Future*, Oxford: Oxford University Press.

Yencken, D. and Wilkinson, D. (2000) *Resetting the Compass: Australia's Journey Towards Sustainability*, Collingwood: CSIRO Publishing.

Young, A. (2000) *Environmental Change in Australia Since 1788* (2nd edn), Melbourne: Oxford University Press.

Notes

1 With the usual *caveat*, I express my gratitude to Kym Anderson, John Nieuwenhuysen, and other participants in the CEDA authors' seminar for helpful comments on a draft of this chapter, and to Mark Diesendorf and Mike Krockenberger for assistance in obtaining data.

2 See, for example, the classic readings collected in Dorfman and Dorfman (1972). For a discussion of some difficulties inherent in the market-failure approach to environmental issues, see Harris (1996), pp. 160–4.

3 See ESD Working Groups (1991) and ESD Working Group Chairs (1992a, 1992b). For assessments of the ESD process as an experiment in policy-making, see Edwards (1992), Wills (1992), McEachern (1993), Kellow and Moon (1993), Lothian (1994), Diesendorf and Hamilton (1997); contributions to Hamilton and Throsby (1998), and Papadakis and Young (2000).

4 See, for example, Tasman Institute (1991), London Economics (1992); several of these reports are critically reviewed in Owen (1992) and Lowe (1992).

5 For further evaluation of Australia's greenhouse response, see contributions to National Academies Forum (1997) and Parliament of the Commonwealth of Australia (2000). On the role of microeconomic reform in various sectors, see contributions to Productivity Commission (2000). For a conservationist perspective, see Diesendorf (1998).

6 Lewis suggested that the advantage of economic growth was not that wealth increases happiness, but that it increases the range of human freedom and choice. But to the extent that growth also causes environmental destruction, it will, ironically, reduce the range of choice available.

7 The introduction of cultural and social capital alongside physical, human and natural capital continues to extend the concept of capital and its role in economic growth a long way beyond the simple capital goods contained in the early Harrod-type growth models. By all means interpret economic development as a process of capital accumulation, but, as Harry Johnson (1964) observed almost 40 years ago, this only makes sense if the concept of capital referred to is one including human, natural, social and cultural dimensions. For further on social capital, see Dasgupta and Serageldin (2000), and on cultural capital, see Throsby (1999, 2001).

PART 3

New Frontiers, Innovation and Governance

8

New Frontiers of Growth

Terry Cutler

Future economic growth and industrial development can be said to evolve along two possible paths. One is incremental, characterised by continuous improvement and adjustment. The other involves abrupt discontinuities, or what *The Economist*, in talking of the digital information revolution, has described as 'tectonic shifts'. Sometimes these paths intertwine; at other times disruptive innovation cuts across established trend lines. In general, we are familiar and comfortable with the processes of continuous innovation; the experience of disruptive change and discontinuities in economic patterns and industry development is more challenging. The latter is a familiar framework in the thinking of biologists or anthropologists, but it proves a singularly difficult topic for discussion at the tables of boardrooms and executive government.

Australian businesses and industries today confront a new landscape, and new frontiers. It is an inescapable reality that the economic landscape is changing because of the transition from a post-industrial scene of the postwar world era to the new information economy. We need to keep reminding ourselves that most of the dominant firms of the twenty-first century do not exist today. The status quo is no longer the natural state of affairs into the future.

In exploring the new economic landscape, two travel guides are most helpful. The first is Clayton Christensen's seminal 1997 text on the impact of disruptive technologies: *The Innovator's Dilemma: When Technologies Cause Great Firms to Fail*. The second is E.J. Hobsbawm's (1999) classic history of the Industrial Revolution, providing useful hints from past experiences.

The new growth sectors we talk about include all the information industries, financial services, health services and biotechnology, education and training, entertainment, tourism and lifestyle services, next-generation transport, environment management systems, transaction management services, and so on (Committee for the Economic Development of Australia 1997). In part these new growth industries reflect the long-term structural changes in industry mix and composition associated with the growing economic importance of the services sector and so-called 'knowledge-based' activities. More importantly, these industries are technology-based, specifically on the technology infrastructure of information and communications technologies. This is the new frontier variously labelled as the Information or Digital Economy.

The information and communications industries are important economic activities in their own right, but they also have a fundamental transformative and enabling function cross-sectorally. In 1997 the Goldsworthy report for the Australian government summarised this point succinctly:

> The information industries have a unique character in that they are not only major industries in their own right, but they are also all-pervasive enablers underpinning the competitiveness of all business activities. The critical infrastructure for businesses of the future will be 'infostructure' (Information Industries Taskforce 1997: iv).

Technology-based firms, or technology-enabled firms, are the firms that are driving business growth everywhere around the world. For example, in the United States between 1995 and 1998, the IT sector – despite contributing only 8 per cent of GDP – accounted for 35 per cent of the nation's economic growth (*The Economist*, 24 July 1999). Information infrastructures not only underpin the economic growth potential of national economies but also redefine economic value drivers globally.

The OECD (2000: 12) has highlighted the crucial role of information and communications technologies in the innovation process through:

- breaking down 'natural' monopolies
- speeding up the innovation process and reducing product cycle times
- fostering industry clusters through the distributed inter-networking of firms
- speeding up the diffusion of technology and ideas
- forging closer links between science and business.

This context suggests two basic propositions about potential growth strategies for Australia. First, that Australia's best economic prospects will revolve around a shift from a reliance on production volumes to a reliance on higher added value, and second, that the main opportunity for new wealth creation lies in the emerging, information-intensive, 'knowledge industries'.

The Information Economy as the new frontier

The basic driver of the Information Economy is the powerful connectivity arising from the linkage of computing power with telecommunications and digital content and services that we call the Internet. Digital networks and information technologies have fundamentally changed the world. They have also made knowledge management the key to wealth creation and the well-being of communities. Human resources – the intellectual capital of the knowledge and skills of a community – are to the Information Economy what natural resources were to the industrial age.

The World Wide Web, which links information, activities and people, grew out of a project to integrate disparate and stand-alone computer systems and work groups within a large research institute in Switzerland (Berners-Lee 1999). The underlying philosophy is both simple and powerful. It involves creating a 'meta system' that enables different systems, networks and structures to inter-work. This is the web of a network of networks. In essence it is a highly organic and social model, not a technical one. In an increasingly fragmented, borderless world the Internet provides the tools for connecting people, firms and markets around their common interests, both locally and globally.

The digital revolution has underpinned and given new potency to a range of global trends shaping our new economic frontiers. These include:

- The globalisation of production and markets, reflected in the internationalisation of trade in goods and services producing new levels of worldwide interdependency. Borderless electronic commerce will entrench this new reality.
- Industrial restructuring, ranging from the trend to privatisation to the emergence of e-businesses.
- Labour market restructuring and the rise of globally mobile 'knowledge workers'.
- The collapse of the twentieth-century 'second world' order of socialist collectivism.
- Radical discontinuities occurring in the technologies and markets of the information industries.
- The rapid emergence of a cadre of 'new economy' firms that have changed stock markets and forced the make-over of traditional enterprises.
- The democratisation of share ownership, with massively increased participation rates, and the growing use of employee stock options, changing the framework of corporate governance and the meaning of employment.

In many areas the eventual impact of the digital revolution is not yet clear. Health services, education, employment, democracy and governance, cities, the state of the environment, and standards of living – the possible changes in each of these areas is likely to be as substantive as the groundshifts that accompanied the industrial revolution (see Hobsbawm 1999), and well beyond the changes already occurring.

A recent state development strategy promulgated by South Australia identifies some fundamental propositions about the new frontiers for economic development (SA Govt 2000). These propositions are that:

- the global information economy, driven by the information industries, has changed the world
- networking allows distributed activity to replace centralisation, and this can free us to redefine Australia's place in the world
- our existing industries will be transformed, and new enterprises will emerge
- the core assets for success will be people, and their skills, knowledge, values and attitudes
- future standards of living and quality of life will entirely depend on how we go about seizing the emerging opportunities now.

Potent factors within the new industrial environment profoundly change the dynamics of the firm and of markets. All businesses will become *e-businesses* (Evans and Wurster 2000). Electronic processes fundamentally change the economics of organisations, affecting both transaction costs and the nature of the value-added processes within the firm that represent its basic purpose.

Transactions are at the core of any market or business operation. Changes in the organisation and cost of transactions now drive structural adjustment at the firm level within the information economy. Douglass North, the noted US economist and Nobel Prize winner, has shown that transactions represent the major – and rapidly increasing – cost function within the US economy (North 1990: 28). Transaction costs include '*search and information costs, bargaining and decision costs, policing and enforcement costs*' (Dahlman 1979: 148). All transactions are information-based, and this is why the impact of information technologies and electronic commerce in all their forms will be so far-reaching. North and others owe their insights into the role of transactions to Ronald Coase, whose seminal article in the early 1930s identified the role of transactions in shaping the firm as an institution. As Coase noted in his 1991 Nobel Prize lecture, his work tackles 'the institutional nature of production' (Williamson and Winter 1993: 227). Information technology and the networking of business functions are now changing the micro-economics of the firm by redefining institutional boundaries within a marketplace and by changing the patterns and dynamics of inter-firm relationships.

Electronic digital interfaces and networking affect every aspect of a firm's operations, from procurement, product design and manufacturing, through to distribution, marketing and customer-relationship management. Electronic processes change all the rules with respect to both a firm's external transactions and its internal processes. It is important to observe that these impacts shape the options for both *existing* and *new* firms in adjusting to the realities of the new Information Economy. There are multiple points of substantive impact on the nature of any firm's operations, as illustrated in Figure 8.1.

Several recent studies have shown that each of these impacts fundamentally changes cost structures and the operating parameters of the firm. Cumulatively, these impacts also make it possible for new firms to enter markets quickly and efficiently, because information-processing and networked operations lower

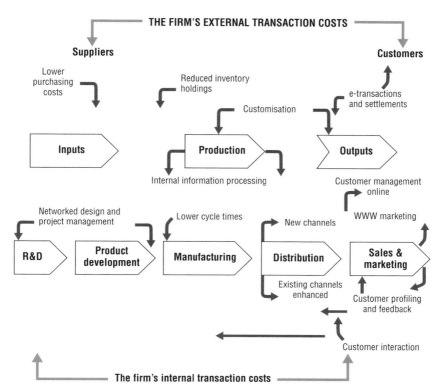

Figure 8.1 Transaction costs and structural adjustment
Source: Cutler and Company (1999).

traditional barriers to entry and, at the same time, facilitate global market access. It is clear that this far-reaching transformation of industrial organisation affects every Australian enterprise.

While considerable attention has been given to the economic impacts of electronic procurement systems on the supply side, probably the greatest overall impact will be driven from the customer interface. In the 'old economy', marketing was predominantly an asymmetrical, asynchronous *push* technology from the firm into a mass market. Digitally enabled marketing transforms the function from a closed system into an adaptive, open system. Customer relationships on the demand side are increasingly driving deep business system redesign. This transformation of the marketing function is based on new digital tools for dynamic, automated, real-time user self-definition, linked to the firm's back office, for optimising the buyer–seller relationship. Customised products and 'just-in-time' manufacturing are early products of this transformation in industrial organisation driven from the demand side.

So-called 'network effects' are another prime value driver in the emerging Information Economy. The law of network effects is that the value of a network increases as more people are connected to it. This is sometimes referred to as Metcalfe's law (after Bob Metcalfe, the inventor of Ethernet): 'The value of a network goes up as a square of the number of users' (Shapiro and Varian 1999, see chapter 7 for network externalities).

The telecommunications industry understood this law long before Metcalfe and networked computing: it was evidenced in the take-up of the telegraph in the nineteenth century and more recent examples include the take-up of facsimile in the 1980s, and now the Internet. Network effects underpin the company valuation models now popular with cellular networks and online services, where value is directly related to the size of the subscriber base. It follows that it is almost impossible for a small network to thrive – unless smaller networks can gain access to a wider user pool through interworking – and this, of course, is the history of telecommunications and now of all the networked activities emerging over online platforms. It is also true of small networked economies and industry clusters.

Behind the economic jargon, three aspects of network effects are crucially important to a consideration of strategies for economic growth.

The first is the importance of achieving the greatest possible participation in order to accelerate critical mass. In an online world, 'you don't get the benefit of change until you do it for everyone'. Critical mass is an important function on both the supply and demand sides of a networked economy, as illustrated in Figure 8.2.

The second important aspect of network effects is the significance of being a first mover. The market innovators who first capture a broad installed base of network users are hard to dislodge or overtake, even with superior services.

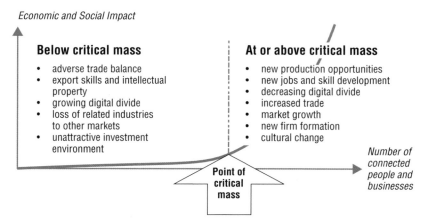

Figure 8.2 The importance of critical mass

Classic examples are VHS versus Beta video recorders, or Microsoft's PC operating system versus that of Apple. Network effects exemplify the Asian proverb: 'The late buffalo drinks muddy water'. The same rule applies to nodes in economic networks; for example, emerging Asian economies have found it difficult to dislodge the role of Singapore and Hong Kong in the regional and global corporate networks of multinationals, and Boston has found it hard to dislodge Silicon Valley in venture capital and as a hub for technology start-ups.

The third important aspect of network-effects is the implication for the role of government. Network effects create wider economic and community benefits – spillovers or externalities – that cannot be expropriated by any individual firm. Such public interest benefits are the classic rationale for direct government intervention in economic development. (A classic case of externalities is government support for research and development, which is also highly relevant to the Information Economy.) Actively promoting widespread online penetration and information industries capability is good public policy in the twenty-first century (see Economides 1996).

The state of play in Australia

Australia has a well-established status as a leading consumer of new technologies. We are fast adopters. The supply side, however, is a very different picture from the demand side. The result is a rapidly growing trade deficit in information and communications goods and services, reflecting the lack of basic capabilities relevant to active participation in emerging global growth opportunities. These shortcomings compound Australia's inherent disadvantages and weaknesses as a small, isolated economy. There is also evidence that Australia's level of investment in key factor inputs such as research and higher education is declining (Prime Minister's Science, Engineering and Innovation Council 2000). In assessing Australia's net economic balance sheet within the emerging global Information Economy, the only possible conclusion is that aggressive and sustained industry development interventions are needed to secure Australia's ability to capture the new growth opportunities and to stake out a position within the new economic frontier.

Australia is at the forefront of international league tables for technology consumption. Australia ranks highly in terms of Internet and computer penetration and usage, the use of online services in education, and in the take-up of electronic commerce. Positive scorecards of adoption and usage are published regularly by Australia's National Office for the Information Economy (National Office for the Information Economy 2000).

Australia's patterns of technology consumption are not matched by production capabilities. A profile of most areas of Australia's information and communications industry shows activity is dominated by a few multinationals (only one or two Australian owned), and a huge tail of sub-scale, under-capitalised small and medium enterprises with a domestic market focus in the areas of product distribution and support services.

Apart from resources and commodities, Australia's chronic problem has always been one of scale and critical mass. Australia is a small economy and a long way from anywhere. It is easy to fall into the trap of concluding that Australia is doing relatively well by reciting good-sounding trend figures based on percentage growth rates and per population achievement. The use of such measures suppresses the harsh reality that these statistical sugar pills disguise low base figures and the small absolute numbers involved. High percentage growth off a really low base is still a really low outcome – in 1997 Australia's share of total OECD country GERD was 1.4 per cent (up from 1 per cent in 1981), and its share of total OECD researchers was 2.2 per cent.

Performance indicators show that Australian industry as a whole is not doing well in research and innovation. According to the Bureau of Statistics (1999), in 1999 there were slightly more than half a million businesses employing staff, excluding farmers and other agricultural businesses, and owner-operated businesses not employing staff. The ABS figures for 1999 show that there were just 3170 businesses undertaking R&D. This represents 0.6 per cent of our pool of Australian businesses employing staff. Not enough are doing their part to build critical mass or to change our industrial landscape. High-technology companies on the Wired Index in the United States had an average investment in R&D of 14.6 per cent of their 1999 sales. The average spend of our Australian companies is 0.5 per cent of turnover.

For three years in a row business investment in R&D has been falling: Australia has slipped back to where it was 10 years ago, at the same time as the rest of the world is moving rapidly ahead (OECD 1999). Some of Australia's traditional industry supporters of R&D, like BHP and Telstra, have drastically downsized their R&D. In Telstra's case, R&D appears to have plummeted from 2 per cent to 0.2 per cent (IAESR and IBIS 1999) of turnover in less than a decade. Over the last three years, a net 3300 research posts have been cut from government, business and private non-profit research institutions.

The situation is worse when one looks at the share of investment directed to the information and communications sector. A recent international survey reported that, on investment in information technology, Australia ranked sixteenth out of seventeen countries (Hindle and Rushworth 2000). Comparable investment in the United States is 24 times greater.

The downsizing of Australia's industrial research is matched by a downward trend in higher education funding, particularly postgraduate research (Australian Vice-Chancellors' Committee 2000). A recent and important survey by the Australian Research Council and CSIRO shows that Australia is falling further and further behind in its share of the world's patented ideas (ARC and CSIRO 2000).

Table 8.1 Import penetration by industry

	High technology industries		Medium-high technology industries		Medium-low technology industries		Low technology industries	
(Imports as a percentage of domestic demand (that is, production plus imports minus exports)								
	1990	1996	1990	1996	1990	1996	1990	1996
Australia	61	68	39	52	13	17	14	16
OECD	29	38	26	30	15	16	15	17

Source: OECD, 2000.

Doing more of the same is clearly not an answer for Australia. More of the same means a worsening balance of trade in the Information Economy. This is an issue that merits some particular attention.

In 1997 an important industry report titled *Spectator or Serious Player?: Competitiveness in Australia's Information Industries* (Charles, Allen and Buckeridge 1997) warned that Australia faced a widening trade gap in the fastest growing areas of world trade: IT&T. Four years later IT&T imports, including services, are continuing to grow at twice the rate of exports (ABS 2000). The resulting deficit is currently the size of our total coal exports (or 10 per cent of our total exports). On current trends it will become $30 billion per annum in 10 years' time. It will get worse: while Australians have taken to the Internet at world's best levels, the Australian economy is not capturing a commensurate share of global e-commerce and is exporting national consumption. Across the board, Australia's import penetration is highest in the high and medium technology intensive industries (Department of Industry 2000: 9) – almost double the average for OECD countries.

On these indicators it is evident that doing more of the same will entrench Australia in a 'second-best' future.

Conclusions: capturing potential growth

The challenges outlined in this chapter are not new. Ten years ago I advocated the development of a national strategy for the information industries, stating:

> Consideration of these new economic realities, and the emerging opportunities . . . raise the question of whether present Government policies go far enough. The right starting point for this assessment is to formulate some possible broad objectives for industry development against which to test the adequacy of possible policy responses. Four broad national goals for this sector can be proposed:
> (i) To facilitate citizens' access to information;
> (ii) To enhance industrial competitiveness through the use of embedded telecommunications and information technology systems;
> (iii) To build distributed information networks that permit the effective clustering of

physically remote activities, supporting continued community cohesion, but also expanding market reach and access internationally; and

(iv) To build telecommunications and information technology industries in their own right that are able to compete worldwide (Cutler 1992, 1994).

Ten years on the challenges remain the same, but the stakes have increased hugely. In 1997 the Goldsworthy report of the Information Industries Taskforce expressed the 'view that Australia's information industries are on the verge of a precipice', and called for a sense of urgency in formulating a National Information Industries Strategy.

The OECD's current Growth project is highlighting the importance of industry networking, collaboration and alliances in capturing sources of innovation and in promoting rapid advance (OECD 2000). What is needed is an Australia-wide web of innovation linking businesses, research institutes and governments within a creative partnership. And this is where government comes in.

Countries that have captured a significant stake in technology and knowledge-based industries, from a low base, have all done so 'by the conscious design and implementation of interventionist public policy' (Green 2000). Australia did just this in promoting the development of the mining industry in the 1960s. Australia did just this in the sports industry, shifting national performance from zero gold medals at the 1976 Montreal Olympics to a global market share of 5.31 per cent in Sydney 2000.

The government's role in funding R&D and high-level skills development is fundamental. Without serious government funding things are not going to change. Without serious government funding there is little prospect for the necessary structural adjustment in Australia's economy and industrial landscape.

To produce results, R&D and high-technology capabilities need sustained, long-term commitment. This is not like tweaking interest rates. Capability takes a long time to build up, to reach critical mass, but it can drain away quickly.

To reverse the decline in our technology and skills infrastructure requires more than just restoring old programs like the 150 per cent tax concession for R&D. One way of being smarter is to link public funding of industry programs to outputs, not inputs. Reward results, whether they be industry R&D levels, new patents, or high-technology job creation. Economic development programs should create the right incentive systems for all players. Industry performance needs to be encouraged and judged on the outcomes produced, not on the resources deployed.

In conclusion, we need to be very conscious that Australia does stand at a crossroad. Australia needs to decide whether it wants to be a spectator or a serious player in the new global information economy, and to have a knowledge-based economy fuelled by high-technology industries. Australia is seriously behind the game in building the industries that are, around the world, creating the new jobs and the new wealth. Its scorecard does not look good.

References

ABS, *Small business in Australia 1999*, Cat. no. 1321.0.

ABS, *R&D expenditure – Business sector 1998–99*, Cat. no. 8104.0.

ABS (2000) Cat. no. 8143.0, May.

ARC and CSIRO (2000) *Inventing our Future: The Link between Australian Patenting and Basic Science*, June.

Australian Vice-Chancellors' Committee (2000) I, an AVCC discussion paper, November.

Berners-Lee, T. (1999) *Weaving the Web: The Original Design and Ultimate Destiny of the World Wide Web*, Harper, San Francisco.

Charles, D., Allen, R. and Buckeridge, R. (1997) *Spectator or Serious Player?: Competitiveness in Australia's Information Industries*, report to the Information Industries Taskforce, Allen Consulting Group and Allen & Buckeridge, Melbourne, March.

Committee for the Economic Development of Australia (1997) *Australia's Emerging Industries*, Growth No. 45, December.

Cutler, T. (1992) 'Telecommunications', in John Carroll and Robert Manne (eds) *Shutdown: The Failure of Economic Rationalism*, Text Publishing, Melbourne.

Cutler, T. (1994) 'Telecommunications in the Future Australian Economy: An Electronic Switzerland or an Electronic Backwater?', in Ian Marsh (ed.) *Australian Business in the Asia Pacific Region: The Case for Strategic Industry Policy*, Longman.

Dahlman, C.J. (1979) 'The Problem of Externality', *The Journal of Law and Economics*, vol. 22, no. 1, April.

Department of Industry (2000) *Science and Resources, Knowledge-based Activities: Selected Indicators*, February.

Economides, N. (1996) 'The Economics of Networks', *International Journal of Industrial Organisation*, vol. 14, 6, October.

Evans, P. and Wurster, T.S. (2000) *Blown to Bits*, Harvard.

Green, R. (2000) 'Regional Innovation: The European Experience', National University of Ireland, Galway, paper presented to the Regional Cooperation and Development Forum, Canberra, 3 December.

Hindle, K. and Rushworth, S. (2000) *Global Entrepreneurial Monitor: Australia 2000*, Swinburne University of Technology.

Hobsbawm, E.J. (1999) *Industry and Empire: From 1759 to the Present Day*, Revised edition, Penguin.

Information Industries Taskforce (1997) *The Global Information Economy: The Way Ahead*, Canberra.

Institute of Applied Economic and Social Research (IAESR) and IBIS Pty Ltd (1999) *R&D and Intellectual Property Scoreboard 1999*, Melbourne.

National Office for the Information Economy (2000) *The Current State of Play: November 2000*, Canberra.

North, D. (1990) *Institutions, Institutional Change and Economic Performance*, Cambridge.

OECD, *Science, Technology and Industry Scoreboard 1999* <www.oecd.org/dsti/sti/stat-ana/prod/scorebd-sum.htm>.

OECD (2000) *A New Economy? The Changing Role of Innovation and Information Technology in Growth*, July.

Prime Minister's Science, Engineering and Innovation Council (2000) *Australia's Information and Communications Technology (ICT) Research Base: Driving the 'New Economy'*, 30 November.

Shapiro, C. and Varian, H. (1999) *Information Rules: A Strategic Guide to the Networked Economy*, Harvard.

South Australian Government, *Information Economy 2002: Delivering the Future*, Adelaide, <http//:www.ie2002.sa.gov.au>.

Williamson, O.E. and Winter, S.G. (eds) (1993) *The Nature of the Firm: Origins, Evolution and Development*, Oxford.

9

Innovation in Australia: Where to Now?

Jane Marceau

Introduction

Innovation has become a much-used word in Australia over the last three years. In contrast, until late 1997 'innovation' was virtually undiscussed in academic circles, especially economics departments, and not at all in public policy circles. This chapter indicates what innovation is and why it can be useful to encourage different forms of innovation in seeking long-term competitive advantage at a time when Australia's commodity prices and output are in steady decline.

The National Innovation Summit held in February 2000 marked the beginning of serious federal government investment in a series of investigations about how to encourage higher levels of innovation in Australia. The recent reports of the Innovation Summit Implementation Group, ISIG, and *The Chance to Change*, released in November by the Chief Scientist, both advocate increased levels of innovation as assured by shifts in 'culture', in 'people' and in the commercialisation of the results of scientific research. Their pleas for more investment in our knowledge bases have come to fruition with the recent Prime Ministerial statement on 'Backing Australia's Ability'. This emphasis, however, comes in counterpoint to the recently released statistics published by the ABS, which show that investment in R&D by Australian companies has dropped again for the third successive year, this time by almost 10 per cent. Analyses in the reports indicate that if Australia fails to invest in innovation it is unlikely to be able to compete in the future in an increasingly globalised world market. In contrast, productivity growth in Australia has risen in recent years with sustained economic growth. So what is happening? Is innovation not so important after all?

Part of the answer to this apparent paradox lies in the many possible interpretations of what is meant by 'innovation' and hence how it is measured and its effects understood. Much also depends on the timeframe considered.

Innovation has been defined in many ways. In the broadest view it means a novelty of economic value. Innovations must have been implemented to be counted so that the economic value is clear. Innovative products need to be distinguished from inventions, many of which stay on the nation's intellectual property storage shelf, even though firmly protected by international patents.

'Innovation' as normally understood has at least three major tenets: first, in products (including services) when firms bring significantly new products or services to market; second, in processes, the significant improvements to the ways in which products are made. This may involve changes to the machinery that makes tangible products or it may be alterations to the ways in which services are developed and delivered to customers; and third, alterations to the organisational arrangements that surround the productive process. These may, for example, be implemented when new machinery is installed, making some previous arrangements redundant and possibly involving broader changes in firms' management. The latter may include shifts towards greater investment in knowledge production in the firm, through greater investment in R&D, or in the firm's knowledge absorption capacity and skill, through extra training for staff or recruitment of staff with higher levels of education. There may also be significant changes to the ways in which firms think strategically about the markets in which they work and on the best ways to improve market position. Such changes may involve decisions to work more closely with other firms and/or with public-sector research organisations in networks of activity that link firms more closely to their customers and suppliers, or even to their competitors.

International work on innovation has explored all these dimensions and there is now considerable empirical evidence showing how firms go about innovating and the factors in their operating environment which encourage or present obstacles to increasing levels of innovative activity.

But why does it matter whether firms are innovative or not? The answer lies in a revised understanding of the dynamics of modern economies. This has been developed through new branches of economics, especially those following some of the insights of Schumpeter early in the last century and now known broadly as innovation economics or, more specifically, as evolutionary economics. These approaches underline the importance of technological innovation as a determinant of competitive advantage and of the shifting bases of production. They show, for example, that firms which innovate on a continuous basis can lead the market in their chosen field and do so for quite considerable periods, sometimes establishing niche positions to provide temporary and possibly long-term monopoly power through the 'lock in' of technologies. These advantages can persist until a major new breakthrough is made or even slow down such breakthroughs through the positions established (see, for example, Metcalfe 1995 and OECD 2000 for a summary of the relationship between innovation and economic growth).

International empirical analysis also shows that revenue from new or substantially altered products accounts for an increasing share of firms' profits in the manufacturing sector. While there is less evidence as yet, it is likely that the same is true of services and very recent evidence (Marceau, Cook and Dalton 2001) shows clearly that many firms in a variety of sectors are innovating by linking old products and new services or new products and existing services, incorporating them in-house and offering 'product–service packages' in successfully bidding to remain competitive in new conditions.

There is also evidence of an increase in the importance of the science component in many product sectors. Thus, biotechnology products and pharmaceuticals link directly to new knowledge generated by science. A country's investment in science may therefore have direct importance for the innovation capacity of its existing and emerging industrial sectors. It is this link that lies behind the oft-repeated emphasis on the growing knowledge-intensity of modern economies referred to as 'knowledge economies'. These economies are 'directly based on the production, distribution and use of knowledge and information' (OECD 1996a: 7).

Innovation becomes more important in the context of a knowledge-based economy. As the new economies develop, high-level skills and competencies are needed to turn information into useable knowledge and knowledge into innovations. Innovation has been shown in turn to flourish most successfully in the context of knowledge-intensive industrial structures (for example, OECD 1996a; 1999). This is a circular positive relationship. Innovation improves the knowledge-intensity of the industrial structure by encouraging the emergence of new innovative businesses and industries while, at the same time, the knowledge-intensity of the industrial structure will feed the innovation process since new innovative businesses interact with other businesses, thereby influencing their capabilities and aspirations.

There is a common misconception that only areas such as information and communication technologies (ICT) are the hallmark of a knowledge-intensive economy. Knowledge-intensive industries are likely to grow more rapidly than other industries in a knowledge economy, but this trend 'does not signal a science-based economy dominated by high-tech firms' (Lundvall 1996: 3). Innovation in traditional raw material-based industries, for example, has been critical to economic growth in some European countries (Smith 1998) and to Australia as the history of mining and agriculture shows.

Recognising the importance of the 'low-tech' fields, a major report has recently concluded that:

> . . . innovation can drive productivity improvement across all industrial sectors. In this sense, there are not 'low tech' industries – only low technology companies that fail to incorporate new ideas and methods into their products and processes. Innovation opportunities are present today in virtually any industry. Although industries

producing enabling technologies such as computers, software, and communications have received much attention, opportunities to apply advanced technology are present in fields as disparate as textiles, machinery, and financial services (Council on Competitiveness 1999: 12).

Nor is innovation tied only to the use of 'advanced physical technologies'. Changes in the way businesses organise themselves may also be highly innovative and yield rapid growth. R&D statistics capture these organisational innovations only to a limited extent. Moreover, recent European research suggests that some low R&D-intensive industries may enjoy strong growth due to high levels of innovation based on non-R&D inputs, finding that '. . . the knowledge bases of apparently low and medium technology industries . . . are in fact deep, complex, science-based and above all systemic (in the sense of involving complex and sustained institutional interactions)' (Smith 1998: 1).

Systems of innovation

International studies have shown both that innovation is not random but patterned and that some countries and regions are better at innovation than are others. Analysts have therefore turned their attention towards looking at *systems of innovation* (Dosi 1999).

This shift is important because it focuses attention on the *context* in which firms work, rather than just on what individual firms do. This context is composed of a broader scientific and technological community and is influenced by relationships with suppliers, customers, regulators and research and training organisations. In particular, many studies of innovation processes point to well-functioning systems of linkages (communication systems) between key players, including both firms and public-sector research organisations as central mechanisms encouraging successful innovation (see, for example, OECD 1997a). Innovation rates are thus greatly affected by the institutional arrangements in which innovative activities take place.

National, sectoral and sub-national innovation systems

This institutional context in which firms work can be viewed as national, regional or local, or existing at sectoral levels. Each one can usefully be viewed as a system of rules, institutions and inter-organisational interactions.

Studies undertaken by the OECD over the last decade into the functioning of innovation systems have led to the development of quite sophisticated indicators of their achievements, although assessment of the effectiveness of different sets of institutional and organisational arrangements requires further refinement and there is still considerable discussion over the impact of globalisation on national arrangements (Lundvall and Tomlinson 2000).

National systems of innovation are composed of '. . . the national institutions, their incentive structures and their competencies, that determine the rate and direction of technological learning (or the volume and composition of change-generating activities) in a country' (Patel and Pavitt 1994).

Their importance is described by the OECD as follows:

> . . . as there is an increasing number of institutions with specialised knowledge of very different kinds, the ability to access different sources of knowledge and to apply these to their own needs becomes crucial for the innovativeness of firms. *It is the configuration of these institutions and the [resulting] flows of knowledge which characterise different national systems of innovation and underlie the innovative performance of countries* (1996b: 3, emphasis added).

Within this framework, recent studies of innovation emphasise the interactions between and integration of different players (for example, AEGIS/Marceau 1999a and AEGIS/Marceau et al. 1999b). Where inter-firm knowledge-generation is concerned, for instance, they demonstrate the feedback processes operating between scientific research, technical development and production, the simultaneity of R&D activities and the interaction among various actors in industrial R&D broadly defined. At the level of localities, regions or nations they emphasise the links between firms (cluster analysis) and between firms and other institutions. Innovation can thus be usefully viewed as a team effort where all aspects of product generation and marketing are considered together.

The core elements of innovation *systems* are therefore constituted by a country's institutions, organisations and the resulting inter-relationships that come into play in the production, diffusion and use of new and existing economically useful knowledge. The elements of the system include the innovation activities carried out by institutions of government and other public-sector bodies, notably universities and other science-intensive institutions, and the different players in the private sector. Innovation is both more frequent and better managed, leading to more substantial national competitive advantage, when the elements of the broader environment surrounding firms' activities are well articulated into a system of information-sharing than in situations where each element works largely in isolation.

A properly functioning innovation support environment provides collectively what firms cannot individually provide themselves in their innovation activities, notably public good research and the development of a broad range of expertise. Such support is especially important in small countries such as Australia and to small firms that have too few resources to meet, for example, the cost of research of a more basic or promising but initially tangential kind or high-level technical or specialist training.

The emphasis on institutions, however, should not exclude recognising that the effectiveness of innovation systems of all levels partly depends on the

strength of the underlying industrial structure since firms and their strategies
are included as a major element in the system. A 'patchy' industrial structure,
for instance, where public-sector research is linked only to a few companies or
industries, means ineffective linkages within the national innovation system
because firms have too few partners to link with and too little research is
undertaken in given fields because there is perceived to be too little demand in
these fields to justify public investment in knowledge-generation and diffusion.

The continuing importance of the nation and its local regions in a globalising world

The nation remains the most important innovation arena (Guerrieri 1999). It
is still what happens inside national borders that largely determines the success
of the national economic endeavour in terms of its capacity to innovate. It is
still within the national arena, for example, that policies for research, for
training, for the protection of intellectual property, for access to finance for
development, and so on, are decided. Two experts in international trade,
Archibugi and Michie (1995), for example, present evidence that, although
transnational firms exploit technological opportunities in a global context and
collaborate internationally, they also rely heavily on home-based technological
infrastructure for the generation of technology.

Innovation 'speed', a reduction in the lead times available for innovations
to reach market if they are to be profitable, is also significantly affected by conditions in the home market because these impact on the ease of creating and
operating various technological developments (Teubal et al. 1996). If the home
market is not appropriate, if it has the 'wrong' industrial, and especially
customer, mix, a poor R&D base or poor provision of finance, initial marketing, sales and product-testing cannot be carried out effectively.

Work over the last decade or so has indicated that not only nations but also
regions that are successful have well-functioning innovation systems. Thus,
for instance, regions, especially those isolated from the central knowledge-
generating and transmitting nodes, may need to develop better functioning
linkages with public-sector research laboratories, technical institutes, government and other regulators. In addition, they may need to make special efforts to
link with specialist firms located elsewhere in the country because they will otherwise lack the industrial partners needed for co-development of new products and
services and find it hard to establish and maintain the close user–producer relations now recognised as a critical part of successful product innovation.

Summary of international conclusions

The discussion above indicates that a number of different trends have been
coming together in the understanding of the dynamics of innovation and of

policy options for furthering innovation. More specifically, there has been increasing international appreciation of five particularly important elements of the ways in which modern economies and the central players in them operate:

- recognition of many firms' need to collaborate in innovation
- the importance of calling on the skills of a variety of players in innovation, most notably other firms, as users of products or suppliers to the innovating firm
- the need for governments, industry and public-sector research organisations to build new organisational links that lead to a virtuous 'Triple Helix' in which the performance of all can be upgraded (Leydesdorff and Etzkowitz 1999)
- the need to build better functioning national, local and regional systems of innovation
- the continuing importance of policies in place in the home nation because these are the basis of institutional and practical arrangements pertaining in the innovation systems most relevant to firms' activities. Such policies include labour market, intellectual property, education and training, R&D and regulatory arrangements and frameworks, and policy-making capacity.

In other words, improving innovation performance depends on putting into place a broad range of mutually supporting policies, not one or a very small set alone.

Encouraging innovation in Australia

Australia has not done well in recent years in the innovation field, being low on many indicators in relation to other OECD countries (Marceau, Manley and Sicklen 1997, Marceau and Manley 2000). There are two major aspects to encouraging innovation in Australia. The first is better understanding of the issues. The second is a policy approach that uses the lessons from overseas on a broader front than just R&D and focuses instead on industry development strategies that recognise diversity and do not seek a 'one best solution'.

If it is generally accepted that innovation is a key ingredient of economies likely to be internationally competitive in the new century, what are the priorities for policy action? Where do we need greater effort? How able is Australia to take policy advantage of what we know about innovation in different industries and where is improvement needed?

New analytical lenses

A first need in developing good policies for the future is greater sophistication in understanding how Australian industry works and hence where the points of greatest leverage for limited dollars and human resources lie. The point of

departure is the recognition of *differences* between industries and sectors. International work shows a very broad range of patterns of innovation in different
sectors or technological fields. Pavitt, for example, in 1984 distinguished four
main kinds of innovation organisation in manufacturing industries alone.
These were:

- Industries dominated by suppliers. These include many of the traditional
  industries found in Australia, notably textiles and clothing, paper and
  printing, and building and construction. In these industries, the focus is on
  process innovation and design, rather than entire new products, and the
  companies in such sectors rely heavily on innovation by manufacturers of
  components, machinery and materials.
- Scale-intensive industries. The central ones in Australia include the auto-
  motive industry, metal goods and processed food, and information-
  intensive industries. These include companies that develop systems and
  engineering software for clients in finance and other service industries.
- Science-based industries. These are the classic industries that governments
  wanting to improve the knowledge-intensive nature of their economies
  usually turn to first. They include pharmaceuticals, chemicals and elec-
  tronics, and cover some of the core technologies of the opening years of the
  twenty-first century. They are heavy users of R&D, both within their own
  and in public-sector research laboratories. Because they are so close to
  science and many of their products change continuously, there is room in
  many of the fields for small firms as well as larger ones to develop products
  at the leading edge of world markets.
- In addition, specialised suppliers of inputs to a wide spectrum of industries,
  but who often succeed through close contacts with specific clients, can be
  found. Innovation here is often design-dependent and involves long-term
  relationships, almost never spot-contracting.

This list, that applies to manufacturing only (the services industries vary
equally) spells out such clear differences that it becomes equally clear there is
no one quick fix, no one best solution or a TINA (There Is No Alternative)
answer. Instead, we need to look carefully at the functioning of each of the
major industries that we have got and understand much better the dynamics
of their development and change. It is what Australia already has that will
provide the base for future development, at least in the short to medium term.
We must maximise their capabilities and efficiency.

Deconstructing the Patel and Pavitt list further indicates where the best
opportunities for innovation may lie. Some may be in the domain of information – about technologies available, customer needs, skills to develop, scientific
research results and areas of regulation that may provide new opportunities
(for example, in energy conservation). There is, for example, international
evidence that firms are very poorly informed of even local client needs in many

complex industries, especially where these may be linked to sub-contracting opportunities (see, for example, a 1993 study of Quebec). Many are too small to know about international marketing possibilities, or even to scan the relevant literature effectively if they do not employ scientific and engineering personnel. Many may need help with understanding and adopting the new management practices that could give them competitive advantage.

But just listing the problems faced by firms in this way is not enough. Good analytical lenses are required through which to view the dynamics of different industries and to ascertain the sources of innovation that are ill-used or need further development. In general, it is useful to distinguish four major sets of players who hold the keys to information about opportunities for innovation and who may hold the key to opening further possibilities or removing obstacles to product development or process or organisational change. There are two ways of approaching this from a policy-related point of view.

The first is developing an analysis of 'product systems' (Gann and Salter 1998, AEGIS/Marceau 1999a). This approach analyses industries in a way that indicates the potential sources of innovation. Thus, in all industries one can modify official statistics to link together a series of players who do not otherwise appear. In building and construction, for example, one can find groups of inputs called 'on-site services', 'client services', machinery and equipment suppliers, and materials and components suppliers. All four sets of players may be innovative and potentially supply ideas and innovative goods and services to the lead firms coordinating work in the industry. In some cases, potential innovation is hard to customise for the lead firms' needs while in others, if attention is paid to improving information flows, quite considerable opportunities may open up. Thus, for example, 90 per cent of equipment is imported to Australia. This means that equipment imports are a major source of innovation for Australia (new to the country), while it also means that local firms are unable to have any input to equipment design. On the other hand, client service firms such as design or IT provide many opportunities for customisation of products and their incorporation on a customised basis to client firms' process needs. Materials and components in some product systems are of great importance, as in the building and construction system, where these producers invest considerable sums in R&D in such areas as cement, solar energy cells or 'clip-on' technologies (see the R&D Scoreboard 1998), often assisted by links with public-sector R&D or lead firms' own changed organisational arrangements. Analysing the workings of the product system in this way indicates where improvements in communication and investment in innovation may need to be made.

The second policy analytical approach involves using the 'complexes' approach developed by Glatz and van Tulder (1989) in Europe and Marceau in Australia (1994 and AEGIS/Marceau 1999a, b and c). This provides a useful framework for analysing information flows between key players and hence a better basis for policy development. The four key sets of players to examine using this analytical lens are user firms, client firms, R&D and training institutions and regulators, mostly but not exclusively government.

Thus, to continue with the building and construction product system as exemplar, a recent study carried out by AEGIS on the capability of local industry to build items using solar energy using the four-players approach showed clearly that the industry had many of the capacities necessary to undertake more projects using sustainable energies. The study showed that the industry's research capability was leading edge in the world in this field, that there were good relations between user firms and producers of the research, that the designers and builders in the system had the skills to design appropriately, to install and maintain the new technologies involved, and that the photovoltaic cells were available, although not produced in Australia. Lack of capacity was thus clearly not the issue.

Using this approach suggests that sometimes it is not users or producer firms that can best stimulate innovation. Rather, the stimulus for innovation should come from the regulatory system. In the case of solar energy, for example, much greater use of solar technologies has been feasible for some time. What has been missing has been appropriate regulation that pushed firms to use the technologies developed and an associated source of easily accessible advice to enable companies to comply with new rules. The industry has been relying solely on individual client acceptance – a very gradual process – instead of being able to operate within a stimulatory framework encouraging full use of the industry's innovative capabilities. As a result, although Australia has the research and the skills to implement new technologies, it is mainly internationally that solar energy research results are being put into practice, encouraging the decision by the key producer of PV cells to produce not in Australia but in Spain.

Figure 9.1 below outlines what a well-functioning complex of information flows between players looks like. The lines between the players, which represent information flows, are all the same 'thickness' and all are interconnected. Figure 9.2 indicates, based on information gathered through our studies, where the information flows are poor and need further development in relation to the solar energy example discussed above. The lines in this diagram are variable in strength and direction.

Policy perspectives: from individual firm to clusters and sectors

International work is moving towards focusing on developing collectivities, both in determining what policy directions to take and assessing their effectiveness. Thus, for example, Klette, Moen and Griliches (2000) found that it could be useful to take a technology *cluster* approach to evaluating whether fiscal interventions worked rather than look simply at the effects on individual firms (emphasis added). They suggested that:

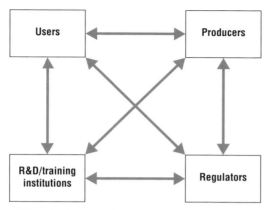

Figure 9.1 A well-functioning complex

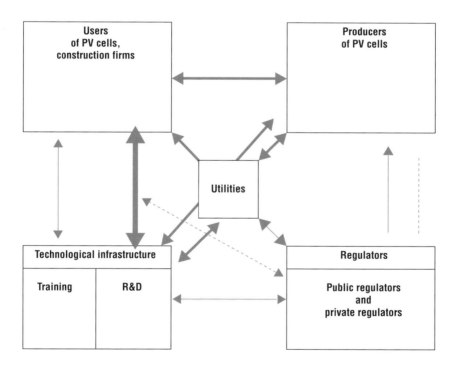

Figure 9.2 Information flows in the energy efficiency segment of the building and construction complex

. . . we need to look beyond the direct impact [of fiscal incentives for R&D in this case] on the performance of targeted firms and *consider changes in the performance of the industries or 'technological clusters' to which the supported firms belong. This may lead us to a more aggregated, industry-level analysis* (2000: 493, emphasis added).

Similarly, David et al. (2000) quote a study by Levin and Reiss that was carried out in 1984 but that has not been widely followed up. The authors found that government R&D investment (rather than an R&D tax concession) has a positive and significant effect on private R&D intensity. This is largely because it can take into account the specific situation of a given industry and relevant aspects of difference with other industries. *The structure of the industry and its opportunities are critical to success.* This point is central to the argument in this chapter.

Such findings again suggest that public policy-making in this field, as in others, needs to develop more sophisticated instruments for understanding the industrial and service-sector environment and the internal dynamics of the sectors before choosing policy approaches. These can provide the context and the basis for a related and more coherent set of policies than are presently available in many countries, including Australia.

In Australia there has been much discussion of industry development strategies in terms of should winners be picked or should the macro environment in which firms operate be improved to enable them to take better advantage of market opportunities. The second view tends to focus on the individual firm as the main unit of analysis and decision-making in relation to innovation when the international evidence on successful innovation suggests rather that *firms operating in conjunction with other firms* working in the same arena need to be the focus of attention.

If groups of interacting firms are critical to successful innovation, policy-makers need to think in terms of improving relationships between key players, and choose investment policies to maximise return through improving the situation of the sector as a whole.

Experience with the R&D tax concession indicates the problem with current policies that do not seem to ensure permanent behaviour change by companies. The R&D tax concession improved investment in R&D in Australia from its inception in 1985–86, both in terms of expenditure by firms on R&D increase and on the numbers of scientists employed, but over a period of 11 years it was not sufficient to embed the need to invest in R&D or in the employment of scientific personnel in long-term firm strategies. This can be seen from the consistent sharp decline in R&D investment once the rate of the concession was reduced in 1996–97. Similarly, once the training levy was withdrawn, firms' investment in staff training, always low but improving from the introduction of the levy, also declined. There was no apparent intention to invest permanently in knowledge-generation or transmission. Moreover, only a few thousand firms out of the tens of thousands of apparently eligible firms ever claimed the tax concession, suggesting that they were not investing at all in R&D. This is confirmed by the two ABS surveys of innovation in Australian mining and manufacturing industry and, to a lesser extent, in services. Small firms that may well be most innovative also rarely meet the criteria for the concession. The Prime Minister's recent package of policies introduced to encourage innovation go some way towards addressing these issues in relation to R&D, notably in relation to small firms, but international evidence on fiscal incentives to firms to invest more in R&D is far from endorsing that approach (see special issues of *Research Policy* in 2000), and the recently selected US Secretary for Commerce indicated that firms who undertook R&D because of fiscal concessions were 'fools'.

So how do we get beyond this? The R&D and training incentive experience suggests that other approaches are needed if Australia is to prepare itself better for the shift in the bases of competition towards greater reliance on innovation. The Australian Science and Technology Budget Statement 2000–2001 suggests that:

> The scene is now set for a further shift in policy thinking. More than ever before, it is now widely accepted that the generation *and application* of knowledge is the key to future prosperity. In recent decades it was widely taken for granted that knowledge developed in universities and research laboratories would be applied in industry as a matter of course. It is now clear that this is not always the case. Application depends on a complex array of interactions between the generators and translators of intellectual capital. It requires a whole host of factors to be present, including, for example, understanding industry needs, access to finance, the ability to negotiate intellectual property rights, effective business management, marketing skills and, perhaps most importantly, vision, leadership and drive. Bringing the necessary elements together requires effective cooperation and high levels of communication. This cooperation may occur within a firm, but it is just as likely to involve outside elements, perhaps other firms in complementary, or even like, industries, universities, research organisations, and government granting and regulatory bodies (2000: 1.3).

A shift towards greater investment not in individual firms directly but in *collective* activities and in the institutions that provide good sources of innovation, knowledge and skills, and the encouragement of their use, thus seems necessary to ensure the application of the knowledge generated, as well as the applicability and relevance of that knowledge to a given sector.

This shift means a move away from simply improving the macro environment as though all industries needed the same things. While all industries could possibly benefit from improved transportation systems, for example, these are not central to the innovation process. Each industry may well need different elements and/or need access to common facilities in different proportions, at different times or in different ways, as work by Pavitt and others has shown. Once the dynamics of different industries are understood, policies can be developed jointly by the users and providers and by the key players in any given sector who are then much more likely to become stakeholders and change their priorities in the desired directions. It is only by overcoming the 'if only . . .' or the 'government oughta' syndromes common in Australia, and understanding the need for many points of assistance for any one sector, that innovation encouragement can succeed.

Key players need to be involved in a continuous discussion of what will be of most value in their industry and of the most effective mechanisms for delivering this. Experience in Quebec, for example, has indicated that collective investments in training and testing facilities would be of great value to many industries, a conclusion reached after extensive discussions between all partners: firms, public-sector R&D providers, unions and government (Government of Quebec 1993). Simple information-sharing through the discussions was also of inestimable value; firms learned of potential new subcontractors on their doorsteps, alleviating the need to go overseas, while smaller or more specialist firms learned more about the need for customisation and developing close relationships with key users.

The benefits of such interaction are permanent and lead to permanently changed practices in ways that government programs developed in isolation or after only superficial consultation or examination of overseas alternatives cannot do. Such interactions also ensure that should government policies change for any reason, good practices will continue because all sets of players have seen the benefit. Once the changes can be entrenched, the need for further support may change and new support systems more suited to the next stage of the industry's development can be instituted.

The current Action Agendas pursued by the federal government through the Department of Industry, Science and Resources are a step in the right direction. The approach partially replicates that taken from the early 1990s by the provincial government of Quebec in Canada and incorporates some of the 'complexes' approach taken by my own earlier research (Marceau 1994).

As the Guidelines indicate, the primary focus of the Action Agendas is:

> to lift the growth prospects of important industry sectors. They offer an opportunity to create long-term sustainable competitive advantage by identifying the actions necessary to lift our innovative and knowledge-creating capacity at the sector level . . . High-level industry commitment is a prerequisite . . . The Government's role is that of a catalyst providing the logistical framework for the process and actions and some direct involvement where necessary . . . Because it is intended that the Action Agendas take a whole of government approach, they will provide a framework for more effective coordination and integration of government policies as they impact on particular industries . . . They will also be an invaluable tool for informing the broader policy development process.

The Action Agendas currently constituted bring together government and industry players in a range of sectors to examine collectively what is needed to improve the competitiveness of the industry sector concerned. The approach is aimed explicitly to recognise the differences between industry sectors. As the Guidelines say, each sector has 'unique characteristics and challenges. Some industry sectors are dependent on large one-off capital-intensive projects while others are best suited to small innovative firms. Some are heavily dependent on science and technology while on others efficiency may be maximised through innovative management and work practices . . .'.

Each Action Agenda has varied somewhat in its methods of work but the common themes include research into the basic parameters of the industry. The parameters include technological capability, skill levels, and R&D infrastructure, and the trade and industry structure (number and size of firms, and so on) of the area, as well as its productivity. The research undertaken by AEGIS also involves reshaping the available statistics to describe the contours of a product system because not all key players are included in studies that take the more usual sectoral approach. Thus, for example, in the furnishings study we included retailers, office designers and architects as the drivers of innovation and not only the furniture-producing firms; in textiles, clothing and footwear the retailers had a key place and in toolmaking the major clients. This is the approach that enables the analyst to understand the *dynamics* of the arena, not just to build a static picture, and therefore improves capacity for judgement about which policies will be most effective in the longer term.

The brief of the Action Agendas participants is, as I have emphasised, to come up with collective suggestions as to how to take the industries forward with an eye on the achievement of specific outcomes. There is a specific section of the Guidelines that indicates the discussions and analysis should consider both the technological strength of the sector and gaps in technological capability, and whether sufficient investment is available for innovative but high-risk projects.

The Action Agendas approach is both innovative and appropriate. There remain, however, two problems with the current Action Agenda framework. Both relate to the range of players included. The first is that, unless the product system approach is systematically used, it may well leave out useful input from the real drivers of innovation who are outside the usual sectoral boundaries as described above. The second is that, while the process brings together officials and industry leaders, it leaves out some other key players. In particular, the process does not provide for involvement by key public-sector researchers, whether in CSIRO or the universities. It also neglects input by the users of the sector's products; for example, in building and construction, the users of key constructed items or by the local regulators, the city planners, who have critical interests in the outcomes of new designs, construction techniques and technologies, or the transport planners who may have to use new technologies to cope with major shifts in population geographies.

If the Action Agenda processes were to be adjusted in a second stage to include R&D personnel and users of different kinds they could provide a powerful mechanism for allowing players to pool their knowledge so as to agree on priorities for research and on the directions for and development of long-term, systematic programs of research and development, and for programs of provision of collective innovation-related infrastructure, such as training and testing facilities. These programs could be financed jointly by industry and government, in whatever proportions were agreed. They would recognise the different needs of different technologies and their producers, as seen, for example, in work by Senker, Faulkner and Velho (1998).

Conclusions

For Australia to move forward successfully and maximise possibilities to innovate and shift to a knowledge economy, a broad package of policies is needed. These should include venture capital (although now the main problem in Australia is finding the firms to support) and a range of measures to better link research and its application and the development of new scientific skills. Again these have been addressed in various policy statements in recent times and the overall situation seems to be improving. There is still one area that deserves special attention, however, despite the work of the Office of the Information Economy. IT is shown by all studies to be critical to the improved communication and knowledge storage and transmission needed for innovation and to enable partners in innovative activity to work successfully together. IT is the key to collaboration between Australia's few large players and numerous small ones. Australia is also a good distance away from our markets overseas. It needs policies to ensure scale for its activities and also that the largest are the best, by encouraging entry of new players. Australia also needs help to overcome the tyranny of distance from users and markets, the essential element of successful innovation, which means that many partners are overseas so the costs of collaboration are greater than for small players in Europe, for instance. Here too IT is critical. Australia is a small country, with a patchy industrial structure and a very large import bill for plant and equipment, especially IT-related equipment. A package of policies for dealing with all the IT issues mentioned above is urgently needed. In this case all sectors, not just some, would benefit.

Using such mechanisms as the Action Agendas and those that ensure Australia develops infrastructure of collective benefit to existing industries, and investing in research in a public sector that is world class will help upgrade established fields of activity and provide the basis for the creation of new industries. This will go a long way towards moving industry forward. It will move firms towards greater understanding of the importance of innovation to their future growth and to the economic betterment of the country. If we can develop a package of coherent policies that recognise fully the limitations of our size and distance from other players and implement them on an efficient and continuing basis, Australia will be well positioned to take full advantage of the native innovation capabilities so often lauded in innovation forums. We will then have a good and sustainable basis for growth in the emerging knowledge economy.

References

AEGIS/Marceau, J. (1999a) 'Mapping the Building and Construction Product System', Sydney: AEGIS/University of Western Sydney and Department of Industry, Science and Resources (ISR), Canberra website.

AEGIS/Marceau, J., Cook, N., Greig, A. and Houghton, J. (1999b) 'Mapping the Textiles, Clothing, Footwear and Leather Cluster', Sydney: AEGIS/University of Western Sydney and ISR website.

AEGIS/Marceau, J. and Basri, E. (1999c) 'The Health Product and Services System in Australia', Sydney: AEGIS/University of Western Sydney and ISR website.

AEGIS/Marceau, J. and Cook, N. (1999d) 'The Capacity of the Building and Construction Product System to Encourage and Undertake Energy-efficient Building Design and Construction': AEGIS/University of Western Sydney and Department of Industry, Science and Resources (ISR), Canberra website.

Archibugi, D. and Michie, J. (1995) 'The Globalisation of Technology: A New Taxonomy', *Cambridge Journal of Economics*, 19: 121–40.

Australian Science and Technology Budget Statement 2000–2001, Department of Industry, Science and Resources, Canberra.

Basri, E. (2000) 'Collaboration in Innovation in Australian Industry: The Results of the Australian DISKO Survey', paper presented to an EU conference on Innovation Indicators, Nice, November.

Batterham, R. (2000) *The Chance to Change*, Final Report of the Australian Science Capability Review, Canberra.

Council on Competitiveness (M. Porter and S. Stern) (1999) *The New Challenge to America's Prosperity: Findings from the Innovation Index*, Washington D.C.: Council on Competitiveness Publications Office.

David, P., Hall, B. and Toole, A. (2000) 'Is Public R&D a Complement or Substitute for Private R&D? A Review of the Econometric Evidence', *Research Policy*, 29 (4–5): 497–529.

Department of Industry, Science and Resources (1999) *R&D Scoreboard 1998*. Canberra: DISR.

Department of Industry, Science and Resources (1999) 'Action Agenda Guidelines'. See ISR website.

Dosi, G. (1999) 'Some Notes on National Systems of Innovation and Production, and their Implications for Economic Analysis', in D. Archibugi, J. Howells and J. Michie (eds) *Innovation Policy in a Global Economy*, Cambridge: Cambridge University Press, pp. 35–48.

Gann, D. and Salter, A. (1998) 'Learning and Innovation Management in Project-based Firms', paper presented to the 2nd International Conference on Technology Policy and Innovation, Lisbon, 3–5 August.

Glatz, H. and van Tulder, R. (1989) 'Ways Out Of The International Restructuring Race?', Project proposal, Annex B, University of Amsterdam.

Government of Quebec (1993) *Quebec: Industrial Clusters*. Quebec City.

Guerrieri, P. (1999) 'Patterns of National Specialisation in the Global Competitive

Environment', in D. Archibugi, J. Howells and J. Michie (eds) *Innovation Policy in a Global Economy*, Cambridge: Cambridge University Press, pp. 139–59.

Hall, B. and van Reenen, J. (2000) 'How Effective are Fiscal Incentives for R&D? A Review of the Evidence', *Research Policy* 29 (4–5): 449–69.

Klette, J., Moen, J. and Griliches, Z. (2000) 'Do Subsidies to Commercial R&D Reduce Market Failures?', *Research Policy*, 29 (4–5): 471–95.

Leydesdorff, L. and H. Etzkowitz (eds) (1999) *Research Policy*, special issue on the Triple Helix.

Lundvall, B.-A. (1996) 'The Social Dimension of the Learning Economy', unpublished paper, Department of Business Studies, Aalborg University, Denmark.

Lundvall, B.-A. and Tomlinson, M. (2000) 'International Benchmarking and National Innovation Systems', draft report for the Portuguese Presidency of the European Union, April.

Marceau, J. (1994) 'Clusters, Chains and Complexes: Three Approaches to the Study of Innovation with a Public Policy Perspective', in M. Dodgson and R. Rothwell (eds) *Handbook of Industrial Innovation*, Cheltenham: Edward Elgar, pp. 3–12.

Marceau, J. and Manley, K. (2000) *Innovation Checkpoint 1999*, Sydney: Australian Business Foundation.

Marceau, J., Cook, N. and Dalton, B. (2001) 'Selling Solutions: Emerging Product Service Linkages in Australia', unpublished manuscript. Sydney: AEGIS and the Australian Business Foundation.

Marceau, J., Manley, K. and Sicklen, D. (1997) *The High Road or the Low Road: Alternatives for Australia's Future*, Sydney: Australian Business Foundation.

Metcalfe, S. (1995) 'The Economic Foundations of Technology Policy', in P. Stoneman (ed.) *Handbook of the Economics of Innovation and Technological Change*, Oxford: Blackwell, pp. 409–512.

OECD (1996a) 'The Knowledge-based Economy', 1996 Science, Technology and Industry Outlook, Paris.

OECD (1996b) 'National Innovation Systems International Mapping Project', Working Group on Technology and Innovation Policy, unpublished work plan. DSTI/STP/TIP (96) 11.

OECD (1997a) *National Systems of Innovation*, Paris.

OECD (1997b) *Industrial Competitiveness: Benchmarking Business Environments in the Global Economy*, Paris.

OECD (1999) *Managing National Innovation Systems*, Paris.

OECD (2000) *Science, Technology and Industry Outlook*, Paris.

Patel, P. and Pavitt, K. (1994) 'The Continuing, Widespread (and Neglected) Importance of Improvements in Mechanical Technologies', *Research Policy*, 23 (5): 533–46.

Pavitt, K. (1984) 'Sectoral Patterns of Technical Change: Towards a Taxonomy and a Theory', *Research Policy*, 13: 343–73.

Senker, J., Faulkner, W. and Velho, L. (1998) 'Science and Technology Knowledge Flows between Industrial and Academic Research: A Comparative Study', in H. Etzkowitz, A. Webster and P. Healey (eds) *Capitalizing Knowledge*, New York: State University of New York Press, pp. 111–32.

Smith. K. (1998) 'Specialization, Innovation and Growth Across Heterogeneous Economies: Issues for Policy', OECD Conference on *Innovation Systems: Growth Engines for the 21st Century*, Sydney, 19–20 November.

Teubal, M., Foray, D., Justman, M. and Zuscovitch, E. (eds) (1996) *Technological Infrastructure Policy: An International Perspective*, Dordrecht: Kluwer.

Unger, B. (2000) 'Innovation Systems and Innovative Performance: Voice Systems', *Organization Studies*, 21 (5): 941–70.

Von Hippel, E. (1988) *The Sources of Innovation*, Oxford: Oxford University Press.

10

Efficiency in Capital Markets

Bill Shields

Introduction

The importance of capital markets to economic growth can be viewed through several dimensions. The fundamental role of capital markets in mobilising and allocating capital to competing economic uses is critical to both enhancing and sustaining an economy's potential and actual growth rate. This was likely to have been more of a constraint in earlier periods, however, particularly for smaller countries such as Australia, when capital was not as freely mobile as in today's 'globalised' economy.

Even if deficiencies in domestic capital markets – whether as a result of size, institutional or policy impediments – can be overcome by access to international capital flows, there is still an important issue of the cost of capital. A higher cost of capital will limit an economy's potential to invest and grow. There is also the more microeconomic dimension of risk management; in particular, whether markets provide adequate financial instruments (at reasonable cost) to help businesses manage the risks inherent in their decisions to allocate capital between alternative uses.

There is an extensive theoretical and applied economic literature devoted to the question of whether or not capital markets are *efficient*. Moreover, the understanding of what constitutes an efficient market has changed over time (Beechey et al. 2000: 2). The efficient market hypothesis was initially developed in the late 1960s and argued that markets are efficient when they adjust rapidly to 'new' information. This definition has subsequently had several versions, which acknowledge that how markets process available information and the associated cost of such information are both important to whether or not the hypothesis is met in practice.

Experience suggests that there is still much to learn about how information impacts on, and is transmitted via markets. This was very apparent during the

1997–98 Asian currency crisis. In particular, there were widespread concerns at the time that financial market 'contagion' from the Asian crisis would engulf not only Australia but also capital markets in the major industrialised economies.

While initially reflecting a lack of comprehensive and reliable information about what was happening in Asia, these concerns continued to affect markets for a considerable time after the initial crisis, even though overall economic performance in other countries, and the stability of their capital markets, were not significantly affected by developments in Asia.

Not only did the Asian crisis highlight how international capital flows can be severely disrupted, it also showed how important expectations can be in influencing financial market responses. Markets today constantly react to developments of all kinds, whether 'new' economic and financial data or more qualitative information such as assessments of business and consumer 'confidence', particularly through expectations of what they are likely to show and their overall impact on the economic outlook – even though these are often based on incomplete information and a sometimes tenuous understanding of their relevance. What constitutes an efficient market in this environment is arguable, and certainly more difficult to test in an absolute sense.

This chapter, after briefly reviewing the development of financial markets in Australia over the past couple of decades, assesses the efficiency of Australia's capital markets *relative to* other recognised capital markets, drawing on available data on size, turnover, volatility and the cost of capital, as well as some key lessons from the experience with the instability in international capital flows in recent years. Finally, some remaining challenges facing domestic capital markets are discussed.

The development of Australia's capital markets

Australian financial markets have expanded rapidly and broadly across a wide range of financial instruments over the past decade or so. As Table 10.1 highlights, all broad market segments have expanded faster than nominal GDP since 1985. This includes markets for physical assets as well as those for derivatives. Even in the bond market, which in recent years has contended with Commonwealth budget surpluses and a marked reduction in Commonwealth government bonds outstanding, turnover has risen at twice the rate of nominal GDP as the expansion in non-government bonds outstanding has accelerated to take up the market slack left by the decline in government securities (Battelino 2000: 5).

This has not been simple coincidence, but followed a period of relatively intense deregulation of Australian financial markets from the late 1970s to the mid-1980s (Jonson and Rankin 1986: 263). That was accompanied by rapid innovation that quickly spread to encompass a wide range of financial transactions across the increasingly deregulated domestic capital markets, although it often involved the application to Australia of techniques or instruments already available elsewhere (for example, cash management trusts in the early 1980s and mortgage securitisation in the late 1980s).

As Table 10.1 also highlights, this expansion was often fastest in futures, or more generally derivative transactions, rather than the physical securities that had dominated domestic capital markets prior to deregulation. Again this covered virtually all markets, although as Figure 10.1 shows, derivative markets are dominated by foreign exchange and interest rate instruments. This partly reflects the relative openness of the Australian economy to international trade and financial transactions.

There has been a range of other important influences on the development of the Australian financial sector over the past decade or so. These were canvassed in the Financial System Inquiry Discussion Paper 1996 (the Wallis Inquiry), and include globalisation, advances in technology, changing consumer needs and demographics. The Discussion Paper also identifies several significant implications for the institutional structure of market transactions, as well as the challenges for economic policy, notably monetary policy.

Table 10.1   Daily turnover in Australian financial markets

	1985 ($m)	1999 ($m)	Average Annual growth (%)
Foreign exchange	5 000	77 000	22
Bond market			
Securities	1 000	4 000	14
Future contracts	100	7 000	35
Money market			
Securities	600[1]	7 000	20
Futures contracts	1 000	30 000	26
Repurchase agreements	200[1]	15 000	18
Equities			
Physical	50	1 000	26
Future contracts	100	2 000	21
Memo item			
Nominal GDP[2]	230 000	600 000	7

1 Estimated.
2 Annual.

Sources: 1999 Australian Financial Markets Report, AFMA; Sydney Futures Exchange; Australian Stock Exchange. Figures for foreign exchange, physical securities and repurchase agreements are on a financial year basis; futures contracts are on a calendar year basis.

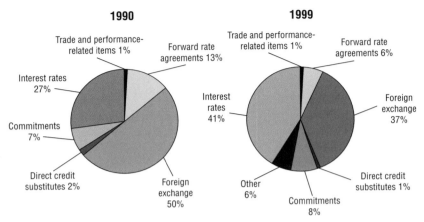

Figure 10.1 Composition of derivative transactions
Source: Reserve Bank of Australia.

The combination of new technology, particularly in computers and associated software applications, and innovation was especially important. Not only did this contribute to the development of more flexible financial products, notably derivatives that became important in extending the limits of risk management, but it also saw a dramatic decline in the cost of financial transactions. Combined with the aggressively competitive markets that emerged from the deregulation process in Australia, this contributed to making transactions in several of these markets (notably that for interest rate futures) as cost effective as any in the world (see also Gizycki and Lowe 2000: 193–8).

This was accompanied by the rapid growth of wholesale markets, such as those for interest rate futures and currency swaps and options, relative to the retail financial markets associated with traditional financial intermediaries such as banks, building societies and insurance companies. The expansion of funds management provided an additional boost to the growth of wholesale markets, and to the so-called 'unbundling' of financial transactions and products (one aspect of which is the charging of explicit transactions fees by banks).

The result of this process is a diversified and well-developed financial market structure in Australia. Comparisons of the size of financial markets usually focus on the volume of transactions, relative to GDP or GDP per capita (a proxy for wealth). For example, Australia's foreign exchange market is ranked in the top 10 markets globally, well above Australia's international ranking based on GDP, while interest rate futures turnover ranks even more highly. In fact, relative to GDP, Australia's foreign exchange market is larger than those in many bigger economies such as the United States and Japan.

Australia tends to rank in the middle of the OECD economies on other measures of financial 'sophistication', such as the share of managed funds as

distinct from traditional intermediaries in total financial assets or the share of
financial intermediaries in financing overall economic activity (Battelino 2000:
8–9). This is well below the most developed capital markets in the United
States but a good deal ahead of several larger European economies and Japan.

One of the ultimate benefits of deregulation and innovation has been the
reduced cost of capital to borrowers. Perhaps the best example of this is the
impact of mortgage securitisation on the margin between the cost of funds to
lenders and the mortgage rates charged to borrowers (see Figure 10.2). There
has been a significant decline in the average interest margin earned by banks
and other traditional lenders, to a level that is now virtually the same as in
comparable mortgage markets outside Australia. Although losing 10 per cent
of their market share to mortgage managers such as Aussie Home Loans,
banks not only remain the dominant lenders in Australia but also enjoy continued profitability from that business. Moreover, the reduction in lending
margins through increased competition subsequently flowed to small and
medium-sized business borrowers.

However, the impact of deregulation and innovation was not necessarily
fast – for example, mortgage managers became a competitive force in the mid-
1990s almost a decade after financial deregulation was substantially completed
– nor without cost. The financial system was faced with several upheavals and
crises over that period reflecting both the swings in general business conditions, particularly in the early 1990s, as well as changes in market structure as
a result of the competitive pressures released by deregulation and innovation.

But there was eventually also a beneficial effect on market volatility, as
shown in Figure 10.3 by the decline in volatility over the decade or so from the
late 1980s to the late 1990s, particularly for the domestic capital markets.
There were periods of heightened instability, but largely as a result of external
shocks – for example, the US stock market 'crash' in October 1987 and the

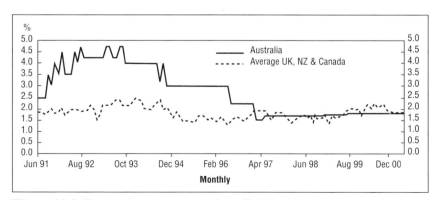

Figure 10.2 Housing interest rate spread to official interest rates
Source: Reserve Bank of Australia.

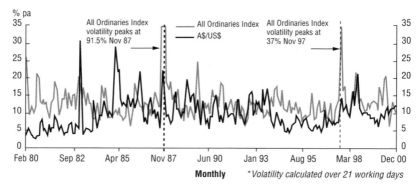

Figure 10.3 Volatility in financial markets
Source: Datastream.

speculative attack on the Australian dollar in mid-1998. The impact of these shocks was heavily absorbed by the floating exchange rate, although its average volatility was little changed over that period and contained within a considerably narrower range than in the second half of the 1980s.

While more balanced macroeconomic policies and outcomes (notably lower inflation) undoubtedly contributed to this trend, it was underpinned by the increasing diversification and depth of Australia's capital markets.

Another important consequence of deregulation and innovation has been the development of a more responsive regulatory framework in Australia. That framework has been changed several times as a result of successive inquiries into the financial system, as well as international developments such as the adoption of the Basel guidelines for capital adequacy. There is little doubt, however, that the regulatory structure that is in place today is more appropriate to the diversity of financial transactions and institutional structures that has developed.

The extent to which any regulatory system is able to effectively contain the impact of severe disruption to capital flows, or 'contagion', is also a valid test of the comparative efficiency of capital markets. Recent experience suggests that Australia's capital markets rank highly in this respect, in that they limit the risks of financial disruption but still allow innovation in financial transactions and the resulting improvement in efficiency over time.

Financial market efficiency

These developments point to three alternative approaches to assessing the efficiency of Australia's capital markets: the first involves testing the various predictions of the efficient market hypothesis against the actual behaviour of asset prices; the second is to assess the ability of financial markets to withstand unexpected shocks such as the Asian currency crisis; and the third is to compare the cost of capital to users, both business and consumers, with that in generally accepted efficient capital markets such as those in the United States.

The empirical evidence

Beechey et al. (2000: 4) provides a useful summary of the results of empirical studies of the financial market hypothesis. In particular, the predictions of the efficient market hypothesis that asset prices should follow a random walk and that 'new' information is rapidly incorporated into asset prices have been found to be approximately true. The same conclusion occurs in regard to the prediction that fund managers cannot systematically outperform the stock market. Indeed, there is some evidence of the opposite.

However, one of the more obvious conclusions of the notion of efficient markets – that asset prices should accurately reflect economic fundamentals – is clearly not supported by the evidence. There are significant examples of actual asset prices deviating from those predicted on the basis of what economic theory would identify as their fundamental influences, often substantially and for extended periods. This is illustrated simply in Figure 10.4, which shows the equity risk premium on the Australian and US stock markets, measured as the per cent per annum margin between the returns on an overall market index and the yield on a *risk-free* government bond.

The charts in Figure 10.4 highlight that the equity risk premium has remained volatile in both economies, irrespective of the apparent (and improved) efficiency of their capital markets. If markets did correctly reflect all available information of relevance to current and future earnings, less (and/or

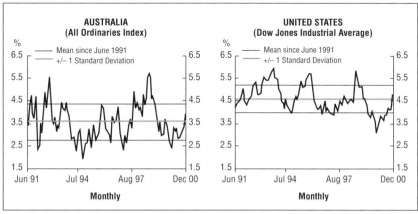

Figure 10.4 Equity risk premium
Source: Macquarie Bank Limited.

a decline in) volatility in that premium would be expected. Although over the past decade, the equity risk premium has generally fluctuated within a band defined by one standard deviation around its mean, that in itself defines a fairly wide range; in Australia, one standard deviation is equivalent to +/– 0.8 per cent per annum compared to the mean of 3.5 per cent per annum.

There have also been several periods of more marked volatility in the risk premium in both countries, often reflecting the tendency for *expected* earnings and, therefore, the prices of stocks, to deviate substantially from what available information would suggest – the euphoria over recent years about 'high-tech' stocks, particularly in the US market, is a case in point. Nevertheless, despite concerns that equity valuations in the United States (and Australia) had become severely misaligned with their fundamental determinants, the equity risk premium has reverted to its average value as investors and markets have 'corrected' the earlier overvaluation of stock prices.

This in itself is not conclusive evidence that financial markets are efficient, at least in some broader sense. Indeed, it does illustrate the apparent failure of even well-developed capital markets such as in the United States to avoid asset price 'bubbles'; that is, periods during which market prices significantly diverge from underlying economic fundamentals. Asset 'bubbles', while notoriously difficult to foresee, are rarely sustained, however, even though market corrections can take considerable time to emerge, and vary in their severity.

This will partly reflect the way in which expectations about likely changes in asset prices are formed, and interact between market participants. For example, while it might be expected that differences in expectations about future earnings would converge over time, this may not always be so, notably when there are substantial structural changes in the economy that can significantly affect the *potential* earnings of companies. Nor is this confined to market participants, who might be accused of being too influenced by day-to-day market developments, or 'noise'.

Take, for example, the assessment in December 1996 by the Chairman of the US Federal Reserve Board of Governors that investors in US stock markets were exhibiting 'irrational exuberance'. In the three years following that assessment, the US Dow Jones index rose to a peak of almost double the level it was in December 1996. While history will ultimately determine to what extent this has represented an extended stock market 'bubble', there is little doubt that some economic fundamentals relevant to equity prices have changed significantly over that period, most particularly the acceleration in US productivity and economic growth, which in turn has raised the actual, and potential, earnings of US companies.

Changes in economic structure and underlying economic relationships are not confined to equity markets. Moreover, as information has become more widely available, and markets become more integrated (or 'globalised'), it is not only changes in economic structure that can influence asset prices. A wide range of other influences, not the least of which are government policies and political developments, can also have a substantial impact on actual and expected asset prices, notably the exchange rates for currencies that many would suggest are determined in the most efficient of financial markets.

Market shocks and contagion

The Australian dollar exchange rate provides a recent test of the relative efficiency of Australia's capital markets, at least in terms of the ability to withstand external shocks.

The Asian financial and economic crisis of 1997–98, which was the latest of several examples of international financial contagion, was characterised by a range of economic impacts (see, for example, International Monetary Fund 1999a: 27–65). It is generally dated from the sharp depreciation of key Asian currencies that began with the devaluation of the Thai baht in July 1997. This spread relatively quickly to several other Asian currencies with the consequence that within six months the currencies of Thailand, Indonesia, Malaysia and Korea had all fallen by 50 per cent or more against the US dollar.

At the time, financial markets were very much focused on fears that the Asian crisis would spread to markets outside the region, including Australia. The channels through which this 'contagion' was expected to be transmitted included established trade and capital flows between those economies, as well as the financial impact on companies (notably banks) operating within and/or lending to the Asian region.

The Australian economy was assumed by many to be particularly exposed, given the relatively rapid development of trade with the region over the years preceding the crisis, and the expected negative impact on Australian financial markets.

In the event, the Australian dollar did come under significant selling pressure in 1998. The nature of that pressure, and the eventual response of the Reserve Bank through direct intervention in the foreign exchange market in July and August 1998, is discussed in Rankin (1999). While that experience appears to reinforce the results of empirical studies that asset prices can become misaligned through speculative activity, it was not inconsistent with the notion that Australia's foreign exchange and capital markets are efficient.

First, a depreciation of the Australian dollar in the first half of 1998 was consistent with changing economic fundamentals, most notably the fall in commodity prices following the Asian crisis (see Figure 10.5). The Reserve Bank's trade-weighted index of US dollar prices for the commodities that Australia exports fell by 13.9 per cent between June 1997 and June 1998, while Australian dollar's exchange rate against the US dollar fell by 18.5 per cent.

While there has been increased conjecture over recent years about whether the Australian dollar is still a 'commodity currency' (see Figure 10.5) – given

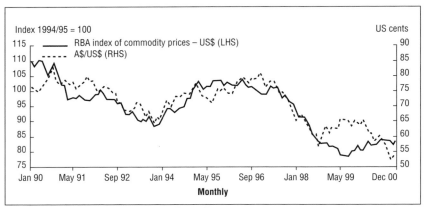

Figure 10.5 The $A and commodity prices
Source: Reserve Bank of Australia and Datastream.

the diversification of Australia's economy and exports away from traditional resource and rural commodities – most empirical research has continued to show that the trend in commodity prices is a major influence on trends in the exchange rate. Many market valuations also still emphasise commodity prices.

This is not to deny that the actual exchange rate fell below what most commodity-based valuations estimated it should have been at that time. However, this clearly reflected the speculative positions taken against the Australian dollar in the foreign exchange market – either as a proxy for illiquid Asian currencies or because of Australia's perceived closeness to Asia. In fact, this arguably contributed to the quick recovery of the exchange rate towards what the consensus of market expectations saw as its 'fair value' (see Figure 10.5), as Reserve Bank intervention led to those speculative positions being unwound.

Second, despite the fears about the impact on Australia's economy of the Asian crisis, it became increasingly clear through 1998 that the decline in the exchange rate provided an effective 'buffer' between the domestic economy and this external shock. This is entirely consistent with both economic theory and the decision to float the Australian dollar (and remove all remaining exchange controls) in 1983. While there had been earlier periods of exchange rate instability that had disrupted the economy, these were often sourced in domestic policy shortcomings (whether perceived or real), rather than a pure external shock.

The deregulation and resulting development of Australia's capital markets over the preceding decade or so undoubtedly contributed to the effectiveness of the exchange rate as a 'buffer'. Not only did the lower Australian dollar provide a substantial offset to the sharp fall in commodity prices and the terms of trade, which transmitted the Asian crisis to Australia, but the remainder of the economy continued to be supported by the largely unaffected domestic capital markets.

While this apparent insulation from 'contagion' surprised many at the time, and was contrary to widespread forecasts of sharply lower growth, it was not necessarily unique. A similar pattern occurred in the United States, even though there were more explicit examples of financial stress as a result of the crisis as it 'spread' to other emerging markets in the second half of 1998.

Both experiences underlined the ability of well-developed capital markets *relative to the size of the economy* to insulate domestic economic activity from individual institutional failure. The net result was a continuation, indeed acceleration, of Australia's overall GDP growth through the Asian crisis.

It also highlighted a third lesson from this experience – the importance of the regulatory system (Financial Stability Forum 2000: 3–6). Although the failure of the highly leveraged US hedge fund Long Term Capital Management (LTCM) in September 1998 resulted in a sharp negative reaction in US capital markets, this was quickly contained by the boost to liquidity provided by the Federal Reserve (a similar policy response to that which followed the 1987 stock market crash), and the Fed-sponsored recapitalisation of LTCM. However, as the experience in Asia and other emerging markets clearly showed, this would not have been as effective if there was not underlying confidence in the regulatory system.

In Australia, there was no such test of the regulatory system, even though some Australian financial institutions were exposed to developments in the region (Carmichael 2000: 167). This partly reflected the different structure of our domestic capital markets (there were no Australian hedge funds), but was nevertheless quite marked in contrast to the more general concerns about, and failures in, banking systems in the surrounding region.

While difficult to quantify, there seems to be little doubt that broad confidence in both the inherent strength of Australian financial intermediaries, and in the regulatory system that supervises them, contributed to the stability in domestic capital markets through that period. This, of course, had not always been the case. The process of deregulation over the preceding two decades, combined with greater volatility in the domestic business cycle, had seen several periods of distress on financial institutions. But it also helped to develop and refine the regulatory system and build confidence in its ability to cope with such periods of stress.

The cost of capital

Another approach to judging the efficiency of Australia's capital markets, at least relative to other markets, is to compare the cost of capital to business and consumers. We have already highlighted one aspect of this in the earlier discussion of mortgage securitisation. Figure 10.2 clearly shows how the lending margin for Australian banks declined to a level that was comparable to those in other countries with a similar market and institutional framework.

Another way to appreciate how much the deregulation of Australia's capital markets has contributed to a lower cost of capital over recent years is to compare *real* borrowing costs (that is, after adjusting for inflation) over time. There has been a marked downward trend in both since deregulation was completed in the mid-1980s, which occurred even as inflation was reduced; in the case of business loans, from an annual average rate of 8.9 per cent in the 1980s to 7.9 per cent in the 1990s.

But to judge whether the cost of capital in Australia is similar to that in other economies it is necessary to use a more comprehensive measure, and preferably one that combines both the cost of debt and equity (which is particularly relevant to financing business expansion over time).

Figure 10.6 compares such estimates for Australia and the United States, and highlights the convergence in the weighted average cost of capital in each country over the 1990s. While there is a substantial margin for error in such estimates, and the aggregate nature of such estimates will not always reflect differences between specific industries or firms (the estimates use average rated corporate debt, for example), the trends in these estimates are consistent with other evidence such as the narrowing spread between yields on Australian and US debt over the 1990s, and the similarity in rates of return on equity (Battelino 2000: 9).

Remaining challenges

A principal aim of the most recent inquiry into the Australian financial system (the Wallis Inquiry) was to achieve a more competitive and efficient financial system. Its final report concluded that 'the financial system is . . . providing in excess of $40 billion worth of services annually to other sectors of the

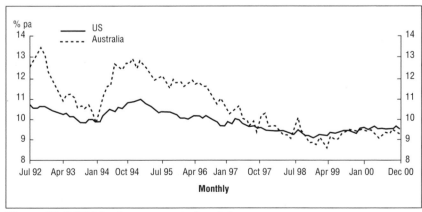

Figure 10.6 Weighted average cost of capital
Source: Macquarie Bank Limited.

economy'. While it did not make a judgment on the efficiency of the system, it did suggest that 'even a 10 per cent improvement in efficiency would translate into cost savings for the economy in excess of $4 billion per annum' (Financial System Inquiry 1997: 15).

In recommending how those savings could be achieved, it focused on improvements to the regulatory system to enhance the competitiveness and efficiency of the financial system. Its specific recommendations included more neutral regulatory treatment of competitors (from different institutional sectors), reducing barriers to entry to promote more contestable markets, and more cost-effective conduct and disclosure regulation.

There is no doubt that these are worthwhile goals. These changes are also likely to improve the overall efficiency of the financial system, although the Inquiry's final report provides little evidence to support the implication that the gains could be as high as a 10 per cent saving in overall costs.

In fact, both the final report and earlier discussion paper provide substantial evidence to support the contention that Australia's capital markets already appear to be efficient, at least relative to other global markets. Whether this meets the more technical definition of capital market efficiency is open to question. However, the available evidence is consistent with a broad under-standing of efficiency in terms of the diversity and availability of financial services, and the (low) costs of transactions and of capital to business and consumers.

Moreover, it is difficult to identify any major improvements that could help to establish the stronger form of the efficient market hypothesis. Improvements in the quality and timeliness of major economic and financial data could obvi-ously help; this has been strongly recommended, for example, in most official responses to the Asian financial crisis.

However, as recent experience highlights, expectations will still play a sig-nificant role in market behaviour. Better information alone is unlikely to either prevent such crises, or asset price 'bubbles' in individual markets, from occur-ring in the future.

Another contribution to improved efficiency that governments can make is through greater transparency in the conduct of economic policies, particularly monetary and taxation policies that can have a direct impact on capital markets. This requires both the clear delineation of the appropriate goals for such policies and the consistent pursuit of those goals through day-to-day policy decisions. Given today's more responsive financial markets, there is also a heightened need for the successful communication to market participants of the reasons for policy changes – or for the lack of a change, particularly when it is widely expected within markets.

As noted in the introduction to this chapter, another dimension of efficiency is the availability, as distinct from the cost, of capital. The discussion here has provided examples of how Australia's capital markets match most other markets in the world in terms of the diversity and the 'sophistication' of instruments available to users.

But that is not to say there are not some deficiencies. One that is often raised is the difficulty in new ventures obtaining adequate capital. Another has been the limited market for corporate debt in Australia. However, both have improved markedly in recent years (see, for example, the *Australian Venture Capital 1999 Yearbook*), although for some businesses, particularly those growing very rapidly and/or utilising new technologies in untried markets, capital can still be difficult to obtain and relatively costly. But this is just as true in most other capital markets, particularly those of a similar size.

Conclusions

On balance, this does not alter the overall conclusion that capital markets in Australia are relatively efficient and, importantly, operate in a framework that generally encourages competition (including from overseas institutions) and innovation. This alone suggests that further gains in efficiency, through the reduction in the costs of transactions and borrowing costs, are also likely.

While the evidence does not support the stronger version of efficiency – in particular, that markets will always value assets consistent with their economic fundamentals – an important question is whether deviations from fundamental values are sustained over time. In this regard the evidence is more mixed. Moreover, the consequences of such deviations will depend not only on the underlying efficiency of capital markets but also on the appropriate and timely response of economic policies.

References

Australian Venture Capital Association Limited (1999) *Yearbook*, Sydney.
Battelino, Ric (2000) 'Australian Financial Markets: Looking Back and Looking Ahead', Australian Finance and Capital Markets Conference, Sydney.
Beechey, Meredith, Gruen, David and Vickery, James (2000) 'The Efficient Market Hypothesis: A Survey', Research Discussion Paper 2000–01, Reserve Bank of Australia.
Carmichael, Jeff (2000) 'Lessons from the Asian Crisis', in *Productivity Commission, Achieving Better Regulation of Services*, Australian Government Publishing Service, pp. 159–69.
Financial Stability Forum 2000, Report of the Working Group on Highly Leveraged Institutions (HLIs), Basel
Financial System Inquiry (1996) *Discussion Paper*, Australian Government Publishing Service.
Financial System Inquiry (1997) *The Financial System: Towards 2010*, Australian Government Publishing Service.

Gizycki, Marianne and Lowe, Philip (2000) 'The Australian Financial System in the 1990s', in Gruen, David and Shrestha, Sona (eds) *The Australian Economy in the 1990s*, Reserve Bank of Australia, pp. 180–215.

International Monetary Fund (1999a) *World Economic Outlook May 1999*, Washington D.C.

International Monetary Fund (1999b) *International Capital Markets: Developments, Prospects and Key Policy Issues*, Washington D.C.

Jonson, P.D. and Rankin, R.W. (1986) 'On Some Recent Developments in Monetary Economics', *The Economic Record*, vol. 62, no. 178, 257–67.

Rankin, B. (1999) 'The Impact of Hedge Funds on Financial Markets: Lessons from the Experience of Australia', in Gruen, David and Gower, Luke (eds) *Capital Flows and the International Financial System: Proceedings of a Conference*, Reserve Bank of Australia, pp. 151–63.

11

Public Governance and Growth

Michael Keating

The relationship between public governance and economic growth has been hotly contested since the Industrial Revolution and the birth of capitalism. Mainstream economics for most of the last 200 years has equated economic growth with the supply potential of the economy. This supply potential is determined by the rate of saving and investment, the allocative efficiency of saving and investment, the growth in the labour force and its skills, and the rate of technological progress. Many orthodox economists consider that government has little direct influence over these key determinants of economic growth. At worst government taxation and expenditures, particularly those aimed at redistribution, will reduce saving and investment, while government intervention in markets risks a loss of allocative efficiency. On this view economic growth will be maximised if government is limited to creating an environment where private saving and investment and trading relations will flourish. Federalist structures and other types of checks on any centralist tendencies are preferred precisely because it is believed that will help limit the opportunities for government intervention, as has largely proved to be the case in Australia.

The alternative view, which was originally associated with Marx, then various forms of under-consumptionists and most compellingly articulated by Keynes, is that capitalist growth is inherently unstable. For various reasons the desired investment may not be forthcoming and/or sustained. Even where aggregate investment is satisfactory its allocation may have a short-term bias, so that government can enhance growth by investing in or otherwise supporting longer term 'national development' projects. Other instances of market failure are expenditures on education and training and R&D, which are likely to be sub-optimal in the absence of government intervention. More generally, government redistribution may be positively associated with economic growth if it encourages a greater willingness to accept change and stabilises the political

environment. People holding these views tend to favour governance arrangements that allow a strong central government to manage aggregate demand,
and to intervene to 'improve' on market outcomes. However, strong government is not always to be trusted, nor is it always capable of acting effectively on
its own, so that frequently these people favour an extension of governance
arrangements to allow for consultation and partnerships, including various
forms of corporatism.

Following the collapse of communism, the world jury has clearly decided in
favour of the market economy, and command and control types of regulation
are out of favour. But systems of governance range well beyond governments
per se and include all those institutions, both public and private, that interact to
manage a nation's affairs. Indeed the World Bank (1992: 1) defines governance
as 'the exercise of political power to manage a nation's affairs', recognising that
not only governments wield political power. Thus the rules and conventions
governing the interactions among businesses and between businesses and their
employees are, for example, an important part of the overall system of governance. Even in market economies, this leaves a considerable range of possibilities regarding the nature and intensity of these interactions, and particularly
the balance between competitive and cooperative relations.

At a minimum, public governance should allow different economic actors to
make *credible* commitments to one another and to resolve their disputes quickly
and satisfactorily. This requires the enforcement of a system of contract and
property law to provide a reasonable level of certainty. Beyond that perhaps the
most sensitive issue that the system of governance must address is how the risks
and gains from collaboration are negotiated and shared. Markets are particularly suited to coordinating most of these negotiations, especially when there are
large numbers of actors. But market relationships are characterised for the most
part by arms' length relations that emphasise competition and formal contracting, and are often less successful where high levels of cooperation and trust are
most helpful. Even in market economies, institutions of governance can be
established that facilitate more cooperative behaviour as a basis for longer term
relations. To the extent that those institutions are able to foster trust, the relationships can be more productive, more flexible and less costly to maintain than
contractual relationships.

For example, Hall and Soskice (2000) describe countries such as Germany
as being 'organised market' economies with a set of institutions that support
forms of relational contracting and technology transfer that are more difficult
to achieve in more 'liberal market' economies such as the United States and
Australia. German firms have traditionally had close relations with banks and
better access to patient capital. This has helped them develop production strategies that take a longer view and are dependent on high levels of skill and commitment from their employees. German workers are less likely to be poached,
but have more job security and receive better job-specific training. By contrast

in the Australian 'liberal market' economy, where employees are more responsible for their own education and training, there tends to be less of it and it is
likely to be more general and less job-specific, allowing those employees greater
mobility. The pace of technological progress may not be much affected by
governance arrangements, but those that reflect organised markets may be
more likely to foster incremental rather than radical innovation.

Most recently East Asia has provided another version of 'organised market'
economies that has sparked a vigorous debate about the influence of governance on economic growth. In the first half of the 1990s it was often claimed
that the East Asian economic miracle partly reflected 'Asian values' that not
only foster close relations between businesses and between business and government, but also allow Asian governments to command more authority that
is then exercised on behalf of the collective interest. This compares with
western systems of governance that give the individual more opportunities to
contest government decisions. Following the East Asian economic crisis,
however, critics have described these same relationships as 'crony capitalism',
leading to poor management and especially to poor risk management, and
have extolled the flexibility and integrity of western liberal democracies.

Despite the variety of views, what stands out is the strong belief that systems
of governance do matter for economic growth. These various hypotheses
about a relationship between forms of governance and economic growth are,
however, largely untested in any rigorous way. Accordingly, the next section
briefly summarises what empirical studies have found regarding the relationship between governance and growth. The following section then discusses the
changes in Australian governance in the last two decades and the reasons why,
and the final section comments on possible future directions.

Empirical findings

There have been remarkably few rigorous empirical tests of the various
theories about the impact of government on economic growth. This is
probably because it is not easy. Most of the studies involve international comparisons, but the results are very different depending upon the specification of
the equations and the countries included. In particular it is important to allow
for the fact that countries' growth rates are converging (Dowrick and Nguyen
1989). After allowing for catch-up by those countries starting from a low base,
Castles and Dowrick (1990: 201) found no econometric evidence of 'a statistically significant negative relationship between the level of government
revenues or the components of government expenditure and medium-term
economic growth'. They also found 'a modest, but statistically significant,
positive effect of non-consumption expenditure, and especially social transfers,
on medium-term growth of productivity' (Castles and Dowrick 1990: 201).

Turning to types of governance arrangements, Lijphart (1999) distinguishes between what he terms majoritarian government and consensus government. Majoritarian government has less need to compromise and may be more effective. By contrast, consensus government has to encompass more separate interests, which may force it to adopt policies that focus on the needs of the wider community, but at the risk of being less decisive. Lijphart found no statistically significant relationships between the position of 36 countries on a composite scale measuring their location on this 'executive-parties' dimension and those countries' economic performance, including their economic growth (Lijphart 1999: Table 15.1). On the other hand, he did find evidence that consensus government outperforms majoritarian government in serving the needs of the wider community as measured by the development of the welfare state, environmental performance, the harshness of the criminal justice system and the generosity of foreign aid (Lijphart 1999: Table 16.2). One might, however, question how far these results apply to Australia; for example, other more important factors, such as our arbitration system and the coverage of its awards, have influenced the development of our welfare system. More generally, Lijphart's work is a reminder how dependent the conclusions from this type of study are on the specification of the model used and the data employed.

Castles has undertaken a more rigorous investigation of the relationship for 21 OECD countries between per capita economic growth over the period 1969–1992 and five measures of decentralisation of governance, including the influence of federal structures (Castles 1999). Only in the case of fiscal centralisation – measured as the share of the tax take going to the central government – did Castles find what he describes as a robust and negative relationship with economic growth (1999: 40). However, if the outlier represented by Japan is excluded and the rate of capital formation is included, even this relation becomes insignificant. For these sorts of reasons Castles himself concludes that this modelling 'is designed to be exemplary rather than comprehensive', and that it does not provide a basis for policy (1999: 50).

In sum, despite the strength of feeling that the system of governance *must* influence the rate of economic growth, there is little objective proof that one set of governance arrangements in a market economy are inherently superior to another in this respect. There are, of course, some clear instances of policy failure that do seem to have affected economic growth, but it has not been shown that different types of democratic arrangements make such failures more or less likely. This suggests that the choice of the system of governance should be made on other grounds than pure economic efficiency.

In this context it is interesting that there has been no rigorous attempt to test whether the more cooperative arrangements that characterise 'organised market' economies, or the Asian emphasis on authority and collective interest, have resulted in better economic performance than achieved by the more competitive arrangements that characterise 'liberal market' economies. Most of the arguments are based on conjecture, and while measurement is clearly a problem, it is probably not the main one. The real difficulty is that each system of governance has its strengths and weaknesses and no particular system may be intrinsically better than another. Rather what works best may depend most on a country's history, geography and culture, and the circumstances of the time.

In terms of Australia's situation what is perhaps most interesting is that many of the proposals for constitutional reform have been directed to strengthening the national government. There have, for example, been referendums covering referral of powers from the states, lengthening of parliamentary terms, and various schemes for reducing the power of the Senate. The evidence cited above, however, suggests that such changes towards an even more majoritarian form of government would not necessarily lead to any improvement in economic performance, even if the Australian public could ever be persuaded to further concentrate power in this way. Rather what is needed is the will to develop cooperative relationships that can allow a consensual model of governance to work. The experience of cooperative federalism shows that Australian governments can work cooperatively, but it takes good leadership.

Changes in Australian governance 1980–2000

Instead of considering how economic growth is affected by the institutional arrangements for governance, an alternative approach is to consider how effectively these arrangements have responded to such determinants of growth as changes in technology and economic and social relations, expectations and values. Is the system of governance in Australia responsive to the changing conditions for economic growth? For example, the means by which Australian governments seek to intervene to stabilise demand, and thus sustain economic growth, have been affected by globalisation and particularly by the massive flows of capital associated with globalisation. Equally the type of services that governments are responsible for has been affected by changing social relations, including more single person households and higher female workforce participation. And the shift in values in favour of neo-liberalism and a more individualistic society has led to changes in how those services are delivered, with greater choice and competition.

In response to these different pressures there have been major changes in Australian public administration since the early 1980s. Initially, the emphasis was on managerial reform to improve efficiency and effectiveness. The implicit expectation was that greater government efficiency would reduce the burden on the rest of the economy and enhance economic growth. Key elements were a focus on program results, as well as the traditional concern for due process. This was matched by improved measures of performance and evaluation to enhance accountability and effectiveness, and devolution to produce a better alignment of authority and responsibility, with less detailed controls by central government agencies. Government budgeting and resource allocation was also improved by the development of forward estimates of expenditure and revenue, improved costing including accrual accounting, and generally greater transparency. Many services were commercialised and government businesses corporatised with any social obligations separately recognised, but these businesses were expected to compete in the marketplace.

Over time the focus of public management reform has extended beyond efficiency to increasing government effectiveness, especially by improving responsiveness to clients. This could be seen as part of a general move in the post-industrial era away from a goods economy to a service economy, with the government being a more dominant player in services, even where it is no longer a direct service provider. Governments are now allowing greater client choice, involving a shift from uniform provision and the notion that one size fits all in favour of service provision that is directed to meeting the specific needs of each individual. Initially this was achieved by offering a choice from a menu of programs, but increasingly contracting out is allowing clients a choice of suppliers. Increased competition and commercialisation of services has also raised the question whether there is any longer a good reason for government ownership, leading to privatisation.

The emphasis on competition and the encouragement of competitive markets has not only applied to the government's own services, but an extensive program of microeconomic reform has spread competition through the broader economy. The nature of government regulation has also changed. The emphasis is more on incentives and disincentives through the use of market-type instruments instead of command and control through quantitative regulation. Together these developments represent a major change to the traditional role of government in Australia in promoting economic growth. Most significantly, the opening up of the economy to external and then internal competition is a repudiation of the previous consensus, forged at the beginning of the twentieth century, and based on the three pillars of (i) industry protection, (ii) (white) population growth, and (iii) major redistribution through arbitrated wages

In order to bring about such a fundamental change in strategy the government had to build a broad basis of support, using such devices as independent reviews and consultation with those most affected. Interestingly, Australia's federal structure did not seriously hinder microeconomic reform. Instead in the first half of the 1990s a form of collaborative federalism was pursued that allowed the state governments to participate in the formation of national policy in return for their support with microeconomic reform. The record is that significant reforms were achieved by governments acting jointly that would probably not have been available if they had acted individually, while at the same time the federalist arrangements allowed a degree of responsiveness to local circumstances (Keating and Wanna 2000).

The challenge of globalisation has helped focus the minds of Australian leaders on the need for microeconomic reform, and is an obvious reason for the adoption of an economic strategy based on competition. But the background to this change dates back before globalisation had become an issue in Australia. By the early 1970s public expectations for living standards, and of government in supporting those expectations, had caught up with and overtaken economic capacity; indeed, capacity even fell as a result of the first oil shock in 1973. As a result, the fight between competing claims over the distribution of the economic cake became more intense. In addition, in a post-material age with a more diverse society, government faces a more difficult political task in mediating claims, such as those on behalf of the environment and the preservation of different cultures, that are not always readily compatible with maximising economic growth.

In the 1970s inflation served to resolve (temporarily) disputes over income distribution. Capital and labour sought to achieve their respective claims by leap-frogging wage and price increases. So long as money illusion prevailed the fundamental nature of this disjunction was masked and the economy continued to grow, though with an increasing tendency to stagflation. Of course, that inflation could only continue while the authorities accommodated it by increasing the money supply, but the authorities accommodated inflation precisely because it represented the most convenient way of resolving the dispute over competing claims. While those claims remained incompatible, the price of bringing inflation down was perceived to be too high in terms of the unemployment and income forgone, at least in the short term. Nor did the government at the time have at hand another more acceptable means of resolving the competing claims.

Following the election of the Labor government in 1983 a new cooperative approach to resolving competing income claims based on the Accord was introduced. The basic aim was to enhance economic and employment growth through wage restraint, with the government 'guaranteeing' workers' incomes by providing enhancements to the 'social wage'. In effect, this cooperative approach attempted to manage people's expectations so as to bring them into line with the capacity of the economy to deliver. For a period at least this did in turn enhance the economy's growth capacity.

The difficulty is whether any such cooperative approach can be sustained in the long run, or whether as memories of unemployment fade, expectations rise and become more difficult to manage. It may also be difficult for government to rely on the 'carrot' of the social wage alone. Indeed the Labor government quickly found that it had to float the Australian dollar in December 1983, and from then on there was continuing pressure to deregulate one sector of the economy after another. In effect, from early on the government reinforced cooperation with the stick of increasing competition.[1] Microeconomic reform has now made the economy less inflation prone and increased income growth, but it has also produced a greater sense of winners and losers, and the distribution of *private* incomes is becoming more unequal. The resulting tensions and other competing claims on behalf of the environment and the preservation of various elements of Australian culture, including Aboriginals and the 'bush', could inhibit growth in the future unless the arrangements for governance can mediate them successfully.

Future directions

Globalisation and technology are already driving governments around the world to rely more heavily on markets. That does not mean there is no scope for effective government intervention, but the means and sometimes the cost of intervention are being reassessed. For example, there has been a change in favour of market instruments in the conduct of macroeconomic policy, but a floating exchange rate has given governments the capacity to maintain an independent monetary policy. This contrasts with the previous fixed exchange rate regime when monetary policy had to target the exchange rate, which meant that Australian monetary policy was effectively determined by US policy in response to US conditions. The issue now is whether the Australian authorities are willing to use the independent capacity that a floating exchange rate gives them. The difficulty is that there is a widespread expectation that the scale and rapidity of international financial flows will on occasions require the authorities to intervene in financial markets; albeit by adjusting interest rates rather than directly. To the extent that the authorities can establish their credibility with markets this will help to reduce such pressures, and that is why governance arrangements have shifted in favour of greater independence for the Australian Reserve Bank. But given this independence and so long as exchange rate movements are not heralding an excessive build-up in inflation there is much to be said for treating those movements with benign neglect. If the fundamentals of the economy are sound, pressures on the exchange rate can be expected to reverse themselves, and if that means that speculators against the currency get their fingers burnt that will be a useful lesson to be more prudent next time.

The need to adapt to new technologies as well as financial flows is also maintaining the pressure on government to pursue more flexible regulatory arrangements for the goods and labour markets. In Australia the principal response at present is more competition and individual or enterprise wage bargaining, rather than collective bargaining or arbitration affecting whole industry sectors or the total economy. Individual contracts and market-based competition are commonly identified with maximum flexibility. This, however, need not always be the case. Unilateral decisions have the advantage that they can be taken quickly, but where implementation depends upon others, cooperation may not cause any delay in implementation and it may achieve more effective results. However, it also has to be acknowledged that where cooperative arrangements have worked best is when change is essentially incremental. The current spate of technological change, which is revolutionising production processes, may be one of Schumpeter's phases of 'creative destruction' where the scale of the uncertainties requires a strong leadership response as the uncertainties do not readily lend themselves to negotiation. This may be a reason why even longstanding relationships in countries like Germany are giving way to more liberal market governance arrangements in order to achieve the desired flexibility in labour and capital markets.

Future governance arrangements may therefore involve more liberal market arrangements in each of the financial, goods and labour markets, with social objectives and any adjustment costs met by using the fiscal system rather than by regulatory institutions directly intervening in those markets. This was clearly the strategy adopted by the Hawke–Keating governments in Australia. It does, however, make a larger call on government for fiscal intervention. One fear is that tax competition in a globalised world will cause a race to the lowest common denominator of revenue-raising, and there will therefore not be sufficient scope to use the fiscal system to mediate competing claims. However, the impact of globalisation on revenue-raising is often exaggerated, and tax competition is not limited to raising revenue, but also to how it is spent. For example, the United States economy is much more integrated than the world economy, yet different US states successfully maintain large differences in their taxation regimes. Moreover, the international evidence so far is that government expenditure on social policy has responded positively, not negatively, to the adjustment costs of globalisation (Garrett and Mitchell 1998).

Projections of future claims on Australian government revenues vary, but there is no consensus that Australia will not have the fiscal capacity to maintain overall income equality in a deregulated market economy (see, for example, Creedy 1998, Keating and Mitchell 2000). The main lesson is that governments should be cautious about reducing their fiscal capacity. In particular, Australia is already a low-tax country and the evidence is not strong that lower income tax rates would have significant incentive effects on economic growth, with the important exception of the very high effective marginal tax rates faced by some part-pensioners and allowees. For Australia the critical issue is not lower taxation, but how revenue is raised. The best tax policy for the foreseeable future would be to allow the necessary time to digest the recent spate of tax reform, especially as any benefits from further changes are likely to be marginal.

The political strain on governments when mediating competing claims can also be relieved if governments are seen to be less directly responsible. Cooperation with other economic actors is of course one way to develop a sense of common ownership and acceptance of policies. In addition, governance arrangements can be structured so that governments achieve their objectives more indirectly, and possibly more effectively by shielding them from the apparent responsibility and criticism that more direct intervention might provoke. Such arrangements can include setting up independent regulatory and advisory authorities, such as the Reserve Bank, the ACCC and the Productivity Commission, and using market-type instruments to manage markets to produce the desired outcome. For example, pollution controls can be maintained by an independent agency at arms' length from government. If the agency auctions the right to pollute, with a control over the total of pollution allowed, this may result in a more acceptable outcome than where the government itself tried to maintain quantitative controls over pollution. Similarly, taxes and subsidies and (partial) user charges can be structured to create a pattern of incentives and disincentives that may be both more acceptable and more effective than the old command- and control-style of regulation.[2]

Overall there is no evidence that government in Australia is reducing its responsibilities – if anything they are increasing as new ones such as the environment are added. Moreover, in a post-industrial society the demand for services is growing relatively, and many of these services are associated with government provision directly or indirectly. Future economic growth and rising incomes are likely to be associated with further pressure to improve and expand government services. Separating the regulatory, purchaser and provider functions for government-financed services can encourage better service delivery and more responsive services. Contracting out is consistent with this type of approach to service delivery. It provides a wider range of choice to more diverse clients and is more responsive to their needs. An emerging problem is the co-ordination of services, and case management is being developed in conjunction with contracting out for health and employment services, so that each individual has convenient access to the package of services that best meets his or her particular needs.

The Australian government is also changing the manner in which it seeks to meet its responsibilities for national development. While there are still examples of intervention to assist or protect specific firms or industries, the balance is shifting in favour of 'creating capability' through generic assistance involving education, research and development, and support for innovation. For example, as Jane Marceau discusses in her chapter, governments can play a critical role in the development of information systems that facilitate interaction among firms and the transmission of new ideas. Governments also support development through the provision of public infrastructure, but with one or two conspicuous exceptions, today this investment is more likely to follow strict appraisal. The intention is that public investment should respond to demand and be justified economically, in contrast to a history of many ill-considered attempts to create new demands through public investment. Generally, the new approach to national development in Australia does not require the government to pick winners and prop up losers, and is more consistent with the norms of the liberal economy.

Perhaps the most important challenge for governance in liberal market economies is that trust and confidence in government seems to be especially low. Whether or not this will affect the pace of economic growth is quite uncertain, but it is affecting the quality of growth and its acceptance in Australia. Some of this loss of confidence may reflect popular perceptions of a loss of effectiveness; that market outcomes are inherently uncertain; and that government has lost control in a more liberal market economy. In that case it has already been argued that government has the means at hand to refute this perception.

In Australia there is also a particular concern that the fruits of what is now clearly better economic performance are not being fairly shared. For example, an opinion poll in 2000 found that 'by a margin of 70–28 per cent, Australians would prefer the gap between rich and poor to get smaller rather than have the nation's overall wealth grow as quickly as possible' (*Australian* 17/06/00: 1). Apparently, this sense of unfairness is combined with a more general angst that government is out of touch and that there has been a loss of social capital as people in a more individualistic society become disengaged.

Market-based competition and contracting out the provision of government services are often associated with this focus on the individual and would seem to downplay the collective interest of society and the imbalances in social and economic power between different individuals (see also Chapter 6). But markets and individual interests need not necessarily clash with community interests and standards. For example, almost half of the contracts for employment servicing are currently to community-based contract agents. These agents are well positioned to both protect their disadvantaged clients from exploitation and to encourage better cooperation and participation at the local level where it is most meaningful for the majority of citizens. The performance of these agents could then be monitored by the state and rewarded accordingly.

Community-based employment agents are cited as one example of how Australian governments could consider more specifically how to achieve a better combination of market liberalism, cooperation and equity. Increased assistance to the 'victims of change' may be necessary, and this could be combined with a restructuring of financial incentives and disincentives by managing markets to achieve social goals. In addition, there are occasions when consultation and participation are appropriate. Such arrangements often result in a loss of immediate efficiency of decision-making and a blurring of accountability. Indeed this blurring, so that the blame is shared, may be one of the attractions if there is opposition. But cooperation and a degree of compromise may be the only realistic way of achieving the desired policy outcome. The challenge is to reap the benefits of cooperation without being captured by vested interests and blunting the advantages of competitive market relationships. This suggests broad-based consultation with all who have a legitimate interest, and wherever possible for government assistance to be generic rather than industry or person/firm-specific. Where tight targeting of assistance is more efficient, the rules determining that targeting may well be the subject of consultation, but they should be as transparent as possible and should ideally be administered at arms' length from ministers, with individual administrators held publicly accountable for any discretion exercised.

Conclusions

Governments have retained their capacity to govern in a more individualistic and globalised world, where the power of markets – and particularly financial markets – is stronger than ever before. On the whole this augurs well for future economic growth prospects. But in a more educated and cynical society, governments are finding it increasingly difficult to maintain their authority. People are more inclined to contest government decisions and voluntary compliance with many laws is less forthcoming.

For these reasons governance arrangements in Australia are shifting in favour of the incentive structures and choice associated with liberal market economies, and involve less direct government intervention. But the responsibilities of Australian governments have not declined, even if their role and the means they employ have changed. Government intervention is switching from command and control regulation in favour of a mix of managed markets, using market-type instruments, and financial assistance to reduce adjustment costs and to achieve social goals.

However, even a liberal market economy cannot rely solely on market incentives and competition to achieve economic growth, especially where there is concern about its quality and its distribution. Other types of longer term relations are also important to reduce opposition and to promote longer term investments, including in education and training. New approaches to seeking cooperation and consultation will therefore need to be part of Australian public governance. The trick will be to respond most effectively to the circumstances of individuals and communities while not becoming captured by vested interests.

References

Castles, F.G. (1999) 'Decentralisation and the Post-War Economy', *European Journal of Political Research* 36: 27–53.

Castles, F.G. and Dowrick, S. (1990) 'The Impact of Government Spending Levels on Medium-Term Economic Growth in the OECD, 1960–85', *Journal of Theoretical Politics* 2(2): 173–204.

Creedy, J. (1998) *Pensions and Population Ageing*, Edward Elgar Publishing, Cheltenham, U.K.

Dowrick, S. and Nguyen, D.T. (1989) 'OECD Comparative Economic Growth in the Post-War Period: Evidence from a Model of Convergence', *American Economic Review* 7(5): 1010–30.

Garrett, G. and Mitchell, D. (1998) Updated version of 'Globalisation and the Welfare State: Income Transfers in the Industrial Democracies, 1966–1990', paper presented at the Annual Meeting of the American Political Science Association, San Francisco, 28 August 1996.

Hall, P.A. and Soskice, D. (2000) *An Introduction to Varieties of Capitalism*, unpublished paper.

Keating, M. and Mitchell, D. (2000) 'Security and Equity in a Changing Society: Social Policy', in G. Davis and M. Keating (eds) *The Future of Governance: Policy Choices*, Allen & Unwin, St. Leonards, Australia.

Keating, M. and Wanna, J. (2000) 'Remaking Federalism', in Keating, M., Wanna, J. and Weller, P. (eds) *Institutions on the Edge? Capacity for Governance*, Allen & Unwin, St Leonards, Australia.

Lijphart, A. (1999) *Patterns of Democracy: Government Forms and Performance in Thirty Six Countries*, Yale University Press, New Haven.

World Bank (1992) *Governance and Development*, Washington D.C.

Notes

1 This summary of economic strategy in the 1980s is drawn from Keating, M. and Dixon, G. (1989) *Making Economic Policy in Australia*, Longman Cheshire, Melbourne.
2 The manner in which managed markets can be used to improve health and allied services is discussed in Keating, M. (2000) 'Lessons from the Market Place for Health and Human Services', *The Australian Economic Review*, vol. 33, no. 2, pp. 198–204.

12

Corporate Governance and Growth

Greg Turnidge

Introduction

During the 1990s there were increasing calls for improved corporate governance in Australia. In part these were in response to high-profile occurrences of unethical business practice, but more recently they have been directed at encouraging improved financial and operating performance of companies as part of improving Australia's overall economic prosperity. The Hon. Joe Hockey, Minister for Financial Services and Regulation, stated that 'we should reflect on the importance of good corporate governance and its critical role in the new economy' (Hockey 2000: 1).

Such calls have not been unique to Australia:

> Chancellor William T. Allen ... urged the leadership of corporate America to recognise the tectonic shift brought about by the evolution of the global market and the growth of the institutional investment funds. He also urged leaders to recognise in corporate governance one source of possible competitive advantage, one way to make the organisation function more effectively. But he did not limit himself to a concern for individual companies: he exhorted company directors to assume their responsibilities in serving the nation (Francis 1997: 4).

The underlying assumption of both of these statements is that good governance provides the basis for good company performance and growth, and by extension broader economic growth and development. However, studies have not been able to substantiate this assumption, partly because it is not agreed what good corporate governance actually is.

One model relates to a concept of 'corporatism' that appears to have become accepted as the key behind success in the modern global economy. Corporatism has been described by John Ralston Saul as organisations acting primarily in their own self-interest, with terms such as business re-engineering and economic rationalism developed to validate public acceptance of the concept (Arbouw 2000: 43–4). This concept refers to the situation where organisations' activities, be they government or private, are dominated by the profit motive.

Within this concept companies operate largely in the financial interests of the shareholders. However, corporatism is increasingly being applied in other organisations, including government-owned ones, with greater emphasis on private interests relative to public good. The principles of corporatism are also being extended into government policy application.

In contrast, this narrow view that a company is responsible exclusively to its shareholders has been challenged by management theorists, who have argued that the model for long-term corporate success requires companies to operate in the interests of all their stakeholders. James Collins and Jerry Porras undertook a case study examination of US companies that demonstrated long-term prosperity and attained extraordinary long-term performance (Collins and Porras 1994). One of the key factors identified behind the success of these companies was that they did not strive for profitability alone, often pursuing higher ideals and seeking to make contributions to society as a whole.

As a consequence of these alternative models, two concepts of the corporate governance have emerged:

> In the first conception, the corporation is seen as the private property of its owners (stockholders); its purpose is to advance the purpose of its owners (usually to increase their wealth) and directors are seen as the agents of owners whose function is faithfully to advance the financial interests of the owners.
>
> The second conception sees the corporation not as the private property of the stockholders, but as an institution; a form of social compact among various constituencies.
>
> The social entity conception sees the purpose of the corporation as not individual but social . . . in this view no single constituency's interests may significantly exclude others from consideration by the board (Francis 1997: 37–8).

This chapter examines the history and recent developments in corporate governance practice in Australia. It reviews recent developments in government policy, and emerging economic and social trends in an attempt to identify the capacity for corporate governance to lead Australia's future long-term economic growth and development.

Evolution of the governance model

The concept of the company, principally as developed in the nineteenth century, has become universally accepted as the basis for business activity. The main principle behind the concept was to limit the liability of the company's shareholders in the case of financial disaster. Since the original conception, through the interpretation of the law, a second principle has emerged that the company be regarded as a separate legal entity or person (embodied in the concept of 'the corporate veil'): separate from its shareholders, directors, creditors and employees. Due to the operation of this principle, company owners and operators have been able to conduct business largely immune from personal liability. The two principles combined have been instrumental in facilitating growth in commerce and trade through the containment of the risks of doing business within the construct of the company.

Within this context, directors have been appointed by shareholders to manage the affairs of the company on their behalf. Under statutory and general law, directors and officers are considered to owe their fiduciary duty (that is, to act with fidelity and trust) to the company which, in terms of the operation of the law, traditionally means the interests of the shareholders (as a group).

Typically this duty involves:

- acting in good faith, and in the best interests of the company
- acting with care and diligence
- avoiding conflicts of interest
- not misusing information obtained as a director (or officer).

The principles of corporate governance have been built around effectively fulfilling this duty, conducting the business on behalf of the owners through appointed management and being able to act largely immune from personal liability.

However the practice of corporate governance, particularly the separation (or lack thereof) of governance duties between directors and management, has differed between countries mostly as a reflection of the national culture and accepted community leadership styles (Francis 1997: 50–1).

In the United Kingdom the board, made up of several executive and several non-executive directors, has been strong and active in company management. In the United States the board is dominated by an extremely powerful individual; the chairman/chief executive, has very few executive directors and is relatively passive, being seen more as a regulator of company management. In Japan the directors are the top management of the company with the chief executive or president all powerful. Each of these models provides a relatively united corporate leadership structure.

By contrast, in Australia there is a much less clear corporate leadership structure. Australia seems to approximate the US model in terms of the board's composition, but with a separation of the chairman and chief executive positions, and consequently a separation of governance and management powers. The link between the board and management decisions is relatively weak, with significant reliance upon delegation.

Australia's corporate governance environment

Governance developments driven by the law

Over the last 20 years, through the courts' interpretation of company law (in the United States, the United Kingdom, as well as Australia), the duty to shareholders alone has been subject to challenge. The consequence has been a piercing of the corporate veil – looking through it to determine who should bear the responsibility for actions taken on behalf of the company. In Australia this is in line with emerging public standards of accountability in respect of a company's responsibilities towards its lenders and credit providers, as well as across a number of areas of the law such as taxation, trade practices, environment, and occupational health and safety.

Increasingly, directors and officers are being held accountable, and hence liable for the consequences of the company's actions (or inactions). This is evidenced in the recent reform of Australia's Corporations Law where the duties of directors and officers have been decriminalised, reducing the standard of proof required to establish a breach of statutory duty. This has been combined with the introduction of substantial penalties that may be supplemented by the Courts with orders for the relevant director or officer to pay compensation to the company. The greater exposure to personal liability implied by these reforms is pressuring directors to extend their fiduciary obligations beyond the shareholders.

These moves have substantially increased the perceived and actual risk of being a company director (or officer). In part this has been offset by the introduction of a US-style 'business judgement' rule into the Corporations Law. This would allow directors to assume that in making business decisions they will not be held liable regarding the fulfilment of their duty of care and diligence if they acted on an informed basis, in good faith and in the belief that the decision was in the best interests of the company.

These legal developments have created strong incentives for corporate governance practice to be increasingly focused upon satisfying statutory obligations; that is, avoiding personal legal and financial exposures by being seen to act within the law. To the extent that the law changes, is reinterpreted or extended, much effort is devoted by directors and their representatives to defining the specific circumstances within which those changes, reinterpretations or extensions apply. In terms of the Australian experience, much work has focused upon the duty of care and diligence, exploring whether directors are in a position, relative to management, to be held accountable for the actions of the company. From this has emerged the concept of reliance upon delegation, and reliance upon information provided by others, with corresponding duties imposed upon directors for placing such reliance. However, directors have not been relieved of the responsibility to demonstrate they have the appropriate skill, experience and capacity to fully understand the commercial, financial and legal risks the company faces in pursuing its business objectives.

The result is that over recent years corporate governance in Australia has increasingly adopted conformance and compliance objectives, to ensure that personal risks confronting directors are minimised. Furthermore, this approach encourages boards to focus their energies on avoiding decisions that generate risk for themselves. This imposes a high level of conservatism on the management of the company.

It is argued that this approach to governance has been undertaken at the expense of focus upon corporate performance. As stated recently by Stan Wallis: 'I note with great interest that some critics of the state of corporate governance are expressing concern that boards are starting to focus on process rather than content. A director can be sued, not for a bad judgement, but rather if it can be shown that he or she didn't take care. Now while this is reasonable, it runs the real risk that boards become overly concerned about ticking off the steps of the due diligence process and spend too little time coming to grips with the business issues involved' (Wallis 2000: 18). By implication therefore, good corporate governance is not defined as simply meaning good governance processes.

Governance developments driven by investors

The conservative governance approach adopted by company boards contrasts sharply with the desires of the increasingly powerful institutional investors, and of the public who are rapidly expanding their involvement in share ownership. Expectations are that companies will grow and provide strong shareholder returns, with these expectations reflected in a company's share price (calculated relative to expected future corporate profitability). It has become accepted that a company's share price fairly reflects the market's assessment of the company's (and hence the directors') performance. This relationship is being reinforced by community expectations that a person's rewards should be closely linked to their performance, and that reputation and status (be it corporate or individual) are no longer a given, but rather are earned and re-earned through effort.

Pressure is now being exerted upon boards, by institutional investors in particular, to improve their performance and the performance of their managers. A key outcome from this pressure is the emergence of executive share and share option schemes, where rewards of the management are linked directly to the company share price. The main rationale for this is that such schemes create an alignment between the interests of the shareholders and the interests of the management, reinforcing the priority of shareholders' financial interests compared to other stakeholders in a company. In contrast, this rationale has not been accepted by institutional investors in relation to the directors themselves.

Directors are expected to be independent and act as regulators of management behaviour. The view is that incentive-based remuneration for directors would cause them to act in concert with management, potentially to the disadvantage of the shareholders.

On the surface, management share schemes seem to conflict with the pressures emerging through the law and professional development for directors to take on duties towards a wider constituency. More significantly they increase the tension between the board and management, particularly in the circumstances where the board is not as familiar with the business as the company executives. As has been pointed out by Stan Wallis, on the one hand the directors are personally exposed to the downside of decisions that work out badly for the company, while on the other they receive no upside for decisions that work well (Wallis 2000: 19).

Share schemes also encourage directors and management to focus upon short-term financial performance. Depending upon how the schemes are structured this focus can in turn encourage companies to concentrate upon revenue growth derived from mergers and acquisitions, or net earnings growth based upon downsizing or tax-driven legal and financial structures. Whether these add fundamental value to a company's performance is a moot point, and questions are now being raised about whether the rewards reaped under these schemes are justified, either in terms of their absolute level, or in terms of the (often poor subsequent) performance of the company. It has also been suggested that the schemes can be manipulated and encourage a 'take the money and run' attitude among the executives privileged to participate in them.

The finance industry generally, and the institutional investors and fund managers specifically, add fuel to this fire by their own emphasis on financial performance and reward. Competition for funds (when fees are related to funds under management) and quarterly or even monthly fund management league tables encourage a focus upon short-term performance, and stimulate a herd mentality among fund managers (for fear of relative poor performance). This can lead to substantial short-term movements of funds, with consequences for share prices, regardless of the fundamental performance of the company. Such volatile market feedback places further pressure on directors and management to adopt conservative or defensive practices. In these circumstances it does not seem that good governance can be defined in terms of a board presiding over a management team motivated by an executive share scheme.

Australia's economic environment

The changing role of government

The role of government and its involvement in the economy has undertaken substantial change over the last 20 years. American-style democracy is now perceived as the model for political success compared to the European model of social democracy, or the Eastern European/Asian models of the planned economy. It has a strong alliance with Saul's concept of corporatism, with its success being reinforced by the emergence of the global economy, where substantial growth in trade and capital flows have created severe problems for governments attempting to manage national levels of economic activity.

In terms of Australia, the acceptance of this essentially corporatist political model has manifested itself in a number of ways:

(i) Through changes in the way government is involved in economic and social activities: privatisation of state-owned businesses and utilities; changed approaches in the means of delivery of public services across a range of areas including education, welfare support and health; changed emphasis in tax with the move towards indirect and away from direct taxation.

(ii) Through changed policy emphasis: increased emphasis on monetary management and inflation containment; reduced emphasis on fiscal policy for economic stabilisation; a movement away from industry-specific policies at both the state and national levels.

(iii) Through deregulation: deregulation of the finance industry and the introduction of foreign banks and financial institutions; deregulation of the traded goods markets with substantial reductions in tariffs and barriers to trade; deregulation of the foreign exchange market with the move to a floating exchange rate and removal of capital controls.

The basis of these manifestations is the decision by Australian governments (both state and federal) to allow the market mechanism (competition based on the pursuit of self-interest) to play a greater role in determining economic and social outcomes. This in turn means that prices, and hence resource and wealth allocation, and environmental outcomes, will be set more by the market.

However, given broad public concerns about the consequences of unregulated private-sector activities (either in the absence of, or during the formative stages of competition), governments have adopted a somewhat prescriptive approach to business behaviour. They have established new, or expanded the powers of existing administrative and regulatory bodies, and introduced legislation intended to monitor and regulate the pricing and competitive strategies of business, with penalties often directed towards holding boards and senior executives personally accountable. In support of this, governments have encouraged and facilitated rising levels of competition through the removal of trade barriers, and exposed companies to the effects of competition through the removal of traditional industry support and assistance programs.

Overall these developments are fundamentally changing the way the government sector influences and impacts the economy. Government now sees its role as less one of actively attempting to minimise variations in economic activity and guide economic growth, and as more one of providing the appropriate conditions and economic environment for growth to occur. The main outcome is that companies and boards are being pressured to respond to the operation of the market mechanism and the associated pricing signals in identifying and pursuing the best business opportunities.

By adopting a corporatist approach the government is sending the signal that this is the preferred model of corporate behaviour. Yet it creates ambiguity and confusion by overlaying that model with a stricter approach towards regulating corporate activity and pressuring directors to accept accountability to the wider community.

Wider economic and social influences

Against this background of a changing government policy environment there are a number of other economic and social trends emerging that are challenging Australian boards and their capacity to lead companies forward. These include:

- the expansion of the Internet as a medium for business and a mechanism for rapid transfer of information, resulting in competition moving from a spatial to a time dimension
- corporate globalisation as communications and information technologies facilitate the achievement of economies of management scale and centralised decision-making, generating potentially enormous economic impacts often beyond the influence of national interests
- the rapid adoption of the communication/media and computer technologies in the home educates and empowers the individual, allowing him or her to exercise preferences and choices more freely, and now on an international scale
- the X (post–baby-boom) and now the Y generation are better educated, less accepting of authority, expect a strong link between reward and effort, and are much less likely to demonstrate company loyalty.

In particular, the world has witnessed the information technology revolution and the emergence of the knowledge economy – the economy within which success is dictated by the ability to manipulate and evaluate information and exploit the knowledge gained. Computers, when combined with the Internet, empower both organisations and individuals, and encourage increased specialisation based upon knowledge-intensity. They facilitate decision-making and the movement of information within companies, eliminating the need for middle management and ending the era of the life-time loyal employee with the potential loss of corporate knowledge. Through enhanced access to information they foster cynicism about organisations, enable greater public scrutiny of corporate activities with the potential to diminish brand loyalty or corporate image. They have opened up the opportunity for new waves of competition (including from departing employees) as they significantly reduce the costs of business entry or substantially alter the costs of operation. They have allowed younger people, the computer/Internet literate, to be extremely well paid without the need of a corporate career.

This development of the 'new economy', which is perceived as operating on different economic principles to the 'old' (increasing compared with diminishing returns to scale), has encouraged major value differences to emerge. There has been a significant decline in the importance of tangible assets relative to intangible assets (knowledge capital) when assessing a company's value. High values are being ascribed to the future growth and earnings potential of 'new economy' companies, so much so that it now appears that world financial markets penalise countries (through the exchange rate) and/or companies (via the share price) dependent upon the 'old economy', leaving them vulnerable to takeover. Australia seems to have been particularly exposed to this.

When combined with globalisation, these trends are placing companies under pressure of an international scale. Australian companies are now facing enormous challenges.

As a result, boards and senior executives are being confronted with high levels of uncertainty about the future with attendant increases in commercial risk. The ability of directors to deal with such complexity and uncertainty depends upon their capacity to assimilate this new environment into their thinking and respond to it. This in turn requires directors and boards as a whole to develop a more complete understanding of their businesses than has been necessary in the past, and to gain a greater appreciation of the value of intellectual capital to the future of their companies. Unfortunately, this requirement is occurring at a time when many companies have downsized in response to intense competitive pressures, and have lost access to significant amounts of corporate knowledge and expertise. The board's traditional dependence upon the chief executive and the senior management team as the means of dealing with these challenges is now being seriously questioned.

The implications for corporate governance and economic growth

What does this mean for governance in Australia? For directors, the trends in policy development and wider economic and social influences are exposing companies to greater commercial risk, while the developments in regulation are placing greater levels of personal accountability on boards and management.

In effect directors are being pulled in two directions: on the one hand, they feel a prime responsibility to their shareholders, and are being encouraged by investors and funds managers to manage the company principally in the financial interests of the shareholders; on the other, developments in the law and legislation are pressuring directors to accept personal accountability for their actions to an expanding number of their company's stakeholders. These pressures in turn are being passed on to the CEO, with that role being seen as more short-term and consequently more mercenary.

To compound this difficult situation, directors are also being confronted with rising levels of uncertainty about the future. On the one hand the governments are increasingly deferring to the power of the market mechanism to determine economic and social outcomes – companies with limited political leverage essentially are expected to fend for themselves. On the other, the information technology and Internet revolutions are totally altering the competitive playing field and compromising the predictability of the sources of future corporate profitability and growth. Deciding what is good governance in this environment is becoming increasingly difficult for directors.

In combination, these developments have significantly altered the risk/reward relationship confronting directors – the risks of business are increasing at the same time that the personal costs of failure are rising. The natural tendency for directors in these circumstances is to respond defensively and conservatively, focusing almost exclusively upon compliance matters, with the consequence that neither of the two concepts of corporate governance referred to earlier is being widely practised.

This would seem to be the opposite of what is required for Australia's economic future. If corporate governance is to provide competitive advantage, directors must be prepared to show effective leadership, demonstrating a willingness to take decisions in the face of uncertainty. For this to happen it will be necessary to diminish the fear of failure, and provide appropriate rewards for success. This can only occur if there are changes in the behaviour of both directors and government, and institutional investors and fund managers adopt a longer term perspective.

From a different but not unrelated perspective the professional bodies are beginning to emphasise the role directors have in adding value to a company. This generally does not favour the purely corporatist model. Ivor Francis has strongly argued that good corporate governance requires directors to recognise the interests of all the company's stakeholders as part of moving beyond conformance and adding value to company performance to deliver long-term shareholder value (Francis 1997: 19). A similar governance approach has been recommended by the UK-based Inquiry into Tomorrow's Company. They concluded that a company's 'license to operate' is granted by all its stakeholders, not just its shareholders (Royal Society 1995). This conclusion not only reinforces the need for a different board structure, it also indicates a basis upon which boards can become more knowledgeable about the key factors driving the future success of their companies, with directors playing a much more active role in understanding the business of the company.

Fundamentally, good corporate governance is defined in terms of the way boards and management make and implement decisions that deal effectively with, rather than avoid, commercial risk. To be confident to take such decisions, directors need to have, or have access to, a detailed independent knowledge and understanding of the business. This need challenges the traditional structure of the Australian company board, as it implies a different relationship between directors and management than currently exists. Furthermore, it places demands on each director's own skill and knowledge, the more so the greater complexity of the business, implying a different basis for determining board composition. It also requires directors to have the capacity to devote appropriate amounts of time and attention to the affairs of the company (and therefore apply realistic limits to the number of directorships they accept).

All of this suggests that there be a careful tailoring of the board composition to the business needs of the company, with more emphasis upon the skills required for future economic success. To support this, there needs to be a much better balance between the risks and rewards facing directors.

Unfortunately, Australian companies have been slow to respond. Board skills continue to reflect legal, financial and engineering backgrounds, often with relatively limited international experience or skills related to the knowledge economy (such as science or technology). This problem is exacerbated by an apparent small pool of experienced directors who end up serving on a large number of boards, a situation seemingly acceptable to institutional investors. In the absence of a diverse and broadly skilled and experienced board it should be no surprise that the focus is upon decision processes rather than content.

On the government side there is also a need for greater economic leadership. Heightened levels of uncertainty about the future long-term economic prosperity necessitate the provision of a stronger sense of direction for the economy. The complexity of the modern world requires the government to clarify its view about a desirable future structure of the Australian economy within which companies and boards can operate. It then needs to integrate that view into its economic policy and legislative strategy. Increasing deferment to the market mechanism by government alone does not create an environment for economic success, but rather enhances the likelihood that the economy will be buffeted about by the forces of change. A strong emphasis on corporatism necessarily does not create the sort of economic and social infrastructure required for corporate growth, and potentially leaves the economy vulnerable to exploitation by the financially powerful.

In many senses the elements of good corporate governance have been demonstrated by the recent emergence of the venture capital industry in Australia. Interestingly, this is the high-risk end of Australia's economic development with its focus upon new technology/knowledge economy organisations. This model, largely adopted from America, reflects a number of the desirable ingredients:

(i) Governments, federal in particular, led the emergence of venture capital through a series of expenditure and tax initiatives aimed at building a financial infrastructure that underpins new venture and innovation capital availability.

(ii)   Representatives of the financial institutions and private investors have adopted a long-term view with respect to investments, and have imposed a strong discipline over the choice of people to manage the investment of venture capital (VC) funds, with a heavy emphasis placed upon the combination of experience and decision-making processes (including governance), ensuring a strong relationship between the fund manager and the fund investor that encourages investor confidence.

(iii)   VC funds managers are expected to have an active involvement in the development of the company, taking a board position and regularly interacting with the investee company management to add value to the business.

(iv)   The fund manager's reward relates directly to how well the investee company performs, not in the short term, but over a number of years, in this way providing a direct link between the role at the board level of the investee company and their responsibilities to the VC fund investors.

(v)   Investee company boards are typically made up of executive directors and investor representatives (such as the VC fund manager), bringing detailed business knowledge and experience to the decision-making processes and building a strong link between the board and company management.

(vi)   Investee company appointments of independent directors typically occur on the basis of the specific value they can add to the performance of the company, usually in terms of desired business skills, international experience or market contacts.

(vii)   VC fund investors accept that individual businesses can fail, as the history of venture capital reveals that only a relatively small percentage of investments will be outstanding successes, yet the fund managers can be regarded as successful if the fund as a whole performs well.

Conclusions

It is still early days in the venture capital industry in Australia. Confidence in the industry is only beginning to build as the achievements (measured in terms of financial returns to investors) are now appearing. They seem to confirm that superior returns for all, including Australia, can be achieved through the adoption of the venture capital approach.

Unfortunately, the VC industry is given relatively small consideration compared to more traditional financial sectors. Institutions have been slow to support its potential due to lack of confidence and knowledge about its relative performance. Furthermore, and reinforcing earlier points, many superannuation fund trustees and their advisers have been reluctant to recommend investments in VC funds for fear that they will be held personally liable if the investment fails (Department of Industry, Science & Resources 2000).

With early signs that this approach can succeed, the challenge facing Australia is how it can translate this success across the economy as a whole. Learning some of the governance lessons may be a good way to start.

References

Arbouw, J. (2000) 'One Individual's Democracy', *Company Director* magazine, Australian Institute of Company Directors, vol. 16, no. 5, June.

Baxt, Professor R. (2000) *Duties and Responsibilities of Directors and Officers*, Australian Institute of Company Directors, 16th edn, March.

Collins J. and Porras, J. (1994) *Built to Last – Successful Habits of Visionary Companies*, Century Business Press.

Department of Industry, Science and Resources (2000) *Benchmarking Australian Institutional Investment in Domestic Venture Capital*, a study prepared by Pricewaterhouse-Coopers, June.

Francis, I. (1997) *Future Directions, The Power of the Competitive Board*, Australian Institute of Company Directors, FT Pitman Publishing.

Hilmer, F.G. (1993) *Strictly Boardroom*, The Business Library.

Hockey, the Hon. J., M.P. (2000) corporategovernance.com, speech to the Sydney Institute, 1 May.

Royal Society for the Encouragement of Arts, Manufactures and Commerce (RSA) (1995) Inquiry into Tomorrow's Company, June.

Wallis, S. (2000) 'The Thoughts of Chairman Wallis', *Company Director* magazine, Australian Institute of Company Directors, vol. 16, no. 6, July.

PART 4

Labour Markets, Human Resources and Demography

13

Unemployment

Jeff Borland

Introduction

For almost three decades now, reducing unemployment has been the primary labour market objective facing policy-makers in Australia. Nor is it a problem that is about to go away. While the rate of unemployment had fallen to just over 6 per cent by late 2000, this is at the end of nearly nine years of economic expansion. Should that expansion be reversed, it seems quite likely that the rate of unemployment would return rapidly to double-digit levels.

This chapter provides an overview of the main features of unemployment in Australia, and reviews evidence on its causes, and policy options for dealing with it. Given its scope, the coverage of many topics is necessarily brief. A range of other recent reviews of the labour market and unemployment in Australia provides more extensive treatments of some of the issues; for example, Borland (1997), Borland and Kennedy (1998), Borland et al. (2000), Debelle and Swann (1998), and Dawkins (2000).

Key facts about unemployment

Unemployment has increased dramatically in Australia over the past three decades. Figure 13.1 shows an upward trend in unemployment from the mid-1970s. Much of this upward shift appears to be accounted for by increases in the rate of unemployment between the mid and late 1970s that were not subsequently reversed. There has also been a strong cyclical pattern to the evolution of unemployment. Cyclical changes have involved sharp increases in unemployment; with subsequent reductions taking much longer. The first cyclical phase involved an increase in unemployment between 1981 and 1983 that was largely reversed by 1989, and the second a rise in the rate from 1989 to 1993 that had been reversed by 2000.

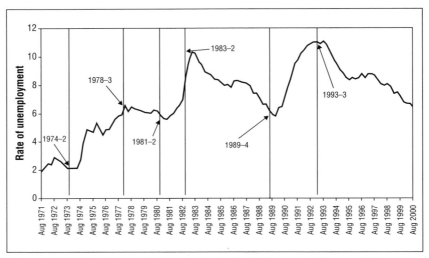

Figure 13.1 Rate of unemployment – Australia (civilian population aged 15 years and over – 1966/third quarter to 2000/third quarter, seasonally adjusted)

Sources: Data for pre-1978 – ABS, *Labour Force Australia Historical Summary 1966 to 1984*, Cat. no. 6204.0 (Table 2); data for 1978–95 – ABS, *Labour Force Australia 1978-1995*, Cat. no. 6204.0 (Table 2); data for 1996–2000 – ABS, *Labour Force Survey Australia*, Cat. no. 6203.0 (Table 2).

Underlying movements in the rate of unemployment are changes in employment and the labour force. Table 13.1 presents a decomposition between these sources. Cyclical phases where increases in unemployment have occurred have been primarily associated with decreases in the male full-time employment/population rate. During the phases where the rate of unemployment has decreased the employment/population and labour force participation rates for females rose strongly. Industry-level factors – declining employment in manufacturing and agriculture and increasing employment in finance, trade and the government sector – are behind these changes in male and female employment/population rates.

High unemployment has of course been a worldwide phenomenon. Cross-country comparisons of the evolution of unemployment can identify whether the Australian experience has simply mirrored that of other countries such as its trading partners. Figure 13.2 presents information on the rate of unemployment for Australia, the United States, Canada, and the United Kingdom. (The other countries have been chosen for the similarity of their industrial structures, and they are commonly chosen in this type of exercise.) Perhaps the most notable feature from the comparison is the reversal of Australia's position – from relatively low rates in the 1960s to the highest rate at the end of the 1990s.

Conventional measures of unemployment do not capture two important dimensions of under-utilisation of labour. First, there may be hidden

Table 13.1 Sources of changes in the rate of unemployment (Australia), 1974/second quarter to 2000/third quarter (seasonally adjusted)

Period	Change in rate of UE:	Males/Females FTE/ Pop.	PTE/ Pop.	Males/Females LFP/ Pop.	FTE/ Pop.	Males/Females PTE/ Pop.	LFP/ Pop.
1974/2–1978/3	+4.4	+6.6	−1.3	−2.4	+2.3	−1.6	+1.0
1978/3–1981/2	−0.9	−0.1	−0.1	−0.7	0	−0.7	+0.5
1981/2–1983/2	+4.7	+5.0	−0.3	−1.1	+1.1	+0.3	+0.1
1983/2–1989/4	−4.5	−1.1	−1.3	−0.8	−3.4	−4.1	+5.7
1989/4–1993/3	+5.3	+6.3	−0.8	−1.6	+1.7	−0.5	0
1993/3–2000/3	−4.7	−1.1	−1.8	−0.6	−2.0	−2.9	+3.0

Note: The decomposition is derived from

$$RUE_t \approx -\ln[\alpha_{mt}((FTE/Pop.)_{mt} \cdot (Pop./LFP)_{mt}) + \alpha_{mt}((PTE/Pop.)_{mt} \cdot (Pop./LFP)_{mt})$$
$$(1 - \alpha_{mt})((FTE/Pop.)_{ft} \cdot (Pop./LFP)_{ft} + (1 - \alpha_{mt})((PTE/Pop.)_{ft} \cdot (Pop./LFP)_{ft})]$$

where α_{mt} = the proportion of males in labour force at time t, $(FTE/Pop.)_{mt}$ and $(PTE/Pop.)_{mt}$ are the full-time and part-time employment/population rates for males, and $(Pop./LFP)_{mt}$ is the inverse of the labour force participation rate for males. The decomposition of the change in the rate of unemployment between periods t and t + 1 is undertaken by sequentially varying components of the expression for the rate of unemployment (from period t to period t + 1 values) in order as shown in the table.

Sources: Data for pre-1978 – ABS *Labour Force Australia Historical Summary 1966 to 1984*, Cat. no. 6204.0 (Table 2); data for 1978–95 – ABS *Labour Force Australia 1978–1995*, Cat. no. 6204.0 (Table 2); data for 1996–2000 – ABS *Labour Force Survey Australia*, Cat. no. 6203.0 (Table 2).

unemployed who remain out of the labour force, but who would like to work. Measuring hidden unemployment as the number of persons who are out of the labour force but report being 'discouraged workers' or being 'marginally attached to the labour force' yields estimates of the rate of unemployment of 8.5 per cent and 15.2 per cent respectively for September 1999 against an actual rate of 7.5 per cent (ABS, *Persons Not in Labour Force September 1999*, Catalogue no. 6220.0, Table 1). Second, some persons may be in employment, but working less hours than they would like. Figure 13.3 presents information on part-time employees actively seeking full-time work. This group represents about 10 per cent and 5 per cent of male and female part-time workers, and does appear to display a slight upward trend over time.

The incidence of unemployment varies between demographic and skill groups in the labour force. Table 13.2 presents data on rates of unemployment for disaggregated demographic and workforce groups in August 2000. It shows that young and less-educated labour force participants, recent immigrants, and persons whose last job was in blue-collar-type occupations account for disproportionately high shares of total unemployment. Figures 13.4a and 13.4b present time-series information on rates of unemployment by age and education attainment. All groups have experienced increases in rates

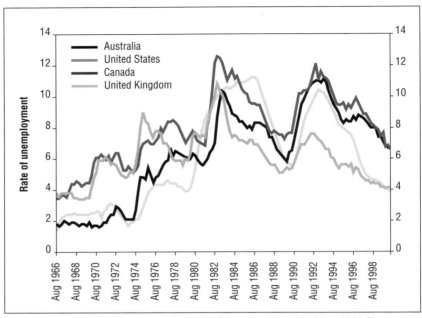

Figure 13.2 Rate of unemployment – OECD countries (1966/3 to 2000/2, season-ally adjusted)

Sources: DX Database – OECD Main Economic Indicators – series USA.UNRTSU01.STSA; AUS.UNRTSU01.STSA; CAN.UNRTSU01.STSA; GBR.UNRTSU01.STSA.

of unemployment over the period since the mid-1970s. The absolute size of increases in the rate of unemployment has been greater for low-skill than high-skill groups, although the ratios of rates of unemployment between the groups tend to be steady over time. The main exception is the period between 1974 and 1978 where the rate of unemployment of 15–24-year-olds increased significantly compared to other age groups.

Another perspective on composition is the distribution of duration of unemployment spells, especially its long-term incidence. In August 2000 about 28 per cent of unemployed persons had been so for more than one year. Figure 13.5 shows the relation between the rate of unemployment and proportion of unemployed with spells of more than 13 and more than 52 weeks. The two series are strongly correlated with movements in the proportion of long-term unemployed slightly lagging behind the rate of unemployment. There was a large shift upward in the proportion of unemployed with longer length spells between 1974 and 1977 that has not been subsequently reversed.

Regional dispersion in unemployment outcomes has also received much attention. Figure 13.6a presents data on the rate of unemployment in each state relative to the national average. State differentials have been relatively

Table 13.2 The distribution of unemployment – civilian population aged 15 years and over (Australia), August 2000

	Rate of UE	Percentage of labour Force	Percentage of unemployed	Percentage of Long-term unemployed
1 Age				
15–19	16.2	8.0	20.6	10.0
20–24	9.6	11.6	17.7	13.4
25–34	5.7	24.6	22.4	22.3
35–44	4.8	25.2	18.9	44.2
45–54	4.3	21.6	14.7	
55–64	4.0	9.0	5.7	10.1
2 Education				
Degree or above	3.5	16.7	7.0	
Diploma	4.7	8.9	5.0	
Vocational qualification –skilled	6.1	12.6	9.0	
Vocational qualification –unskilled	8.6	9.6	9.7	
Completed HS	8.9	18.7	9.6	
Not completed HS	12.5	33.5	49.7	
3 Occupation				
Manager/administrator	0.7	6.9	1.8	1.3
Professional	1.1	17.9	7.0	6.7
Associate professional	1.8	11.4	7.4	6.1
Trades persons	3.1	13.3	14.0	18.5
Advanced clerical/service	1.4	4.5	2.2	1.0
Intermediate clerical/sales/service	2.5	17.1	14.5	6.4
Intermediate production/transport workers	5.1	8.8	15.4	17.9
Elementary clerical/sales/service	3.1	9.8	10.6	8.6
Labourers and related workers	7.7	10.3	27.1	33.5
4 Industry				
Agriculture	4.0	5.1	6.8	12.0
Manufacturing	4.2	13.3	18.5	21.9
Construction	4.4	8.3	12.1	9.5
Wholesale trade	2.7	5.2	4.6	3.2
Retail trade	2.7	14.9	13.1	13.3
Accommodation etc.	5.6	5.4	9.9	8.6
Transport/storage	3.2	4.8	5.1	9.2
Finance	8.6	4.0	11.3	10.5
Business and property services	0.6	12.0	2.6	3.8
Government administration	1.6	3.9	2.0	1.3

Education	1.6	7.2	3.8	2.5
Health and community services	0.8	9.5	2.6	1.6
Recreation services	1.7	2.5	1.4	0
Personal services	4.8	3.9	6.2	2.6
5 Immigrant status				
Australian-born	6.1	74.4	75.5	
Immigrant	6.5	25.6	24.5	
Time of arrival:				
Pre-1976	4.7	40.1	28.7	
1976–1985	6.0	20.8	19.1	
1986–1995	7.9	26.4	31.9	
Post-1995	10.4	12.7	20.3	
6 Family status				
Family				
Husband/wife	3.6	61.2	35.9	
With dependants	3.9	34.1	21.6	
Without dependants	3.2	27.1	14.3	
Sole parent	10.8	4.4	7.8	
Dependent student	15.7	4.9	12.5	
Non-dependent child	10.1	11.4	18.0	
Other family member	11.2	1.9	3.5	
Non-family	8.1	16.2	21.5	

Notes: Unemployment rates by education are for the civilian population aged 15 to 64 years and for May 1998. Labour force and unemployment by occupation and industry include as employed all persons employed in the respective occupation or industry at the time of the survey, and as unemployed all persons who were unemployed at the time of the survey, who had worked for at least two weeks full-time in the previous two years and whose last job was in the respective industry or occupation.

Sources: ABS, *Labour Force, Australia*, August 2000, Cat. no. 6203.0; and ABS, *Education and Training in Australia, 1998*, Cat. no. 4224.0.

small with rates for all states for the most part remaining within a one percentage point band around the national average. Unemployment rates in Victoria, New South Wales, Queensland and Western Australia have fluctuated around the national average (with the largest fluctuations occurring for Victoria); whereas in Tasmania and South Australia rates of unemployment have remained persistently above the national average over the past two decades. Figure 13.6b provides an alternative measure of regional dispersion – the distribution of rates of unemployment between 186 DEETYA labour market regions in 1996. Dispersion in rates of unemployment is far higher at this level of region than at the state level—less than 10 per cent of the overall variation in rates of unemployment between DEETYA regions can be explained by between-state variation.

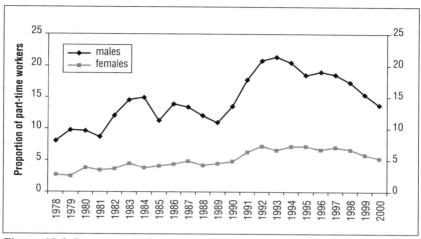

Figure 13.3 Proportion of part-time workers actively seeking full-time work (1978 to 2000, August)

Source: ABS, *Labour Force, Australia, August 1978–2000*, Cat. no. 6203.0.

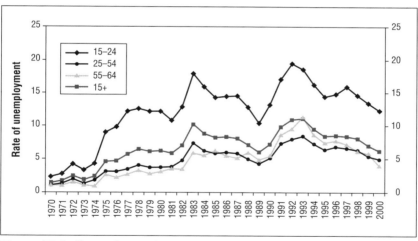

Figure 13.4a Rates of unemployment by age – Australia (civilian population, 1970 to 2000, August)

Unemployment has a range of important consequences for welfare, through its effect on economic growth and distribution. Obviously, there is a direct relation between growth and unemployment – to the extent that if there are unemployed labour resources then society is not achieving its maximum potential output. As well, some recent studies have suggested that societies with

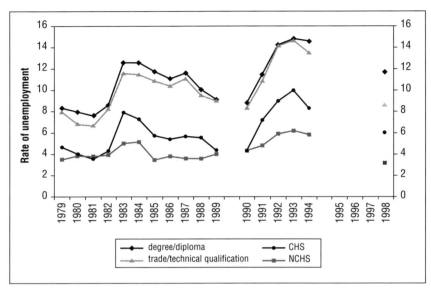

Figure 13.4b Rate of unemployment by educational attainment – Australia (civilian population, 1979 to 1998)

Notes: Data on rate of unemployment by educational attainment between 1979 and 1989 are for the civilian population aged 15+ years; for 1990 to 1994 for the civilian population aged 15 to 69 years; and for 1998 for the civilian population aged 15 to 64 years.

Sources (Figures 13.4a–b): (a) Age – data for pre-1978 – ABS, *Labour Force Australia Historical Summary 1966 to 1984*, Cat. no. 6204.0 (Tables 6 and 32); data for 1978–1995 – ABS, *Labour Force Australia 1978–1995*, Cat. no. 6204.0 (Table 6); and data for post-1995 – ABS, *Labour Force Survey Australia*, Cat. no. 6203.0; (b) Education – ABS, *Labour Status and Educational Attainment, Australia*, Cat. no. 6235.0, 1979–1994; and ABS, *Transition from Education to Work, Australia*, Cat. no. 6227.0, 1998.

lower levels of inequality are able to achieve higher rates of economic growth – due, for example, to the greater social cohesion that comes with lower inequality (for example, Benabou 1996). With regard to the effects on distribution, there are now several Australian studies showing how unemployed persons are concentrated disproportionately at the bottom of the distribution of household income (Borland and Kennedy 1998; Harding and Richardson 1998). Moreover, the burden of unemployment appears to have become increasingly concentrated over time; for example, the share of unemployment among couple families accounted for by family units where both husband and wife are unemployed tripled between 1979 and the mid-1990s (Miller 1997). There is also evidence that there is a causal relation between unemployment and poor health outcomes, and that the unemployed have significantly lower levels of 'life satisfaction' than others (Borland and Kennedy 1998).

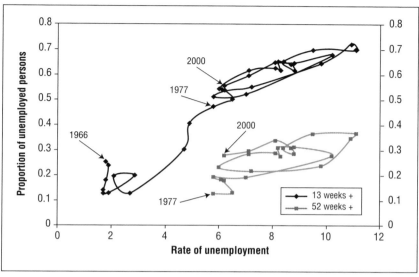

Figure 13.5 Rate and distribution of unemployment – Australia (civilian population, aged 15 years and over, 1966 to 2000 August)

Sources: Data for 1966–1977 – ABS, *Labour Force, Australia*, August 1966–2000, Cat. no. 6203.0; data for 1978–1995 – ABS, *Labour Force Australia 1978–1995*, Cat. no. 6204.0; and data for post-1995 – ABS, *Labour Force Survey Australia*, August, Cat. no. 6203.0.

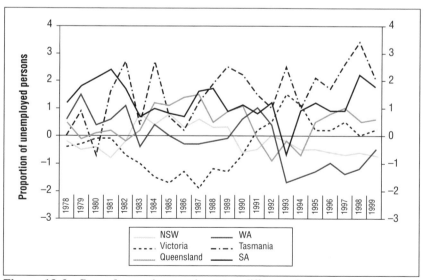

Figure 13.6a Rate of unemployment by state – difference from rate of unemployment for Australia (persons, 1978 to 1999, August)

Sources: Data for 1978–1995 – ABS, *Labour Force Australia 1978–1995*, Cat. no. 6204.0; and data for post-1995 – ABS, *Labour Force Survey Australia*, August, Cat. no. 6203.0.

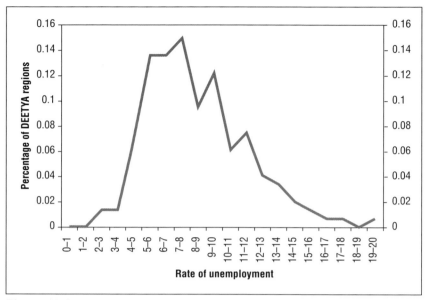

Figure 13.6b Distribution of rates of unemployment by DEETYA regions (Australia), June 1996

Source: Department of Employment, Education and Youth Affairs, *Small Area Labour Markets Australia*, June quarter, various issues 1984–1997.

The 1980s and 1990s

Another perspective on unemployment is through comparisons between the expansionary period of the 1990s, and the similar phase in the 1980s. Figure 13.7a shows changes in the rate of unemployment for the two time periods. The expansion in the 1990s has seen a similar magnitude of reduction in the rate of unemployment as over a comparable period in the 1980s expansion. However, the similarity in the evolution of the rate of unemployment disguises some significant differences in employment and labour force participation growth. Figure 13.7b shows the change in employment and labour force for males over the 1980s and 1990s periods. There are not large differences between the series, although growth has been slightly slower in the later stages of the current expansion than in the 1980s. Figure 13.7c shows the same series for females. Here, large differences are apparent. Employment and labour force participation growth have been much slower in the 1990s than 1980s period. This gap emerged (from a 1990s perspective) between November 1995 and May 1999, and thereafter has narrowed slightly.

Analysis of the possible causes of slower employment and labour force participation growth for females suggests that both demand and supply-side

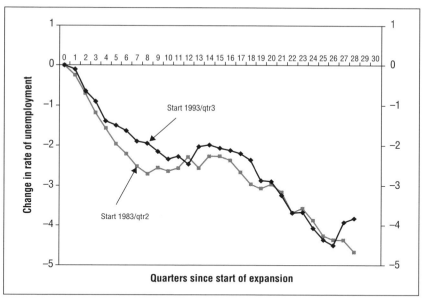

Figure 13.7a Comparison of expansions – males and females (rate of unemployment)

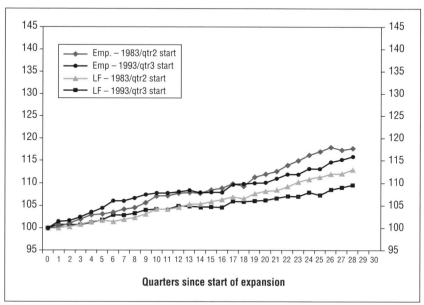

Figure 13.7b Comparison of expansions – males (employment and labour force)

Sources: (Figures 13.7a–c): Data for 1983–1995 – ABS, *Labour Force Australia 1978–1995*, Cat. no. 6204.0; and data for post-1995 – ABS, *Labour Force Survey Australia*, February/May/August/November, Cat. no. 6203.0.

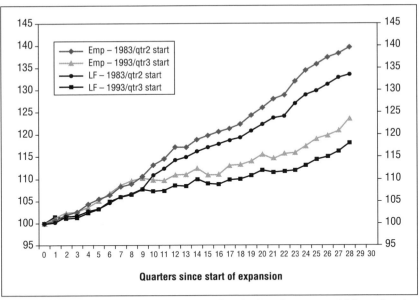

Figure 13.7c Comparison of expansions – females (employment and labour force)

factors are likely to have been important (see Borland and Kennedy, 1998). On the demand side slower growth in female-dominated industries (finance/insurance/property; retail; and health and community services) can explain about one-half of the relative fall in female employment growth. (However, differences in the rate of growth in output between the 1980s and 1990s do not appear to explain the difference in employment growth rates. Figure 13.7d shows that growth in non-farm GDP has been very similar between the 1980s and 1990s expansions.) On the supply side it is possible that increasing competition for part-time jobs from male labour force participants, reductions in average mortgage repayments, and changes in government benefits for childcare and parenting allowances have played some role.

One important issue in the 1990s is whether there has been more 'churning' of persons into and out of unemployment than at previous times. Figures 13.7e and 13.7f present information on the monthly rate of inflow to unemployment. The series exhibits substantial seasonal variation, but it is still possible to discern two main features from the data on inflows. First, for males and females, and in the 1980s and 1990s, the rate of inflow to unemployment declines during the period of expansion. Second, for males, but not for females, the rate of inflow to unemployment during the 1990s has been higher than during the 1980s. Thus far there does not appear to have been any analysis to explain why this shift might have occurred.

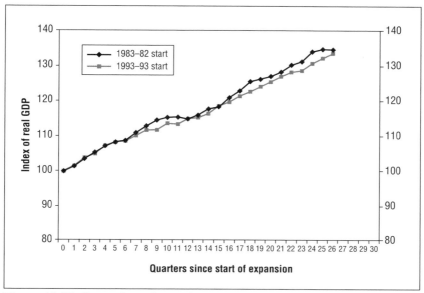

Figure 13.7d Comparison of expansions – males (employment and labour force)
Source: DX database – Series GGDPNFSA.

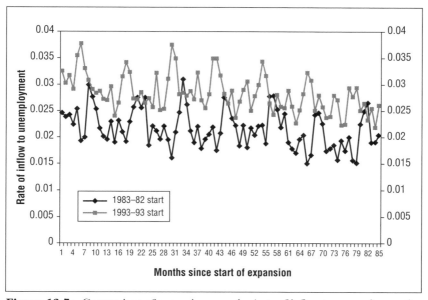

Figure 13.7e Comparison of expansions – males (rate of inflow to unemployment)

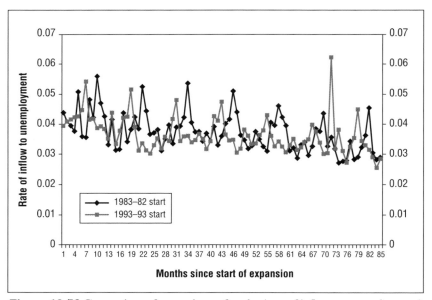

Figure 13.7f Comparison of expansions – females (rate of inflow to unemployment)
Sources: (Figures 13.7e–f): Data for 1983–1995 – ABS, *Labour Force Australia 1978–1995*, Cat. no.
6204.0; and data for post-1995 – ABS, *Labour Force Survey Australia*,
February/May/August/November, Cat. no. 6203.0.

What has caused high unemployment?

An explanation for high unemployment in Australia is perhaps best thought of
in two parts. First, why have episodes of increases in the rate of unemployment
occurred in the 1970s, early 1980s, and late 1980s to early 1990s? And second,
why were those increases in the rate of unemployment either not reversed, or
only reversed after prolonged expansions?

Studies of the causes of unemployment in Australia have applied a range of
methodologies, and examined different time periods, so that it is a challenging
exercise to draw general conclusions. Nevertheless, it does seem possible to make
some synthesis from the existing studies. (For a recent detailed review of the
literature on the causes of unemployment in Australia, see Borland et al. 2000.)

First, periods of increase in the rate of unemployment seem to have been
associated primarily with reductions in the rate of output growth or with very
high rates of wage inflation. Most studies of the increase in unemployment in
1974 to 1976 conclude that the primary cause was the rapid rate of wage inflation. The increase in unemployment between 1981 and 1983 is attributed to
both wage inflation and a fall in the rate of growth in output. And the rise in
unemployment between 1989 and 1993 is generally attributed to a reduction

in the rate of output growth due to international factors and domestic monetary policy. Changes to institutions do not seem to have been an important causal factor for increases in unemployment – apart from the rise in unemployment benefit payments in 1973 that seems to have accounted for some part of the increase in that period.

Second, persistence in unemployment during periods of economic expansion seems partly related to declines in search efficiency of the unemployed. As the distribution of unemployment spells shifts towards longer length durations during a recession it is likely that the average 'job readiness' and skills of the unemployed fall. In a subsequent expansion this will act as an impediment to reducing unemployment – directly through the reduced efficiency of job matching, and indirectly through the consequences for wage inflation and hence the rate of output growth that can be sustained. Regional dispersion in employment outcomes could also be a source of reduced search efficiency following an increase in the rate of unemployment.

Third, cross-country studies suggest that some features of Australia's institutional structure – together with macroeconomic conditions – may explain differences in unemployment outcomes between Australia and other OECD countries. Institutional factors that are particularly important appear to be the unemployment benefit system in Australia, and aspects of the wage-bargaining environment. Cross-country studies have been influential in forming the policy recommendations of international agencies such as the OECD, but there are several important reasons why it is necessary to be cautious in interpreting the findings of the studies.

Policies to reduce unemployment

It is sometimes said that 'If we knew how to reduce unemployment, it would have been done long ago'. This implies that there exists great uncertainty or lack of knowledge about how to reduce unemployment. In fact, although debate remains, there is a high degree of consensus about what are appropriate strategies for countering unemployment. The problem for policy-makers has been not being able to implement those strategies in a sustained manner.

This section describes some of the main issues about policies to reduce unemployment. It is organised as a series of questions that face policy-makers.

How important is maintaining high rates of economic growth for achieving reductions in unemployment?

A first point of consensus is that the main mechanism for achieving reductions in unemployment is to maintain high rates of economic growth. Studies of the causes of unemployment in Australia suggest that reductions in aggregate demand have been one of the two main factors associated with periods of

increases in unemployment in Australia in the 1980s and 1990s. Simple modelling and simulation of employment and labour force participation in the Australian labour market support this view suggesting, for example, that
maintaining a rate of growth of 4 per cent per annum over a five-year period,
rather than 2 per cent per annum over the same period, would result in a rate
of unemployment that was 2 percentage points lower (Borland 1997).

The importance of avoiding recessions is another point of consensus. This
may sound like a trite point. Of course, if there were no recessions then for that
time unemployment would be lower. But there is a further point. Where
unemployment changes the labour market environment – for example, by
lowering the skills of those who become unemployed – avoiding a recession
can also mean lower unemployment tomorrow. To illustrate: one reason why
Australia's average rate of unemployment during the 1990s has been higher
than in the other countries is that the initial increase in the rate of unemployment in the early 1990s was also higher.

While there is substantial agreement on the primacy of policies to maintain
high rates of output growth, there are, however, two issues on the relation
between output growth and unemployment where there is less consensus. One
issue is how high a rate of growth is sustainable in Australia while keeping price
inflation within the target range of the Reserve Bank of Australia. Dungey and
Pitchford (1998) argue that the rate of growth in GDP consistent with steady
inflation is about 4.4 per cent. However, this has proved to be contentious with
suggestions that this objective would not be consistent with steady inflation. In
discussions about what constitutes a 'steady inflation rate of growth' one
important point is that this rate of growth should not necessarily be expected
to be constant over time. Structural changes such as improvements to the efficiency of operation of labour markets or the wage-bargaining environment
should change the rate of output growth that is sustainable.

The second issue concerns the weight that should be attached to policies
that promote economic growth relative to other types of policies for dealing
with unemployment. Dawkins provides a neat summary of the contrasting
views:

> The Green Paper on unemployment, and the resultant Working Nation policy,
> strongly emphasised the rate of economic growth as a determinant of the rate of
> unemployment, and its main conclusion was that the rate of economic growth
> needed to be increased to substantially reduce unemployment . . . Since that time,
> the unemployment debate seems to have reflected a growing view that while raising
> the rate of economic growth is a good aim, we should not place too much emphasis
> on this as a solution to the unemployment problem (1998: 310).

Instead, there has been a shift in focus to policies designed to improve
'employment absorption' from output growth – such as changes to the wage

structure or labour market programs to enhance the efficiency of operation of the labour market. As an example of this shift in perspective, in the Policy Forum on Unemployment published in the *Australian Economic Review* in December 1997, only one of the three commentators considered in any detail how to promote economic growth in Australia.

The right weight to attach to growth and to other types of policies probably lies between Working Nation and the more recent perspective on policy. Policies to maintain growth must remain the primary method for dealing with unemployment; and it would be unwise to emphasise other types of policies at the expense of measures to maintain high rates of output growth. At the same time, policies designed to improve the efficiency of operation of the labour market can be an important complement to policies for higher rates of economic growth. For example, such policies can reduce inflationary bottle-necks that arise from shortages of suitably skilled labour during economic expansion, and hence allow high rates of output growth to be sustained over a longer period than would otherwise be the case.

Do we have a wage-setting system that is consistent with moderate rates of growth in wages?

Analysis of the causes of unemployment in Australia suggests that an important factor behind increases in unemployment in the mid-1970s and early 1980s was the high rate of wage inflation in those periods. From this experience a second point of consensus has emerged: that maintaining a moderate rate of wage inflation is a necessary condition for achieving reductions in unemployment.

During the 1980s it seemed generally accepted that a high degree of wage moderation was achieved through the centralisation of wage-bargaining via the Prices and Incomes Accord (Chapman 1998). However, the wage-bargaining system that exists today is very different. Political and economic forces have caused a gradual evolution towards a system where the locus of wage-bargaining is decentralised to the enterprise level, although a significant fraction of workers unable to enter into enterprise bargaining still receive wage increases through centralised safety-net wage adjustments.

Whether the new decentralised wage-setting system is consistent with moderate rates of growth in wages has very important implications for unemployment. In recent decades, decentralisation of the locus of wage-setting has been a recipe for rapid wage inflation. With decentralisation strong unions have been able to obtain large wage increases. Those increases then generally flowed on with some short time lag to most workers in the economy. Hence, this past experience suggests that key issues in assessing the implications for wage inflation of the current system of wage-bargaining are: first, whether strong unions have been able to achieve large wage increases; and second, to what degree flow-ons to other workers are likely to occur. In this context it is important to note that decentralisation of wage-bargaining is taking place in a very different environment in the 1990s than 1980s; for example, the more limited role of the Industrial Relations Commission may have consequences towards the extent of flow-ons in wage-setting.

Should changes to the wage structure be part of a policy to reduce unemployment of low skill labour force participants?

Probably no policy for dealing with unemployment has received more attention in the past few years than the proposal by the 'Gang of 5' economists (see Dawkins 1999) for a four-year freeze on safety-net wage adjustments to promote employment growth, with adverse distributional consequences being offset by a program of earned income tax credits.

My assessment is that there are three main difficulties with this proposal:

(i)   There is little direct evidence to support the underlying rationale that is necessary for adjustments to relative wages to be an appropriate policy response to unemployment.

(ii) The employment (and unemployment) consequences of the proposal may not be substantial.

(iii) There may be better means of adjusting the relative cost of low-skill and high-skill labour than through changes to wages; for example, changes in payroll tax.

In what follows the second and third points are taken up in more detail (for a more detailed treatment, see Borland 1999).

To estimate the effects of the policy it is important to recognise that the employment consequences of a safety-net wage freeze will depend on three factors:

• the proportion of workers affected
• the average percentage reduction in real wages for those workers
• the elasticity of employment with respect to wages.

The magnitude of each of these factors cannot be known with certainty. However, it is possible to make reasonable estimates. I argue that the proportion of workers affected will be between 25 and 40 per cent; that the rate of inflation (and hence the rate of decrease in real wages for workers affected by the wage freeze) is likely to be between 2 and 3 per cent; and that reasonable bounds for the wage elasticity of employment are −0.5 and −1. Using a combination of the lower bound estimates, the effect of the safety-net wage freeze is estimated to increase employment by 1.0 per cent over four years; alternatively using the upper bound estimates the effect is to be an increase of employment by 4.8 per cent.

To give some further perspective to these magnitudes what would be the effect on the rate of unemployment of each scenario? Using August 1998 as the benchmark, and assuming that increases in labour supply offset two-thirds of the increase in employment (Dixon 1994), the following results are obtained: for the lower bound scenario the rate of unemployment would fall over four years from 7.8 per cent to 7.5 per cent as a result of the adjustment in real wages. For the upper bound scenario the rate of unemployment would fall from 7.8 per cent to 6.4 per cent over the four years. On the principle that 'the truth lies somewhere in between', a best guess might be that the safety-net wage freeze would reduce the rate of unemployment by about one percentage point over a four-year period.

In choosing how many workers to hire, employers are concerned with the overall cost of labour – not just wage payments. This raises the possibility that adjustments to relative wages of low-skill and high-skill workers may be done through changes to labour costs apart from wages. For example, one possibility would be to exempt wages of some groups of low-skill employees from payroll tax. (This is already done for junior workers and apprentices in some states, see Dixon et al. 1988: 298.)

One advantage of using payroll taxes to adjust relative labour costs would be that it may allow the adjustment to be targeted more specifically at low-skill workers; on the other hand, the 'Gang of 5' proposal involves reductions in relative labour costs for workers receiving safety-net wage adjustments, not all of whom may be low skill. Arguments against the payroll tax proposal would be that it may be administratively complex, would only affect employment in larger size businesses, and that the equity consequences of a wage freeze/earned income tax credit scheme are superior to using the wage-regulation system to achieve distributional goals. On the latter point, the latest evidence does seem that any increase in wages for low-wage workers due to wage regulation in Australia does not have much effect on the distribution of income (Harding and Richardson 1998). By contrast, an earned income tax credit can be targeted at workers who are in families at the bottom of the distribution of income. Of course, there is no necessary connection between a freeze to safety-net wages and introduction of an earned income tax credit scheme. Using payroll tax changes to adjust relative labour costs, and an earned income tax credit scheme to improve equity outcomes is an equally feasible policy combination.

How much use should be made of active labour market assistance as a method of achieving reductions in the rate of unemployment?

Active labour market assistance is intended as a means of improving employment outcomes and skills of unemployed persons. During the period of operation of labour market programs there may be some direct effect on unemployment through the additional employment that the programs provide. An indirect – but more permanent – potential effect comes where labour market programs enhance the 'job readiness' or skills of unemployed persons, thereby expanding effective labour supply and lowering the rate of unemployment at which excessive wage inflation will begin to occur.

Despite the potential benefits of labour market programs, evidence on their effectiveness is very mixed. Based on this evidence there can certainly not be a general presumption that labour market programs will always be a useful policy mechanism. In fact, the strongest positive statement that it seems can be made is that such programs are *sometimes* useful for *some* groups of unemployed (Heckman et al. 1999). Following on from this type of evidence Martin (1998) argues that the use of labour market programs should be selective, with specific types of interventions targeted at groups that will benefit from the programs (for example, early intervention to reduce school-leaving for students identified as 'at-risk').

During the 1990s in Australia, labour market programs have received significant attention as a policy for dealing with high unemployment. The most recent manifestation of these programs has been the Job Network model. The model was introduced in May 1998, and the first phase of operation covered the period to February 2000. The second phase will cover from February 2000 to March 2003. The main aspects of the Job Network model are the establishment of a single agency, Centrelink, to administer income support and to undertake registration, eligibility assessment and provision of job-seeker services to the unemployed; and the establishment of a competitive services market for provision of active assistance with three levels of service provision: job matching, job-search training, and intensive assistance for disadvantaged job-seekers.

Unfortunately, an absence of publicly available information has made it almost impossible to make any comments on the performance of the Job Network. One point that is evident is that there were significant problems with the structure of incentive payments to service providers in the initial phase. For example, it appears that the design of the payment structure for Intensive Assistance was such that a significant number of providers chose to collect the up-front fee for referrals for some clients but to provide no substantial assistance to those clients, for the reason that the subsequent incentive payments for placing the clients in employment would not cover the costs of achieving that outcome (DEWRSB 2000: 79). In the second phase of the Job Network there has been an attempt to deal with this problem by changing the payment structure (that is, the balance between up-front and outcome-contingent payments), and by introducing explicit criteria for services that should be provided to IA referrals (DEWRSB 2000: 89).

Conclusions

Unemployment has been a significant problem for policy-makers in Australia for a considerable period of time. Its persistence might be thought to indicate an absence of solutions to unemployment. This chapter has argued that such a perception is not correct. Policies for dealing with unemployment do exist; and based on historical experience these policies can achieve reductions in unemployment. First, the primary means to achieving reductions in unemployment is to maintain high rates of economic growth, and to avoid recessions. Second, maintaining a moderate rate of growth in aggregate wage inflation will assist in reducing unemployment. Third, policies to promote the efficiency of operation of the labour market – such as labour market programs – can potentially assist in reducing unemployment. But such policies need to be carefully designed and targeted.

The main difficulty in dealing with unemployment is not that we do not know what to do in order to reduce unemployment, but that it is extremely difficult to implement policies – such as maintaining high rates of output growth – over a sustained period of time. This is the real challenge for policy-makers.

References

Benabou, R. (1996) 'Inequality and Growth', in B. Bernanke and G. Rotemberg (eds) *NBER Macroeconomics Annual 1996*, Cambridge Ma., MIT Press, pp. 11–74.

Borland, J. (1997) 'Unemployment in Australia – Prospects and policies', *Australian Economic Review*, 30, 391–404.

Borland, J. (1999) 'Will Lowering Wages Reduce Unemployment?', *CEDA Bulletin*, July, 18, 20–1.

Borland, J., J. Freebairn, I. McDonald, P. Summers and J. Thomson (2000) 'Unemployment in Australia: Economic Analysis and Policy Modelling – A Review of the Literature', Melbourne Institute of Applied Economic and Social Research, University of Melbourne.

Borland, J. and S. Kennedy (1998) 'Dimensions, Structure and History of Australian Unemployment', in G. Debelle and J. Borland (eds) *Unemployment and the Australian Labour Market*, Reserve Bank of Australia, Sydney, pp. 68–99.

Chapman, B. (1998) 'The Accord: Background Changes and Aggregate Outcomes', *Journal of Industrial Relations*, 40, 624–42.

Commonwealth Department of Employment, Workplace Relations and Small Business (DEWRSB) (2000) *Job Network Evaluation Stage One: Implementation and Market Development*, Evaluation and Monitoring Branch Report, 1, Canberra.

Dawkins, P. (1998) 'Solutions to Australian Unemployment', in G. Debelle and J. Borland (eds) *Unemployment and the Australian Labour Market*, Reserve Bank of Australia, Sydney, pages 309–28.

Dawkins, P. (1999) 'A Plan to Cut Unemployment in Australia: An Elaboration of the Five Economists Letter to the Prime minister, 28 October 1998', Mercer–Melbourne Institute *Quarterly Bulletin of Economic Trends*, 1: 48–59.

Dawkins, P. (2000) 'The Australian Labour Market in the 1990s', in D. Gruen and S. Shrestha (eds) *The Australian Economy in the 1990s*, Reserve Bank of Australia, Sydney, pp. 316–52.

Debelle, G. and T. Swann (1998) 'Stylised Facts of the Australian Labour Market', Research Discussion Paper 9804, Reserve Bank of Australia.

Debelle, G. and J. Vickery (1998) 'The Macroeconomics of Australian Unemployment', in G. Debelle and J. Borland (eds) *Unemployment and the Australian Labour Market*, Reserve Bank of Australia, Sydney, pp. 235–65.

Dixon, P., D. Prentice and L. Williams (1988) 'Wages and On-Costs in Australian Industries: 1968–69 to 1985–86', *Journal of Industrial Relations*, 30, 294–310.

Dixon, R. (1994) 'Apparent Asymmetries between the Participation Rate and Employment Rate in Australia', mimeo, Department of Economics, University of Melbourne.

Dungey, M. and J. Pitchford (1998) 'Prospects for Output and Employment Growth with Steady Inflation', in G. Debelle and J. Borland (eds) *Unemployment and the Australian Labour Market*, Reserve Bank of Australia, Sydney, pp. 208–34.

Harding, A. and S. Richardson (1998) 'Unemployment and Income Distribution', in G. Debelle and J. Borland (eds) *Unemployment and the Australian Labour Market*, Reserve Bank of Australia, Sydney, pp. 139–64.

Heckman, J., R. Lalonde and J. Smith (1999) 'The Economics and Econometrics of Active Labour Market Programs', in O. Ashenfelter and D. Card (eds) *Handbook of Labor Economics Volume 3A*, North Holland, Amsterdam, pp. 1866–2097.

Martin, J. (1998) 'What Works Among Active Labour Market Policies: Evidence from OECD Countries' Experiences', in G. Debelle and J. Borland (eds) *Unemployment and the Australian Labour Market*, Reserve Bank of Australia, Sydney, pp. 276–302.

Miller, P. (1997) 'The Burden of Unemployment on Family Units: An Overview', *Australian Economic Review*, 30, 16–30.

14

Efficiency in Markets:
Labour and Industrial Relations

Mark Wooden[1]

Introduction

The institutional arrangements that regulate employment relationships in Australian workplaces changed markedly during the 1990s.

The tribunal-based systems of conciliation and arbitration that have shaped labour–management relationships since the turn of the century now play a less pivotal role, and the systems of awards that continue to be administered by the various tribunals are less central to the determination of wages and conditions (Hawke and Wooden 1998: 74).

Instead, enterprise bargaining has supplanted arbitration as the dominant industrial relations paradigm. The new industrial relations landscape in Australia is one where national and industry-wide considerations are more likely to be subordinate to the needs of enterprises, and where employers and employees are expected to determine their own arrangements without any significant involvement from industrial tribunals.

Importantly, prior to the late-1990s, all the major parties including employer groups, the union movement and governments, at both the federal and state levels, and of both of the major political persuasions, strongly endorsed the enterprise-bargaining approach. The main reason for this consensus appears to have been the widely held view that workplace and enterprise bargaining would stimulate greater levels of productivity, facilitating both increased real wages and increased employment. In other words, reform of Australia's industrial relations structures was seen as an important prerequisite for creating an economy capable of delivering more efficient outcomes.

In this chapter Australia's experience with industrial relations reform during the 1990s, and especially its impact on productivity, is briefly reviewed. It is concluded that while the case for change is still far from proven, the weight of evidence suggests that reform has been conducive to the achievement of higher levels of productivity growth. Moreover, these gains appear to have been achieved without marked adverse impacts on job security, working time and income distribution.

The changing industrial landscape

Enterprise bargaining

By far the most significant feature of the reform process has been the downward shift in the level at which wages and employment conditions are determined. Prior to the late 1980s, employment conditions for the large majority of Australian employees depended heavily on highly prescriptive, multi-employer awards, determined on their behalf by tribunals and commissions that had little or no direct knowledge of individual enterprises. Today the situation is far different. Legally enforceable enterprise-based collective bargaining arrangements are widespread, and most awards provide only a benchmark above which wages and other conditions can be negotiated.

Survey-based data, reported in Table 14.1, suggest that 42 per cent of Australian employees in June 1999 were paid according to rates set in registered collective agreements. A further 22 per cent relied on over-award payments or unregistered agreements. With 14 per cent of employees described as not being covered by either awards or collective agreements, this leaves only 22 per cent of Australian employees as reliant on arbitrated awards as the main mechanism for obtaining variations in their wages and conditions.

The data reported in Table 14.1 also indicate that coverage by registered collective agreements is far more pronounced in the public than the private sector. Private-sector firms are instead relatively more likely to rely on less formal arrangements. Indeed, coverage by registered collective agreements within the private sector is, at less than 30 per cent, relatively modest. As such, it could be argued that changes in the nature of bargaining activity within the private sector at least are not as marked as often assumed. There are, however, good reasons to suspect that the character of these less formal arrangements has also been changing. For example, it can be expected that the award simplification process,

Table 14.1 Award and agreement coverage (% of employees) by sector, June 1999

	Private sector	Public sector	Total
Awards only	26	13	22
Over-awards/unregistered agreements	30	1	22
Registered collective agreements	29	76	42
Other arrangements	15	10	14
Total	100	100	100

Source: Joint Governments' Submission (2000) *Safety Net Review – Wages: 1999–2000*, Commonwealth Department of Employment, Workplace Relations and Small Business, Canberra.

by rendering awards less prescriptive, will have enhanced the significance and scope of these informal arrangements.

Non-union bargaining

Another significant change in the character of bargaining concerns the role of trade unions. Prior to 1993, any agreement certified by an industrial tribunal would almost certainly have required a union as a party. Today, provisions for bargaining collectively with employees without the involvement of a trade union exist in all jurisdictions except New South Wales. Within the federal system, for example, certified non-union agreements first became possible under the *Industrial Relations Reform Act 1993*. This provided for non-union agreements in the form of Enterprise Flexibility Agreements (EFAs), though this provision was not well used, with just 261 EFAs covering only 23 200 employees approved (Department of Employment, Workplace Relations and Small Business 1998: 16).

The *Workplace Relations Act 1996*, however, strengthened the non-union bargaining stream. Specifically, the requirement to notify relevant trade unions that negotiations were being undertaken as part of the agreement-making process was removed, and non-union agreements were made subject to the same compliance tests as the union agreements. As a result, the incidence of certified non-union collective agreements increased. For example, by 30 June 1998, 576 agreements had been made under section 170LK of the Act (the non-union bargaining stream), and in total covered just over 75 000 employees (Department of Employment, Workplace Relations and Small Business 1998: 16). Further, the number of non-union agreements approved continues to grow rapidly, rising by more than three-fold by the end of March 2000.

Individual agreement-making

In addition to promoting enterprise-based bargaining, legislative changes have been introduced in some jurisdictions that provide greater scope for employers to use individually negotiated employment agreements to supplement or replace awards. Most obvious here is the introduction of Australian Workplace Agreements (AWAs) as part of the *Workplace Relations Act 1996*.

As noted above, around 14 per cent of Australian employees currently have their pay determined by individual arrangements. Relatively few of these workers, however, are actually covered by individual agreements formalised under industrial legislation. Within the federal system, for example, data from the Office of the Employment Advocate (OEA) indicate that 107 745 AWAs had been approved as at 31 May 2000 (see <*http://www.oea.gov.au/*>). To these we must add workers covered by formalised individual agreements within state systems (mainly Western Australia) – about 95 000 workers. The total number of employees covered by individual agreements that have been certified by industrial tribunals would thus appear to number around 200 000, or about 2.6 per cent of the employee workforce.

Individual agreement-making thus remains concentrated on a minority of employees, most of whom are outside the awards system and, in all likelihood, would have been beyond the regulatory sphere of awards even without the reforms of the last decade. Interest in individual agreements among employers, however, seems to be growing (see Wooden 1999).

The changing role of industrial tribunals

The role for industrial tribunals has also been much changed, with their powers increasingly curtailed. In part, this is simply a reflection of the shift towards enterprise-based bargaining structures, embodying the hope that employers and employees (or their representatives) can determine arrangements without third-party intervention. Tribunals continue to retain responsibility for administration of awards, but in most systems, and especially federally, awards are becoming less prescriptive. Under current federal legislation, for example, the Australian Industrial Relations Commission (AIRC) can only make awards with respect to a relatively small number of 'allowable matters' (covering, for example, minimum rates of pay, hours of work, leave arrangements, types of employment and termination). Furthermore, since July 1998, non-allowable matters in existing awards ceased to have effect.

Of course, the AIRC now has responsibility for certifying enterprise agreements, but the conditions under which it can refuse to certify are quite limited. As discussed by Stewart (1994: 142), legislative provisions introduced by the Commonwealth Labor government as part of its *Industrial Relations Reform Act 1993* deliberately targeted the AIRC's ability to use the public interest test to refuse to certify agreements. Before this, it was not enough for the AIRC to be satisfied that any agreement was reached by mutual consent; it also had to be convinced that the agreement was not contrary to the public interest. With the introduction of the new legislation this power to refuse to certify was removed so long as the agreement involved at least one union, was confined to a single business, and did not reduce the employment conditions of the affected workers (the no-disadvantage test). Changes introduced by the Coalition government as part of its *Workplace Relations Act 1996* further tightened the conditions under which the AIRC might refuse an agreement. In particular, the public interest requirement was also removed from non-union agreements.

Finally, the role of the AIRC in the arbitration of disputes has also been reduced, now seemingly confined to those that relate to matters in awards and that threaten essential services. The AIRC still retains considerable powers over the conduct of bargaining – that is, it has wide-ranging powers to terminate bargaining periods – but in most instances it no longer has the power to make arbitrated awards.

Enterprise bargaining and productivity

One of the interesting features of the reform process is that, for a time at least, all the major parties including employer groups, the union movement and governments, at both the federal and state levels and of all political persuasions, strongly endorsed the enterprise-bargaining concept. As noted earlier, the main reason for this consensus appears to have been the widely held view that workplace and enterprise bargaining would stimulate greater levels of productivity.

So how do these productivity-enhancing effects arise? Following Dowrick (1993), there are at least two avenues through which a shift away from centralised determination of wages and conditions towards enterprise bargaining might facilitate higher productivity. First, firms are assumed to be not operating as efficiently as they might be and that enterprise bargaining can help them move closer to best practice by enhancing the incentives to introduce more efficient work and management practices. Where wage determination is relatively centralised, with rates of increase bearing little or no resemblance to the performance of either the firm or the individual, there is little incentive for workers to cooperate in the removal of inefficient work practices. In contrast, enterprise-based bargaining provides an opportunity for employers to trade off wage increases for changes in work practices, thereby potentially leaving both individual workers and the firm better off. In this view, enterprise bargaining is largely about negotiating the removal of inefficient work and management practices. Efficiency gains from this process will thus be reaped once only.

Very differently, the second avenue raises the possibility that enterprise bargaining may have a sustained impact by raising the long-term rate of productivity growth. This might arise if enterprise bargaining is able to promote more cooperative relations in the workplace, thereby potentially encouraging innovation, facilitating greater acceptance of new technology and promoting the development of worker skills, thus enabling a shift outwards in the production function. However, it does not necessarily follow that changing bargaining structures will have this effect. For example, if enterprise bargaining leads to an enhancement in managerial prerogatives at the expense of consultative modes of practice, a climate of resentment and distrust among workers might be fostered.

So has productivity increased and is any of the increase attributable to changes in industrial relations arrangements? As previously discussed in this volume by Dowrick, at the economy-wide level, national accounts data suggest that a marked pick-up in productivity has occurred. This is illustrated in Figure 14.1 that, following Parham (1999), plots an index of labour productivity (output per hour) against the capital–labour ratio. These data, covering the period 1964–65 to 1998–99, reveal a distinct upward movement in Australia's productivity growth during the 1990s. Further, the productivity surge only becomes noticeable from about 1994–95 on. This is entirely consistent with the possibility that enterprise bargaining is partly responsible for the improvement, with coverage by agreements only beginning to assume significant proportions after 1993.

However, while suggestive of an association between enterprise bargaining and productivity, these data are hardly conclusive. Other explanations for the rise in productivity cannot be discounted. As discussed by Dowrick, perhaps most obvious are other microeconomic reforms intended to facilitate the more effective operation of market forces, especially in the delivery of government services. During the 1990s, for example, major changes have occurred in the way many services are delivered, especially in the telecommunications and electricity, gas and water supply industries.

Some of the other usual suspects for productivity growth, however, are not strong candidates for explaining the upsurge. The process of trade liberalisation, for example, has been very gradual and dates back to at least the early

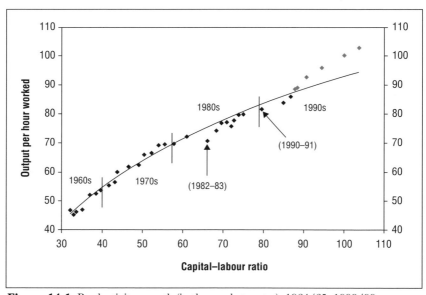

Figure 14.1 Productivity growth (in the market sector), 1964/65–1998/99

Note: As defined by the ABS, the market sector only covers those sectors in which output can be meaningfully measured. Industries not covered by this definition are: property and business services; government administration and defence; education; health and community services; and personal and other services.

Source: ABS, *Australian System of National Accounts, 1998–99*, Cat. no. 5204.0, Table 1.17: 28.

1970s – it cannot, therefore, explain the relatively sudden improvement during the 1990s. A similar line of reasoning can be applied to the role of rising levels of workforce skills. While higher skills undoubtedly contribute to economic growth, this is not a new trend. The education level of the workforce, for example, has been rising since at least the 1970s, and hence it is difficult to see how changes in the quality of labour could account for more than a small proportion of the recent rise in productivity growth.

Very differently, if the explanation lay in more rapid rates of adoption of new technology, then surely we would expect to see similar changes in many other industrial nations. As documented in Parham (1999: 33–8), the shift in the productivity growth path appears to be peculiar to Australia. Elsewhere in this volume, for example, Dowrick identified only Ireland and Norway as experiencing similarly large shifts in productivity performance. Somewhat differently, perhaps the acceleration in productivity growth reflects some lagged response to increased levels of innovation? Here the evidence appears to be more persuasive. Not only is there evidence of a rising relationship between productivity growth and the intensity of R&D expenditure in cross-country data (Bassanini, Scarpetta and Visco 2000: 26–9), but a marked increase in business expenditure on R&D did occur in Australia during the late 1980s and mid-1990s that, given the long lags between innovation and productivity, is consistent with a productivity pick-up beginning around 1994.

Finally, it might be argued that the recent rise reflects nothing more than the usual cyclical movements in productivity. The problem for this explanation, however, is that the response appears to be more sustained than we might expect if it were solely a response to business cycle variations. Further, it is again instructive that the recent pick-up in productivity growth is not a feature Australia shares with many other developed economies, even though all industrial economies went through the same recessionary episode in the early 1990s.

The economy-wide evidence is thus entirely consistent with the claim that changes in bargaining structures facilitated higher productivity growth. However, the evidence could hardly be described as conclusive. More convincing would be evidence that connects enterprise bargaining to productivity improvements at the firm or workplace level. Unfortunately, in Australia we run into major data problems. There are only two publicly available micro data sets that provide any information about productivity growth and both are far from ideal.

The first is the 1995 Australian Workplace Industrial Relations Survey (AWIRS). These data are problematic for at least three reasons. First, growth is assessed retrospectively. Second, the only productivity measures available are based on subjective data provided by managers. Third, the data were collected too soon to assess the impact of changing enterprise-bargaining structures.

The second data source is the Business Longitudinal Survey (BLS) conducted by the Australian Bureau of Statistics (ABS) over the period 1994–95 to 1997–98.

These data have the distinct advantages that they are longitudinal, they provide detailed financial information about output and inputs, and they cover a period when bargaining structures were changing. However, and in stark contrast to the AWIRS, these data are dominated by very small businesses, which are unlikely to have been much affected by industrial relations reform. Furthermore, coverage by agreements and awards is poorly defined and measured.

Investigations of these data sources have thus not been able to conclusively establish whether changing bargaining structures have had any significant impact on productivity. Analysis of the AWIRS data, for example, revealed some evidence that, among poor performers, labour productivity growth may have been higher where enterprise agreements were present, but not in the total sample (see Wooden 2000: 175). Very differently, within the BLS data there is evidence of up to a 9 per cent productivity premium associated with coverage by registered agreements (Tseng and Wooden 2001). That said, despite the longitudinal nature of these data, we have been unable to establish whether agreement-making *per se* is the source of this productivity advantage.

Ultimately, the hypothesis that enterprise bargaining has resulted in the enhanced productive performance of Australian enterprises is still yet to be proven. The weight of evidence, though, leads me to lean in favour of supporting this hypothesis.

The changing nature of work

According to many critics, even if reform has had these beneficial effects for productivity, they have come at a cost. The Australian Centre for Industrial Relations Research and Training (1999), for example, has claimed that industrial relations reform has exacerbated trends towards rising job insecurity, longer working hours, and widening wage inequality.

Job security

While the view that employment is far less secure today than in the past has widespread currency, the proportion of workers who believe that their own jobs are at risk has not changed much. This is demonstrated by an opinion poll data collected on an annual basis by the Roy Morgan Research Centre. These data, summarised in Figure 14.2, indicate that worker perceptions about job security tend to rise and fall with aggregate unemployment, but do not reveal a marked downward trend.

Such findings are consistent with other more objective data collected by the ABS as part of its labour mobility survey (see Wooden 1998: 186–93), which indicate that, compared with 1975:

(i)   the average worker today has been in his or her current job slightly longer (about six months longer)

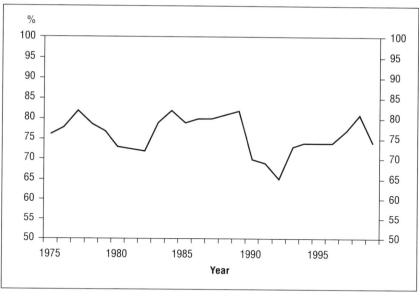

Figure 14.2 Job security, 1975–1999 (% of employed persons reporting their current job is safe)

Note: With the exception of 1981, 1982, 1983 and 1996, all data were collected in the month of November. The data for 1982 and 1983 were collected in December and October, respectively, while the data for 1981 and 1996 have been interpolated.

Source: Roy Morgan Research Centre.

(ii)   the proportion of persons in short-term jobs (less than one year) is smaller
(iii) the incidence of job-changing has declined (from 25 per cent of employ-
        ees in 1975 to 21 per cent in 1998).

Further, the slight decline in job mobility is not a matter of falling rates of voluntary mobility disguising a rise in dismissals and retrenchment – retrenchment rates were also lower in the most recent data (1998) when compared with data for 1975.

Working hours

A lengthening in the work week for full-time workers has also been linked to the industrial relations context (ACIRRT 1999: 112–14). For example, Table 14.2 shows that just over 28 per cent of the employed workforce were recorded as working 45 hours or more during the survey week in the August 2000 Labour Force Survey, which compares with less than 21 per cent in 1975.

Growth in the incidence of persons working long hours, however, was actually very pronounced during the 1980s when bargaining arrangements

Table 14.2 Composition of employed workforce by hours actually worked (%), 1970–2000

Year (August)	Zero hours[1]	1–29 hours	30–40 hours	34–40 hours	41–44 hours	45 hours or more
1970	5.2	10.2	5.3	51.2	5.2	23.0
1975	6.4	12.6	4.6	51.5	4.3	20.5
1980	5.2	17.1	7.1	43.3	5.4	21.9
1985	5.1	19.4	8.6	39.2	5.3	22.4
1990	4.5	21.5	7.1	36.6	5.3	24.9
1995	4.3	23.9	6.7	32.1	5.1	27.9
2000	4.3	25.1	6.9	30.5	4.9	28.4

Note: [1] Includes, for example, persons on recreation leave, on sick leave, on strike, and those who did not work any hours during the reference week because of shift arrangements.

Source: ABS, *The Labour Force, Australia,* Cat. no. 6203.0, various issues.

were highly centralised. In contrast, and despite the spread of enterprise- and individual-level agreements, the period since 1995 has actually been associated with only a small increase in the proportion of the workforce working very long hours. Such observations are thus inconsistent with the claim that industrial relations reform has necessarily facilitated longer working weeks.

Earnings inequality

Perhaps the most voiced criticism of enterprise bargaining concerns its impact on the distribution of earnings. However, while there can be little doubt that the earnings gap between the most highly paid and the most lowly paid has been widening over the last few decades (see Borland 1999, Norris and Mclean 1999), it is difficult for critics to attribute the majority of the blame to changing bargaining structures. First, the widening in the gap between the most highly paid and the most lowly paid can be traced back to at least the mid-1970s, and hence has occurred under both highly centralised structures and highly decentralised structures. This can be seen in Table 14.3, which summarises how the ratios between the earnings of workers at the 9th and 5th deciles, and between the earnings of workers at the 5th and 1st deciles, have been changing. For both men and women these ratios have been rising fairly steadily over time. Second, part of the increase in earnings dispersion will be the result not of changes in wage relativities, but instead of changes in the composition of labour demand favouring more skilled and hence more highly remunerated jobs (Norris and Mclean 1999).

Nevertheless, it is still very unlikely that earnings inequality has not increased further under enterprise bargaining. After all, one of the objectives of bargaining is to increase the degree of diversity of wage outcomes. But does widening earnings inequality provide an argument for returning to more centralised wage

Table 14.3 Trends in earnings dispersion, 1975–1998 (full-time non-managerial adult employees)

Year (May)	Males		Females	
	D9/D5	D5/D1	D9/D5	D5/D1
1975	1.48	1.33	1.37	1.27
1980	1.49	1.36	1.43	1.28
1985	1.54	1.38	1.48	1.29
1988	1.56	1.42	1.49	1.33
1990	1.56	1.44	1.48	1.34
1992	1.58	1.42	1.53	1.33
1994	1.58	1.45	1.50	1.34
1996	1.60	1.50	1.48	1.38
1998	1.63	1.52	1.50	1.39
2000	1.63	1.54	1.52	1.40

Note: D9, D5 and D1 refer to the upper limits of the 9th, 5th and 1st deciles, respectively, in the earnings distribution.

Source: ABS, *Employee Earnings and Hours*, ABS Cat. no. 6306.0, various issues.

mechanisms? The answer, at least in my view, is no. First, wage regulation is a very poor device for redistributing income, with many low-wage earners found to live in households with relatively high disposable incomes (Harding and Richardson 1998). Second, surely what matters most to workers is not the wage paid, but net income received, and this depends on both the wage and taxes and social transfers. Any efficiency benefits from more decentralised wage bargaining thus do not have to come at the expense of greater income inequality provided the tax-transfer system is used in a way to cushion the effect of increasing wage inequality. Indeed, this is exactly the way the tax-transfer system has been used in Australia, and is reflected in evidence based on data from the Income Distribution Survey, which shows negligible change in the distribution of after-tax disposable incomes between 1982 and 1996–97. These data are summarised in Table 14.4, which reports Gini coefficients for a selected range of income measures. As can be seen, both tax and government benefits have an ameliorating effect on income inequality. Thus, despite a marked rise in the inequality of the distribution of both earned and total private income, the inequality in the distribution of total disposable income has hardly changed.

Conclusions

Overall, it is very difficult to make strong statements about the impact of the industrial relations reforms that have taken place over the last decade or so. While many of the adverse consequences that were predicted have failed to transpire, it is also true that the case for reform, particularly in terms of its impact on workplace productivity, is still far from proven. Further, it is not at all clear that any significant benefits in terms of improved employment

Table 14.4 Changes in income inequality across income units, 1982 to 1996–97 (Gini coefficients)

Income measure	1982	1996–97	Change	Verdict
Earned income	0.477	0.538	0.061	Sharp inequality increase
Private income	0.457	0.511	0.054	Sharp inequality increase
Total income	0.386	0.398	0.012	Inequality increase
Disposable income	0.337	0.346	0.009	No real change
Henderson equivalent income	0.290	0.287	−0.003	No real change

Source: A. Harding, 'Income Distribution Trends 1982 to 1996–97', The Australian Advance Australia Where website, June 2000,
<http://highered.theoz.com.au/flathtml/extra/where/data/trends.pdf>.

outcomes have yet to be delivered (Gregory 2000). As a result, resistance to yet more change might be expected to be greater than in the recent past.

That said, the downside to any attempt to reverse the current direction of industrial relations reform is still considerable. One of the major achievements of the economic recovery of the 1990s is that real wage growth has been delivered without generating any significant additional inflationary pressures. In my view, this has been due in no small part to the fragmented nature of our enterprise-based bargaining structure. Any return to a system where multi-employer agreements are dominant has the potential to generate wage claims in many sectors of the economy that are not matched by improvements in productivity. This, in turn, would be met by a tightening response from the Reserve Bank, effectively putting a brake on economic growth.

References

Australian Centre for Industrial Relations Research and Training [ACIRRT] (1999) *Australia At Work: Just Managing?* Prentice-Hall, Sydney.

Bassanini, A., Scarpetta, S. and Visco, I. (2000) 'Knowledge, Technology and Economic Growth: Recent Evidence from OECD Countries', paper presented at the 150th Anniversary Conference of the National Bank of Belgium, Brussels, 11–12 May.

Borland, J. (1999) 'Earnings Inequality in Australia: Changes, Causes and Consequences', *The Economic Record*, 75, June, pp. 177–202.

Department of Employment, Workplace Relations and Small Business [DEWRSB] (1998) *Update: Collective Agreement-Making Under the Workplace Relations Act, January to June 1998*, Commonwealth of Australia, Canberra.

Dowrick, S. (1993) *Wage Bargaining Systems and Productivity Growth in OECD Countries* (EPAC Background Paper No 26), Australian Government Publishing Service, Canberra.

Gregory, R. (2000) 'A Longer Run Perspective on Australian Unemployment', *Queensland Economic Review*, 4: 12–15.

Harding, A. (2000) 'Income Distribution Trends 1982 to 1996–97', The Australian Advance Australia Where website, June, <http://highered.theoz.com.au/flathtml/extra/where/data/trends.pdf>.

Harding, A. and Richardson, S. (1998) 'Unemployment and Income Distribution', in G. Debelle (ed.) *Unemployment and the Australian Labour Market: Proceedings of a Reserve Bank of Australia Conference*, Reserve Bank of Australia, Sydney.

Hawke, A. and Wooden, M. (1998) 'The Changing Face of Australian Industrial Relations: A Survey', *The Economic Record*, 74, March, pp. 74–88.

Joint Governments' Submission (2000) *Safety Net Review – Wages: 1999–2000*, Commonwealth Department of Employment, Workplace Relations and Small Business, Canberra.

Norris, K. and Mclean, B. (1999) 'Changes in Earnings Inequality, 1975 to 1998', *Australian Bulletin of Labour*, 25, March, pp. 23–31.

Parham, D. (1999) *The New Economy? A New Look at Australia's Productivity Performance* (Productivity Commission Staff Research Paper), AusInfo, Canberra.

Stewart, A. (1994) '*The Industrial Relations Reform Act 1993*: Counting the Cost', *Australian Bulletin of Labour*, 20, June, pp. 140–61.

Tseng, Y. and Wooden, M. (2001) 'Enterprise Bargaining and Labour Productivity: Evidence from the Business Longitudinal Survey', Melbourne Institute Working Paper Series.

Wooden, M. (1998) 'Is Job Stability Really Declining?', *Australian Bulletin of Labour*, 24, September, pp. 186–93.

Wooden, M. (1999) 'Individual Agreement-Making in Australian Workplaces: Incidence, Trends and Features', *Journal of Industrial Relations*, 41, September, pp. 417–45.

Wooden, M. (2000) *The Transformation of Australian Industrial Relations*, The Federation Press, Sydney.

Note

1 Some parts of this chapter have appeared previously in an article by the author published in the *Mercer–Melbourne Institute Quarterly Bulletin of Economic Trends*, No. 3.00.

15

Human Capital Accumulation: Education and Immigration

Bruce Chapman and Glenn Withers[1]

Introduction

This chapter examines the role of human resource development as a driver of growth for Australia. The focus is upon education and immigration as sources of human capital formation and upon associated policies for economic growth.

While the chapter is ambitious it is not a truly comprehensive treatment, so that issues such as labour market programs, labour market structure, informal skilling and short courses, human resource management, overseas student markets, refugee issues and some others are not covered.

These latter issues are each important but the position taken here is that formal education and skilled migration are the core human resource concerns for building national capability to perform well in the liberalised environment created by the economic reform of recent decades. In a global knowledge economy, smart growth in human resources is likely to be the key to being able to realise the benefits of new technology and of the more open global and domestic market environment.

People are ultimately the source of national capability and differential achievement in a globalised world. Education and skilled migration foster that capacity to capitalise on change and to benefit from it while muting the social costs. Indeed the building of human capital and social capital can be seen to be highly correlated, and are vehicles whereby both economic advance and improved equity can be complementary outcomes given good policy design. This chapter focuses on economic issues, but the broader context for these particular policies does deserve prominent recognition in policy development.

Improvement in Australian productivity growth in recent years has come from microeconomic reform (Productivity Commission 2000). Such reform has been beneficial because it has shaken up 80 years of institutional sclerosis. But growth by 'shake-out' cannot, by its nature, be a sufficient source of sustainable growth. Instead, new attention is required to capacity-building to enable ongoing and equitable productivity-enhancement in a competitive and globalised environment. In this chapter education and migration are affirmed as core sources of sustainable productivity growth – and they are, arguably, core sources of social equity.

Education: a human capital approach

Education as investment

Mainstream economics considers educational outcomes to be the result of choices, at the margin, involving the costs and benefits of the alternatives. For individuals the major costs of the investment are the earnings forgone while learning (plus fees and other direct costs of education), and the major benefits accrue in the form of higher earnings than would otherwise have occurred.

For governments the issue is societal investments in education. The costs are outlays to education with the benefits being societal advantages above and beyond what accrue directly to the recipients of the education. Net societal benefits imply a role for government: subsidies to education should ensure that the right amount is delivered.

The human capital approach is adopted in what follows. We start with theory and an exploration of the individual perspective, with respect to Australian experience over the last two decades. The basic human capital predictions are supported, which suggests that the framework is useful. Changes in Australian education levels are then explored, as are variations in public/private-sector financing. These areas are then put in an international context. A final section addresses several selective policy issues: how the recent Australian experience might be interpreted; and a way to improve current policy arrangements with respect to financing.

Individual education outcomes: 1982 and 1995

The outcomes of the individual investment process are illustrated in Table 15.1. They reflect annual pre-tax levels of individuals' earnings by age, for different levels of education and by sex for two periods of time, 1981–82 and 1994–95 – to show the extent to which the relationships have changed recently. The data are comparable and use two of the ABS Income Distribution Surveys.

In exercises such as these hypothetical individuals are constructed. In our examples, individuals have the choice at age 17 of: leaving school and undertaking no further education; leaving school and undertaking a Year 12 certificate followed by a two-year diploma, both being undertaken at TAFE; completing high school and taking a four-year degree at university; or doing the last and undertaking a two-year Masters.

Table 15.1 Marginal internal rate of return calculations (%)

	1981–82 males	1981–82 females	1994–95 males	1994–95 females
TAFE Qualification	5.2	6.6	11.8	13.0
Degree	10.1	11.6	13.2	11.3
Higher Degree	9.3	9.0	9.0	9.0

The table shows the nature of the costs and benefits of further educational investments, summarised as marginal rates of internal return; that is, the financial reward to educational choices.

The major results are:

- educational investments have high returns for both men and women, in the range of 5–13 per cent (real) per annum
- the returns were higher for women than men in 1981–82 for TAFE and undergraduate degrees
- there is broad stability in returns to education across the 13-year period, with the major exceptions of returns to TAFE, which have more than doubled for both sexes to be more in line with other education returns, and an increase in male benefit from a university degree.

Overall, for individuals, the data are supportive of the human capital perspective. This offers some confidence that the approach can be useful in an analysis of Australian educational experience and its relationship to economic growth. The more difficult issues concern societal benefits, the role of government and linkages with economic growth.

Education as social investment: theory

Critical issues for policy concern the nature of social benefits and their likely size, given economic theory suggests that answers to the latter should form the basis of the level of government subsidy. With respect to policy the essential concern is thus: what, and how valuable, are education externalities?

The externalities have been argued traditionally to include, among other things: reduced criminal activity, more informed public debate, better informed judgements with respect to health, and more sophisticated voting behaviour.

However, the value of these particular externalities is likely to be small and debatable relative to the externality effect of education on economic growth. Since the early 1960s it has been argued that in a world of rapidly changing information, more highly educated workers have an advantage in adapting to different environments, in 'dealing with disequilibria' – the capacity to adjust to unanticipated shocks (Schultz 1975, Huffman 1974, Fane, 1975).[2]

Related issues have emerged in new growth theory, in which educational improvements are seen to facilitate technological progress, the engine of growth – Dowrick in this volume acknowledges the potential role of education in economic growth. There are several (highly related) ways education is seen to impact on technological change:

- high levels of formal education are necessary for the successful introduction of capital equipment (Bartel and Lichtenburg 1987)
- during periods in which a population is undergoing increases in education there will be an effective increase in the size of the labour force, so long as education raises productivity (Barro 1991)
- education disseminates knowledge and through this adds to growth because death does not result in knowledge loss (Lucas 1988).

These notions have received wide acceptance in the economic research community. Their likely empirical importance is now considered.

Education as social investment: evidence

Measuring the impact of education on economic growth is not straightforward. An important reason is that the growth impact of education on the skills of the labour force will be determined by both its quantity (higher participation rates) and its quality (the amount of knowledge imparted at any given schooling level). Understandably, given data availability, most analyses focus on the former.

The best example in the Australian context is from Pope and Withers (1995). It suggests that in Australia over the last century or so economic growth (as measured by changes in output per head) has been influenced importantly by changes in aggregate skill levels. They find that in the 1930 to 1990 period, increases in school enrolments, university enrolments and years of labour market experience led to significant increases in annual per capita growth.

The role in economic growth of both the quality and quantity of education internationally are compared in Hanushek and Kimko (2000). They test the extent to which educational quality, as measured by standardised scores for mathematical and scientific literacy, has contributed to economic growth differences averaged over 30 years across 139 countries. The test results are compared with the effect of changes in schooling quantities (as measured by the number of years of schooling).

They find that increases in workforce quality have a profound influence on economic growth, and by much more than quantities – where these can be measured separately. For example, on average a one standard deviation increase in test scores adds about 1.0 per cent to a country's GDP per capita annual growth rate. By contrast, increases in the quantity of schooling required to match this growth rate change seem to be very much higher; that is, to achieve a 1 per cent increase in the annual growth rate of a country's GDP per capita would require on average that workers had nine additional years of education.

The Hanushek and Kimko analysis says little about the sources of labour force quality; that is, the determinants of test scores. And it is very possible that these are correlated over time with rising school participation rates, which suggests that Pope's and Withers' conclusions concerning the role of educational quantities in Australian growth over time are robust but require unbundling, as indeed they were able to do for migration numbers and skill levels.

The Hanushek and Kimko main international result is nevertheless insightful in relation to this issue for Australia, since Australia has in fact had test scores below the average. Indeed their results imply that if Australian workforce quality had been the average of other countries over the 30 years from the 1960s, we would have experienced about a 1 per cent higher average GDP per capita annual growth rate,[3] which is a large increase.

It is important therefore to examine trends influencing the quantity and quality of education for Australia more closely. This is done in the next two sections.

Australian educational experience: aggregate changes over time

This section shows recent aggregate changes in Australian levels of education, with respect to secondary schooling, TAFE diplomas and certificates, and higher education. These data help motivate our main concern: government involvement in education and its implications for growth.

Year 12 retention rates

Figure 15.1 shows Year 12 retention rates, measured as the proportion of a Year 7 cohort enrolled in Year 12 five years later, for the years 1980 to 2000.

The main points are: there has been a very significant increase in retention rates for both males and females in the 1980 to 2000 period, from about 35–40 per cent in 1980 to about 65–75 per cent in 2000; the pattern of change is very similar for boys and girls; and the rates of increase were very rapid for both sexes from 1980, but in 1993 both stopped growing, and even fell back a little.

TAFE enrolments

Figure 15.2 shows enrolments in TAFE vocational courses in the 1990–2000 period. The focus is on professional courses: those taking at least one year and which lead to a certificate or diploma.

The data from Figure 15.2 suggest: there has been a large increase in TAFE vocational enrolments over the last two decades; and the increase for females has been relatively high – from about 20 per cent lower than males in 1980 to equality in 2000.

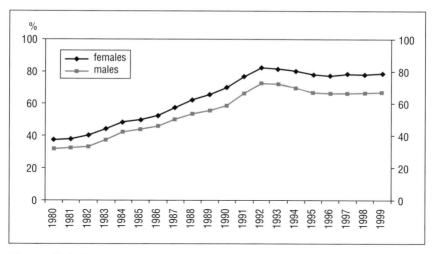

Figure 15.1 Year 12 retention rates, 1980–2000

Source: National Schools Statistics Collection and DETYA, Retention and Participation in Australian Schools, 1967–1992.

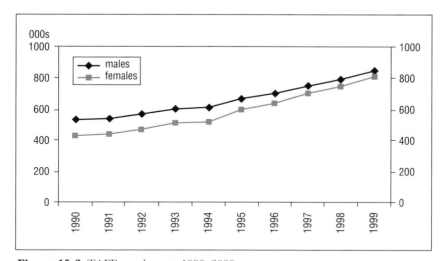

Figure 15.2 TAFE enrolments, 1990–2000

Source: Australian VET Statistics at a Glance 1999, National Centre for Vocational Education Research, Leabrook, South Australia, 2000.

University enrolments

Total university enrolments since 1989 are shown in Figure 15.3. The obvious point is that higher education enrolments have expanded considerably over the last decade or so, by around 50 per cent, or around 5 per cent a year. This has occurred in spite of the introduction of the Higher Education Contribution Scheme (HECS) in 1989; that is, a (deferred) fee to be paid by students themselves or their families. The annual increase for women has been slightly but consistently higher than has been the increase for men, and at the end of the 1990s there were more women than men enrolled in university courses.

In general Australian education enrolments have increased in all areas over recent periods, and the increases have been very significant – particularly for women. These outcomes imply that private rates of return to education have remained strong over the last two decades, which is precisely the finding of the earlier analysis, and/or that quotas on entry to education places have been eased. Both are likely to have contributed.

The increase in quantities levelled off for schooling from 1993, and there is a need to monitor boys' participation, which has recently declined. TAFE and university enrolments have continued to rise for more than a decade. Whether or not these quantity changes have been associated with changes in educational quality is now considered.

Australian government educational inputs

A critical issue in assessing the stance of government educational policy in relation to quality relates to expenditure per student. This reflects the extent to which government is prepared to subsidise education in terms of per unit

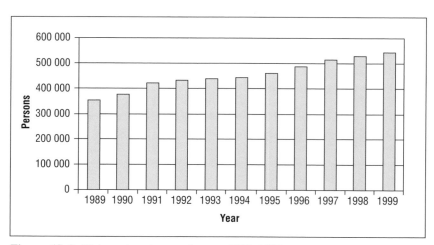

Figure 15.3 Higher education enrolments, 1989–1999

inputs. It is not a direct measure of quality, of course, but it is a possible indirect indicator for consideration when consistent and agreed direct measures are not available.

Primary and secondary per student government expenditure

Figure 15.4 shows government outlays per student for various years over the last two decades. There has been a very small increase in government outlays per student. However, this result should be treated cautiously given the large compositional changes in school enrolments; that is, governments subsidise private schools but at a lower level than for public schools. Hence, a change in the public/private mix of students will influence these data.

Higher education per student government expenditure

Figure 15.5 shows real governmental outlays per university student, and reveals that since the mid-1990s there has been a consistent decline, in total of the order of 20 per cent. This could reflect compositional changes, such as between disciplines with different cost structures, but it is much more likely to be the result of increased private payments for university services.

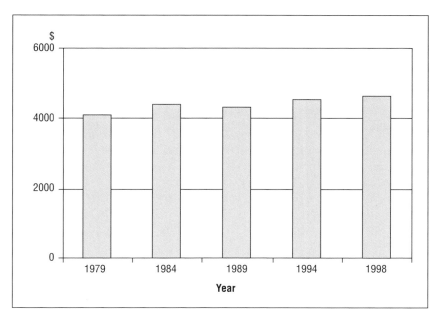

Figure 15.4 Real government expenditure per school student (1998$)
Sources: Calculations using Burke and Spaull (2001) and ABS educational expenditure data.

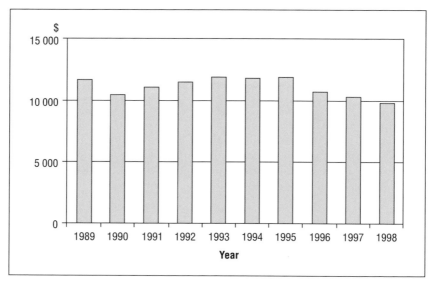

Figure 15.5 Real government expenditure per university student (1998$)
Source: Private correspondence from the Australian Vice-Chancellors' Committee (2001).

We conclude that over the last decade there has been some increase in government outlays per school student and a fall in government outlays per university student. Some part of this is reflected in the private/public proportions of educational expenditure, which are now considered.

Australian educational experience: public/private changes over time

The section on Australian educational experience showed that there have been considerable increases in educational enrolments in all areas, and the section on educational inputs suggested that this has been accompanied by a small increase in government outlays per school student, but decreases for university students. What now follows offers complementary data illustrating the extent to which the picture presented by public spending is altered by examining how private funding as a proportion of all expenditure has changed. This helps us to understand the extent to which educational enrolment levels have been the result of the increase in private funding.

Total educational expenditure

Figure 15.6 shows changes in total Australian educational expenditure over the last 20 years or so in terms of the public/private division. Government

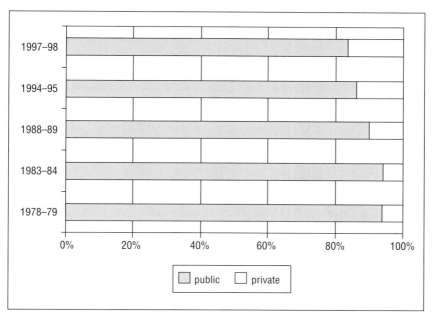

Figure 15.6 Public/private Australian total education expenditure, 1979–1998
Source: Bourke (1999).

remains the dominant contributor of funding for education, although there has been a very significant decrease in the relative extent to which the public sector has subsidised total education, with the increase in private-sector support being around four-fold – however, the data could be understating changes in the extent of private-sector support since it is unclear how HECS revenues have been included.

Schools expenditure

One dimension of the public/private split for primary and secondary school-ing is the proportion of public recurrent outlays going to government and private schools. The basic message is that there has been a consistent decrease in the proportion of schools expenditure in government schools, from 81 per cent in 1979 to 69 per cent in 1999.

This situation can be understood to be a reflection in part of the very large changes that have taken place in the composition of school students, now illus-trated in Figure 15.7. It shows changes in primary and secondary school enrol-ments over the last 20 years or so, for government, non-public (Catholic) and non-public (other) sectors.

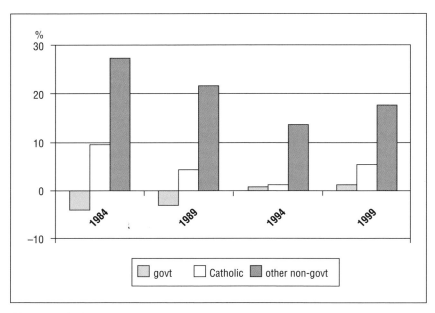

Figure 15.7 Percentage change in enrolments by school type (after periods of five years, starting in 1979)
Source: Calculations from the data presented in Bourke (1999).

We note that there has been a slight decrease in government enrolments; there has been an extremely large increase in non-Catholic private enrolments (averaging about 20 per cent for every five-year period); and there has been a moderate increase in Catholic school enrolments (averaging about 4 per cent for each five-year period).

Higher education

Figure 15.8 illustrates changes in public/private-sector financing of higher education over about the last 20 years or so.

After 1989 (when private contributions began through the HECS system), there has been a marked decrease in the direct government financing proportion in higher education. From 1989 to 1992 the fall in public-sector financing was around 20 percentage points, and the decrease in years after that has averaged around two percentage points per year.

In general, therefore, over the last 20 years Australian governments have decreased their education total expenditure in proportionate terms, from about 95 per cent to just over 80 per cent of all education outlays, public and private. The biggest change has occurred with respect to university funding,

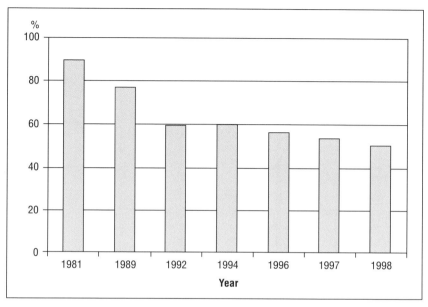

Figure 15.8 Proportional federal government expenditure in higher education, 1981–1998 (selected years)
Source: Prior to 1993, DEET 'National Report on Australia's Higher Education Sector', May 1993 (Table 4.6); from 1993 onwards, DETYA Selected Higher Education Finance Statistics.

where the government decline has been from about 90 to less than 60 per cent of total funding.

Australian education financing experience in international context

To understand further the policy position of Australian governments it is instructive to consider our expenditure levels and the public/private split with reference to similar countries.

While some limited comparisons are possible for different periods, the general paucity of data has meant that much of what now follows relates to single snapshots for 1997.

Public/private total educational expenditure proportions

Figure 15.9 shows the private/public mix for total educational expenditure for selected countries for 1997.

The data reveal that with respect to total educational expenditure the Australian public-sector proportional contribution is now around about

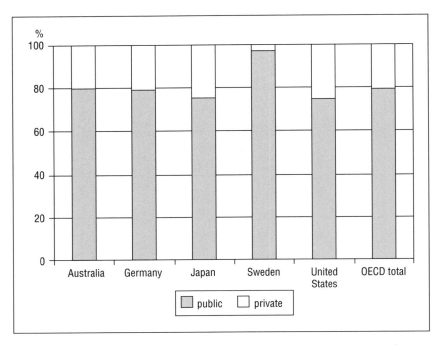

Figure 15.9 Public and private expenditure as proportion of total educational expenditure in 1997 (various countries)
Source: OECD (1998) *Education at a Glance*. OECD indicators, Paris.

the average for the OECD, though we have seen that over the 1990s the Australian public-sector contribution fell by about five percentage points. At the beginning of the period Australia had a relatively higher public-sector contribution, but this had disappeared by the late 1990s.

In terms of sectors, for schools the Australian experience lies in the middle of the countries considered for schools, at about 85 per cent, and this is about the same as the OECD average.

For tertiary education, there are very large differences between countries in relation to public/private splits, from just over 40 per cent government for Japan, to about 90 per cent for Sweden. Again Australia lies in the middle, at just over 60 per cent, which is slightly higher than the OECD average.

The remaining issue is how the balance of public and private outlays add up to total national commitment to education. This is indicated for selected OECD countries (and the OECD average) for 1998 in Figure 15.10. It is here that Australia is a little behind the average and significantly behind countries such as Canada, Sweden and the United States. Such comparisons can be bedevilled by statistical quirks such as how training is measured and by factors such as disparate phases of the business cycle, but as a country with a relatively

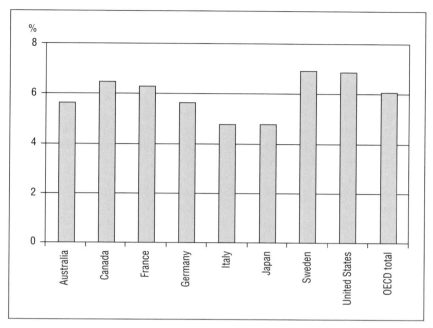

Figure 15.10 Total expenditure on all education as a percentage of GDP, 1998
Source: OECD (1998) *Education at a Glance*. OECD indicators, Paris.

younger age structure than most OECD countries it seems likely that our outlays are at best average. Unless, therefore, other countries are over-spending (that is, reaping lower net marginal benefit), or we are a more efficient provider than most, then Australia's performance may be sub-optimal.

Interpreting the current role of government in education

Given data limitations, much of the information presented above should not yet be considered to be definitive evidence of the changing role of government in Australia with respect to education. In particular, international real unit total outlay data for the various levels of education are needed, as is comprehensive incorporation of TAFE-type studies on a consistent basis. With that said, six points can be noted:

- individuals have decided that there are continuing benefits to increases in educational investments, and this is supported by analysis of individual rates of return to education
- expansion of enrolments has been very significant over the last several decades

- this significant expansion has been accompanied by stable or increasing private rates of return, implying that expansion to date has not at all diluted private net benefit
- schooling expansion has been supported by some increased public and, even more, increased private real unit outlays
- university expansion has been accompanied by much-reduced public real unit outlays and substantially increased private revenue
- in a current international context, Australian educational outlays in total are slightly below the OECD average, but the public/private funding mix broadly conforms to the OECD average.

These results are suggestive of the following. One is that Australian governments remain prepared to finance most educational expenditure. However, there has not been a willingness in the public sector to substantially increase real unit subsidies for schooling, and the extent to which governments are prepared to subsidise unit costs in tertiary education has fallen.

Private-sector expenditure on education has changed significantly over the last two decades, with there being a marked increase in private schooling, and also a considerable increase in higher education external funding, including student contributions. It is likely that these tertiary changes reflect the equity responses of the Labor government to 'free education', which led to the introduction of HECS in 1989 (Chapman 1997).

There are significant issues for policy. The first relates to the implications for income distribution of an education system moving increasingly away from public funding. While educational expansion is arguably very healthy from a societal point of view the implications for inter-generational opportunities and intra-generational social justice may not be. As is increasingly understood, social capital influences growth in many ways along with direct investment in physical and human capital. Thus, the expansion of private schooling under new funding arrangements needs close scrutiny for this reason, including in relation to the extent to which any perception of growing unfairness undermines cooperation with change in a dynamic economy.

Further, in the tertiary education sector there is a tendency to impose up-front student fees. This is, in fact, an inappropriate mechanism increasingly likely to limit the educational chances of prospective TAFE students in particular. Income-contingent charging mechanisms, such as HECS, can be used for improved social and economic outcomes from education, and assessing their suitability for a range of educational pathways should be given policy priority.

Next, the question arises as to whether the quantity expansion in enrolment levels has come at the expense of education quality. As indicated in the section on education and the human capital approach above, this is likely to be the key parameter in the role of education in productivity-driven economic growth. To determine this requires closer review of trends in cost per student, their linkage to educational outcomes and Australia's position on such indicators relative to other industrial nations.

Finally, the combination of public and private funding for educational expenditure now prevailing still leaves Australia in the middle level of industrial countries, even though its relatively younger demographic profile should lift it higher than most, other things being equal. It will therefore be important to determine the extent to which these trends are having negative impacts on Australia's capacity to compete globally and deliver increased living standards.

Withers (2000) has argued that an increase in total outlays on education, training and R&D from 8 per cent to 11 per cent of GDP is required if a sustainable growth target of 3 per cent per capita growth is to be achievable. This is not to say that funding increases are the only requirement. Ongoing structural reform is also urgently needed. And one central requirement here is for more flexible and responsive government schooling. Recent path-breaking US work (Hoxby 2000) has shown that greater choice and competition within government education systems can jointly limit the outflow to private providers and improve educational achievement substantially – thus arguably advancing both efficiency and equity or social cohesion at the same time. Sims (2000) provides a reform agenda for Australian universities.

Economic issues in migration

Migration as individual investment

Immigration, like education, is often viewed by economists as an investment: current consumption is forgone by incurring costs in moving location so as to increase future earnings and other benefits. And this is indeed the outcome of the migration process to Australia. Earlier research established that both the average income levels and their growth across the countries of origin for Australian migrants were below those of Australia. For example, for the first 40 years of the postwar period the migrant opportunity cost was an average growth rate for per capita income of 1.52 per cent as opposed to an actual growth rate of 3.38 per cent in average incomes achieved by relocating to Australia (Withers 1985).

Migrants themselves have therefore gained through their international mobility, and this point is relevant to evaluation of the outcomes of Australia's immigration program: one-quarter of Australia's present population has improved its economic position as a direct result of the act of immigration to Australia.

It is also interesting to note that the one global econometric study of the welfare consequences of free movement of people across borders found that world GDP would double (Hamilton and Whalley 1984). In economic terms this would be predicted in the same way that removal of barriers of trade in goods and removal of capital controls lead to improved resource allocation and associated higher average incomes.

Migration as social investment

However, it is a fact that population movements remain more regulated and controlled than do trade and capital movements. And this is true even for a so-called 'settler' nation such as Australia.

Why might this be so? The basic reasons are probably to be found in the following popular beliefs variously present in the public or political mind:

- Migrants create unemployment, crowd out local training and reduce per capita income.
- Migrants create balance of payments deficits, induce inflation and are a drain on the public purse.
- Migrants compromise Australia's carrying capacity, deplete resources, crowd cities and endanger ecosystems.
- Migrants create ethnic enclaves and undermine social cohesion.

Under the National Competition Policy that became pervasive in Australian microeconomic policy in the 1990s, a general presumption is that a legislative restriction on competition (for example, migrant entry controls) should be repealed unless a public interest case to the contrary can be made. This is to say that the benefits of the restriction to the community as a whole should outweigh the costs, and the objectives of the legislation can only be achieved by that restriction.

In the case of some perceived costs of immigration that would, if valid, compromise the public interest, there is evidence that the perception is incorrect. With unemployment, for instance, there is a good amount of empirical evidence for Australia that immigration of the kind we have experienced has not added to the unemployment rate and indeed is likely to have reduced unemployment for the native population, including the long-term unemployed. Originally established in Pope and Withers (1985), the most recent documentation of this is in Shan and Sun (1998) and Konya (2000), and similar findings apply to the other economic effects; for example, public budget effects (ACIL Consulting 1999, Richardson 2001).

Other possible negative costs in areas like the environment are complex to analyse and a rich research base on population–environment linkages in Australia does not exist. The House of Representatives Long-Term Strategies Committee (1994) and the State of the Environment Advisory Council (1996) emphasised the knowledge gap. But even where demonstrable linkages do exist, for example urban congestion, it remains important to establish that population restriction is the most effective means for reducing such costs, relative to other approaches and with due attention to balancing both losses and gains. A recent report by the Australian Academy of Technological Sciences and Engineering (2001) finds that rarely is population the most suitable mechanism to gain relevant environmental benefit.

Naturally the further area of social cohesion is harder to quantify than others in effects. But even there a body of research challenges some common propositions about possible community cost. For example, claims of urban segregation and ghetto-formation have been examined using residential concentration and mobility data and determined to be ill-founded for Australian experience, as are claims of disproportionate ethnic contribution to crime rates. Castles, Foster, Iredale and Withers (1998) provide a survey of the literature on these issues.

Any wholesale deregulation, however, is unlikely, despite such evidence. Contrary to the formal Competition Policy process applied to much legislation, the onus still seems to be on proponents of liberalisation to make a public interest case for deregulation. This may reflect some public attitudes and values not necessarily easily influenced by analysis and evidence. It is therefore not sufficient to disprove the negative views or to document better policy levers. Rather, the political economy seems to require that a positive case be developed.

An older 'nation-building' case was previously accepted in a more pioneering Australia. The resonance of that in terms of raw labour power for clearing land and building cities, and for working in factories and defending a continent on the fringe of populous Asia, has dissipated in modern times. Instead, a new approach based on notions of global integration is emerging that is more supportive of a contemporary expansionist position.

On the economic front, a scale effect is fairly self-evident. But it can be given a quantitative illustration. Without migrants and the children of migrants over the postwar period, our GDP would be more like $265 billion than $550 billion today. Migrants and their children have provided almost 10 per cent of the postwar growth in the Australian workforce. Taking this forward, a 1 per cent population growth will add about $600 billion more to Australia's GDP by 2051, as shown in Figure 15.11.

But what of per capita benefit? Importantly, endogenous growth theory adds a new understanding of how such benefit may indeed be derived from population scale expansion – especially via skilled labour and with complementary physical investment. In earlier work anticipating the endogenous approach, John Nevile (1990) had found Australian population expansion to be a major source of technological change for Australia. In particular, he concluded that a 1 per cent increase in total output increased the rate of innovation by 0.6 per cent and that this benefit in terms of translation into per capita growth was optimised with a little over 1.25 per cent population growth. Australia currently has a 1 per cent population growth rate and that is gradually declining on present trends.

Similarly, work by Brain et al. (1979), Baker (1985), the Centre for International Economics (1988) and Withers (1987) had all shown a significant per capita pay-off from skilled migration. And, using an explicit modern endogenous

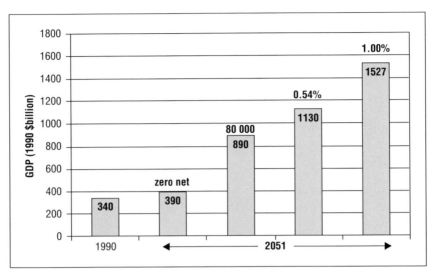

Figure 15.11 Aggregate growth effects (alternative migration options)
Source: Withers (1999).

growth model, Pope and Withers (1995) found high per capita pay-offs to both migration quantities and skills – as they did also for domestic education and workforce on-the-job training and experience.

Murphy (2001) and Access Economics (1998) provide recent supporting empirical micro-foundations for these results. For instance, Access Economics found that business migrant firms have a consistently better rate of exporting – with small firms exporting 10 times the value of other equivalent-sized Australian firms.

In common-sense terms what is said to be happening is that:

- a growing market, outstripping capacity, engenders confidence for investment;
- an increasingly large and skilled labour force ensures the capability to best add value to physical investment;
- fresh perspectives and new ways of doing things enhance innovation; and
- a culturally diverse population promotes trade links and global integration.

And new international economic research is backing this up too and providing insight into the underlying mechanisms; for example, Collier (2001) on cultural diversity and Quigley (1998) on agglomeration. For instance, for the United States, each extra two million people add about 8 per cent to average productivity for a city. These effects of scale, diversity and agglomeration are missing in some earlier Australian studies, which lead them to reach conclusions that the positive per capita effects are not clearly demonstrated.

Once such effects are acknowledged it is less surprising to find a recent London *Economist* survey of Australia offering a final section titled 'Is anybody there?', and concluding its survey with the proposal that 'perhaps this is the moment for (Australia) to start thinking about a new project: matching its population more closely to its size' (9–15 September, 2000: 16).

That said on the economics front, it is arguable that there are also social benefits in terms of migration assisting with reduced health costs, retirement support costs and education costs, as well as providing reunification and support for families otherwise separated, itself an intrinsically desirable outcome in a society that sees families as the basic social unit, including for the care of dependants.

In this context the impact of immigration on reducing the adverse consequences of population ageing has attracted particular attention. There is a view among many demographers, however, that immigration can contribute only a small benefit there (McDonald and Kippen 1999), and a view among some economists that the problem is anyway exaggerated in fiscal terms, too, or can readily be accommodated by policy (Banks 1999). But there is an alternative view that sees an expansive immigration program as a useful component of the package of policy response to the ageing population; for example, Alvarado and Creedy (1998), Guest and McDonald (2000), Richardson (2001), Withers (2001) and Murphy (2001), though there is no suggestion that it is a single or simple solution, nor that it should fully turn back rather than merely mute the demographic trend.

It is estimated that a migration-based 1 per cent population growth rate, compared to the present migration level and fertility trend, can halve the extra share of GDP otherwise needed for aged support under present support policies – a saving of perhaps \$25 billion in 1999 dollars (Withers 2000). Figure 15.12 illustrates this.

Migration rates: changes over time

Despite the claims made for potential benefits of migration, Australia has been steadily reducing the rate of migration. Naturally, there are fluctuations up and down from time to time in annual migration rates but the high and low migration points in the cycle have been getting lower almost continuously (Sims 2000). The trend is down.

The decline in permanent entry rates is complemented by a growing rate of emigration. Permanent departures have now reached 41 000 per annum in 2000, and they are even more skewed to high skills than is the entry program.

Nevertheless, while the postwar migration program has always delivered an average skill level ahead of the domestic Australian average (Withers 1989), this skill content has been further enhanced in recent years. According to the Immigration Department (DIMA 2000) the skill stream in migrant entry has

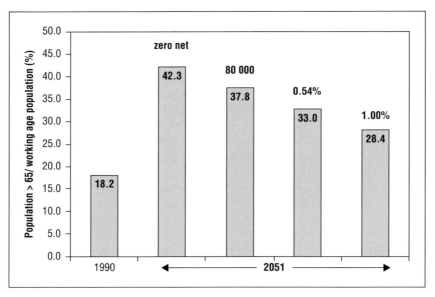

Figure 15.12 Age dependency effects (alternative migration options)
Source: Withers (1999).

risen from 29 per cent of the program in 1995–96 to a proposed 53 per cent in 2000–01. Birrell (2001) shows that it is the skilled entry program that prevents a major 'brain-drain' from otherwise emerging for Australia.

While the settler arrivals rate has been declining, non-permanent population inflows have grown substantially. This is especially so for tourists and other visitors, but this trend also includes steady expansion in business and skilled categories. Nevertheless, the stock (as opposed to flow) of all such persons as residents at any fixed time is only currently around 120 000.

The large magnitude of movements recorded, for example four million tourists, therefore implies substantial turnover in both directions. It is in the nature of such movements that most are short-term and that even when long-term they still do mostly leave. So it is perhaps premature to shift primary policy focus yet to short- and medium-term entry, and ignore settler movements, even though temporary entry is correctly seen as of increasing importance and of considerable value for skill transfer and flexibility (Ruddock 2000).

Policy for smart growth

Determining the precise levels of immigration required into the future is a challenge. Illustrative long-term population consequences of alternative migration options are outlined in Figure 15.13.

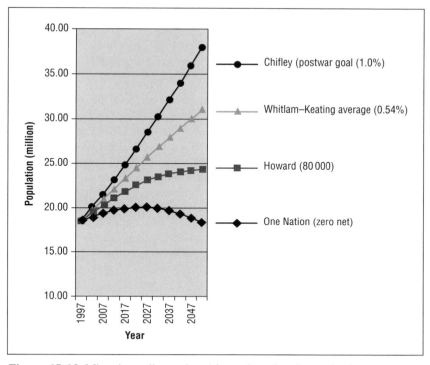

Figure 15.13 Migration policy settings (alternative migration settings)
Source: Withers (1999).

One benchmark for choosing is offered above in the work of Nevile (1990). It is found that the optimum population growth historically for purposes of enhancing per capita income growth has been a rate of a little over 1.25% per capita. Rates very much higher or lower were less beneficial. In the presence of a reducing fertility rate this implies increasing the migration rate over time to achieve this total population growth rate. Currently, population growth is around 1 per cent and falling.

While future fertility is difficult to predict, present trends would imply a migration program of 115 000 rising to 250 000 by mid-century to match the Nevile target. This requires a migration rate averaging around or a little above the Whitlam–Keating average, starting below and rising above that average over time. Such levels could also contribute to social savings in relation to demographic ageing, perhaps by several percentage points of GDP relative to present migration settings, if the 'alternative view' projections cited earlier are correct.

A key question is whether such an inflow can be achieved without reducing the economic skill quality of the intake. There is some concern that expanding migration must come at the expense of skill quality, particularly in the presence of growing international competition for skilled migrants (Cobb-Clark and Connolly 1997). Yet a balanced program is important for economic, social and political objectives to all be served.

There are reasons, in fact, why expansion may be possible without unacceptable reduction in skill composition:

- The broad parameters of the present points test used for selecting independent entrants (economic migrants) were set arbitrarily to deliver intake numbers around the then current level. Withers (1988) in particular a weighting given to each component – for example, age, spouse skills and settlement capital – was quite arbitrary. The age weight could be reduced and the other two increased without any demonstrable loss.
- The present points test is set so high that the great majority of Australians would not be eligible. In fact, it need only ensure no dilution of average skill to be beneficial.
- The government does not undertake, encourage or support the sustained, professional promotion of skilled and business immigration to Australia. It could.

Of course, to return to the National Competition Policy framework adopted earlier in this chapter, greater liberalisation need not mean full deregulation. The evidence on benefit and on limited adverse consequences from some expansion is drawn empirically from the range of Australian migration actually experienced. To go beyond this would be risky, in terms of known consequences. It is reasonable to believe that a rapid acceleration of immigration levels, for instance, could well stretch Australia's economic, social and urban environmental capacities for healthy adjustment; that is, there may be genuine speed limits. Nevile's work cited above does show this for per capita income growth, quite apart from other criteria. He stresses that population growth that is too high (greater than 1.75 per cent) and too low (less than 0.75 per cent) may come at severe cost in living standards.

Conclusions

In summary, an expansion of migration may help enhance Australian human resources development and economic vigour. The migration program could be set to underpin a 1.25 per cent population growth path, and be focused on 'smart growth' and program balance and not just growth in numbers. For this to pay off, appropriate national policy settings for complementary investment in education, innovation, infrastructure and ecological sustainability are also required, as are the family-friendly workplace policies that will help reduce the decline in fertility and increase the labour force participation rate, including for older workers (McDonald and Kippen 1999). Some of the education policy directions needed have also been discussed earlier in this chapter.

Such a package could significantly enhance Australian human resource development. Above all it should be stressed that immigration and education are complementary. Neither is a substitute for the other and their joint advancement will underpin growth and equity for a better future for the country.

References

Access Economics (1998) *Evaluation of the Contribution of Business Skills Migrants to Australia*, Canberra: DIMA.

ACIL Consulting (1999) *Impact of Migrants on the Commonwealth Budget*, Canberra: DIMA.

Alvarado, J. and Creedy, J. (1998) *Population Ageing, Migration and Social Expenditure*, Cheltenham: Edward Elgar.

Australian Academy of Technological Sciences and Engineering (2001) *Population Futures*, Canberra: ATSE, March.

Baker, L. (1985) 'The Orani Simulations', in N.R. Norman and K.F. Miekle (eds) *The Economic Effects of Immigration on Australia*, Melbourne: CEDA, vol. 2: 370.

Banks, G. (1999) 'Introduction' in Productivity Commission, Microeconomic Reform and Australian Productivity: Exploring the Links, Supporting Research, Canberra, AGPS.

Barro, R.J. (1991) 'Economic Growth in a Cross-Section of Countries', *Quarterly Journal of Economics*, 106: 407–44.

Bartel, A. and Lichtenburg, F.R. (1987) 'Education and Technical Efficiency', *Review of Economics and Statistics*, vol. 69, February: 108–27.

Birrell, R. (2001) *Skilled Labour: Gains and Losses*, Canberra: DIMA, February (mimeo).

Brain, P.J., Smith, R.L. and Schuyers, G.P. (1979) *Population, Immigration and the Australian Economy*, London: Croom-Helm.

Burke, G. and Spaull, A. (2001) 'Australian Schools: Participation and Funding 1901–2000', *Year Book Australia*.

Castles, S., Foster, W., Iredale, R. and Withers, G. (1998) *Immigration and Australia: Myths and Realities*, St Leonards: Allen and Unwin.

Centre for International Economics (1988) 'The Relationship Between Immigration and Economic Performance', in *Immigration: A Commitment to Australia*, Consultants' Reports, Canberra: AGPS.

Chapman, B. (1997) 'Conceptual Issues and the Australian Experience with Income Contingent Charges for Higher Education', *Economic Journal*, vol. 107(442), May: 738–51.

Cobb-Clark, D. and Connolly, M.D. (1997) 'The Worldwide Market for Skilled Migrants: Can Australia Compete?', *International Migration Review*, Vol. 31 (Fall): 670–93.

Collier, P. (2001) 'Implications of Ethnic diversity', *Economic Policy*, April, 32: 127–66.

De Meulemeester, J.-L. and Rochart, D. (1995) 'A Causality Analysis of the Link Between Higher Education and Economic Development', *Economics of Education Review*, vol. 14(4): 351–61.

Deparment of Immigration and Multicultural Affairs (DIMA) (2000) *Population Flows: Immigration Aspects*, Canberra: DIMA.

Doyle, C. and Weale, M. (1994) 'Education, Externalities, Fertility and Economic Growth', *Education Economics*, vol. 2(2): 129–68.

Fane, G. (1975) 'Education and the Managerial Efficiency of Farmers', *Review of Economics and Statistics*, LVII (November): 452–61.

Guest, R.S. and McDonald, I.M. (2000) 'Population Ageing and Projections of Government Social Outlays in Australia', *Australian Economic Review*, vol. 33(1): 49–64.

Hamilton, R. and Whalley, J. (1984) 'Efficiency and Distributional Implications of Global Restrictions on Labour Mobility: Calculations and Policy Implications', *Journal of Development Economics*, 14: 61–75.

Hanushek, E.A. and Kimko, D.D. (2000) 'Schooling, Labor-Force Quality, and the Growth of Nations', *American Economic Review*, December: 1184–208.

House of Representatives, Standing Committee on Long-Term Strategies (1994) *Australia's Population Carrying Capacity; One Nation–Two Ecologies*, Canberra: AGPS.

Hoxby, C.M. (2000) 'Does Competition Among Public Schools Benefit Students and Taxpayers?', *American Economic Review*, vol. 90(5), December: 1209–38.

Huffman, W.E. (1974) 'Decision Making – The Role of Education', *The American Journal of Agricultural Economics*, February: 85–97.

Konya, L. (2000) 'Bi-Variate Causality Between Immigration and Long-Term Unemployment in Australia, 1981–1998', *Department of Applied Economics Working Paper*, Victoria University, No. 10/00.

Krueger, A.B. and Lindahl, M. (2000) 'Education for Growth: Why and For Whom?', *NBER Working Paper Series*, Working Paper 7591, March.

Lucas, R.E. (1988) 'On the Mechanics of Development', *Journal of Monetary Economics*, 22: 3–42.

McDonald, P. and Kippen, R. (1999) 'Ageing: the Social and Demographic Dimensions', in Productivity Commission, *op.cit*: 47–70.

Murphy, C. (2001) *The Economic Impact of 2000/01 Migration Program Changes*, Canberra: DIMA, February (mimeo).

Nevile, J. (1990) *The Effect of Immigration on Living Standards in Australia*, Canberra: AGPS.

Pope, D. and Withers, G. (1995) 'The Role of Human Capital Accumulation in Australia's Long-Term Economic Growth', paper presented to 24th Conference of Economists, Adelaide.

Productivity Commission (1999) *Policy Implications of the Ageing of Australia's Population, Conference Proceedings*, Canberra: AGPS.

Productivity Commission (2000) *Microeconomic Reform and Australian Productivity: Exploring the Links, Supporting Research*, Canberra: AGPS.

Quigley, J. (1998) 'Urban Diversity and Economic Growth', *Journal of Economic Perspectives*, vol. 12(2): 127–38.

Richardson, C. (2001) *Impact of Immigration and the Age Criteria on the Commonwealth Budget*, Canberra: DIMA, February (mimeo).

Romer, P.M. (1990) 'Endogenous Technological Change', *The Journal of Political Economy*, vol. 98, no. 5, Part 2: The Problem of Development: A Conference of the Institute for the Study of Free Enterprise Systems, October, pp. S71–S102.

Ruddock, P. (2000) 'Australian Immigration in a "DotCom" World', *Australian Economic Review*, vol. 33(3), September: 257–61.

Schultz, T.W. (1975) 'The Value of the Ability to Deal with Disequilibria', *Journal of Economic Literature*, September: 827–43.

Shan, J. and Sun, F. (1998) 'Immigration and Unemployment: New Evidence from Australia and New Zealand', *Department of Applied Economics Working Paper*, Victoria University, No. 2/9.

Sims, R. (2000) *An Agenda for a Strong Australia*, Sydney: Port Jackson Partners (mimeo).

State of the Environment Advisory Council (1996) *Australia: State of the Environment*, Canberra: Department of Environment, Sport and Tourism.

Withers, G. (1985) 'Immigration and the Measurement of Income Growth', *Department of Economic History Working Paper*, Australian National University, no. 62.

Withers, G. (Chair) (1988) *Immigration Selection Systems, Report of Committee of Inquiry, National Population Council*, Canberra: Department of Immigration.

Withers, G. (1987) 'Immigration and Australian Economic Growth', in Department of Immigration, Local Government and Ethnic Affairs, *The Economics of Immigration: Proceedings of a Conference*, Canberra: AGPS: 29–70.

Withers, G. (1989) 'The Immigration Contribution to Australian Capital Formation', in Pope, D. and Alston, L. (eds) *Australia's Greatest Asset: Human Resources in the Nineteenth and Twentieth Centuries*, Sydney: Federation Press: 53–71.

Withers, G. (1999) 'Australia's Need for a Population Policy', *BCA Papers*, vol. 1(1), May: 21–29.

Withers, G. (2000) 'Population Issues and Options: Investing in People', *Australian Economic Review*, vol. 33(3), September: 265–71.

Withers, G. (2001) 'Population Ageing, and Immigration' *Australian Economic Review*, Forthcoming.

Withers, G. and Pope, D. (1985) 'Immigration and Unemployment', *Economic Record*, 61: 554–63.

Notes

1 Thanks are due to David Throsby, as designated discussant, and to other contributors to this volume for their helpful comments on the preliminary version. Helpful comments were also received from participants in the ANU Public Policy Seminar. Responsibility for the final contents nevertheless must still rest with the authors.

2 For education to result in social, as well as private, gains requires that the rents from the process are not captured completely by the educated individuals or the firms employing them. However, this will be the case if technological change flows easily from one workplace to the next (Romer 1990).

3 Our estimate comes from the fact that the measure of quality for Australia is about one standard deviation below the average of the data.

16

Demography and Growth

Vince FitzGerald

The range of issues that could be canvassed under the heading 'demography and growth' is very broad, and needs to be narrowed here so as to focus on some key ones for Australia's growth, especially looking forward – in particular, ageing and some other aspects of the *composition* of the population. Also, related topics are covered elsewhere. In this chapter, the first few sections dispose of relevant aspects that will not be covered in depth.

The rate of population growth

A country's overall *rate* of population expansion *per se* can affect its growth in productivity, and real income, per capita (the economic growth measure of most interest here being per capita rather than absolute). On the negative side, rapid population increase may reduce productivity growth through dilution of the available capital and the country's resource base generally. On the positive side, there may be economies of scale effects.

Steve Dowrick (1995a) has examined the interaction of population growth and economic growth in a cross-country study of the experiences of Asia-Pacific nations since 1960 (with reference to a global set of over 100 countries). The common pattern exhibited was a *decline in fertility* as incomes increased, and hence rising working age proportions of populations (or falling 'dependency ratios'; that is, proportions of populations younger or older than working age). Dowrick found that as well as a strong *transitional* effect of declining fertility on output per capita (and hence on its rate of growth over the transition period) via the effect on the dependency ratio, there was evidence of an effect on *long-term* growth via capital deepening.

These findings concerning the economic effects of demographic transitions, specifically major changes in fertility, are nevertheless consistent with a low observed correlation between per capita economic growth and the rate of population growth *per se*. In other contributions, Dowrick has set that research in the wider context of the general determinants of economic growth – not only population and labour supply, but investment, education, research and development, and so on (see Dowrick 1995b: 31–2). In that wider context, the overall rate of population growth in itself does not nowadays present as an important determinant of economic growth for a country such as Australia.

Migration

Overseas migration

Overseas migration and fertility (hence, natural increase), together with mortality, are the main proximate drivers of population growth, and it is best to look at each of these separately.

Because fertility cannot be readily influenced by government, and mortality not much more so, it is not surprising that overseas migration has been the main focus of debate on population policy, including the recently revived debate that continues today.[1]

It is also not surprising that in forward-looking studies of demography and its influence on age structure, labour supply, dependency, and so on, only limited attention is given to alternative fertility scenarios. Virtually all the action in such studies is generated by alternative migration scenarios.[2]

Migration has had significant effects on Australia by any measure, particularly in the years following World War 2, certainly via its effect on overall population growth, but perhaps more so through its association with the industrial and geographic pattern of economic growth within Australia. A classic example is the attraction of British and other European immigrants to work in the motor vehicle and other manufacturing industries, generally under relatively high tariff protection, particularly in South Australia and Victoria. The more direct effects on aggregate productivity growth and per capita income growth seem, in retrospect, problematic and now may (arguably) be seen as a less important legacy than the wider effects on the diversity and character of Australian society.

Commentators such as Glenn Withers argue at least those positive societal effects, but add that the postwar waves of migrants to Australia have contributed significantly to the dynamism of the Australian economy and so indirectly, as well as directly, to real output per worker. Those now proposing a strong immigration policy over coming decades make similar points about the prospective contribution to economic dynamism (as well as more direct effects on age structure – lifting the proportions at younger ages – and on the dependency ratio), in the future context (see, for example, Withers 1999a, 1999b; Pope 1999).

The in-depth analysis of overseas migration and its interaction with growth is, however, the subject of a separate chapter and will not be examined further in this one.

Internal migration

Interstate migration, and for that matter *intrastate* migration and the *regional dimension* of Australian demography generally, are also important from some economic (and other) perspectives, but are also omitted from any detailed consideration here. Some states are certainly growing faster than others, and the same is true at the regional level within states. While *labour mobility* among regions is no doubt a significant factor in absolute levels of productivity, it is not clear that it has changed enough in recent years, or will do so over coming years, to merit deep consideration.

Fertility and participation in the workforce

Fertility

Fertility has changed significantly over past decades (see Figure 16.1) and its key drivers are inherently difficult to understand – notwithstanding that there are plenty of 'plausible' explanations (including changing social attitudes, especially among women, the greatly increased availability of reliable and convenient means of contraception, and so on).

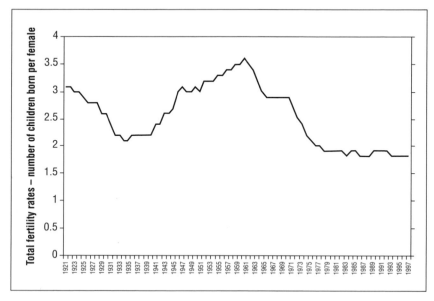

Figure 16.1 Fertility
Source: ABS Cat. no. 3301.0.

The 'baby-boom' and future fertility

One of the most important postwar demographic phenomena, the 'baby-boom', can be seen in the broad fertility measure depicted in Figure 16.1. The main relevant movements have been:

- the steady rise in the fertility rate during, and particularly after, World War 2 – from 2.2 births per female at the war's onset to 2.7 in 1945 and then up to a peak of 3.6 in 1961
- the steep decline (with a 'pause' in the late 1960s) to just below 2 at the end of the 1970s – and a subsequent steady 'floor' of 1.8 or so since: a level below replacement rate.

The figure serves to illustrate that any direct relationships between fertility and economic circumstances, in both directions, must be complex; for example, fertility has both fallen and risen in good (or improving) times. It would thus be hazardous to predict, on economic or other grounds, any definite future trend different from the recent flows, and as noted earlier, few contributors to current debates on population policy are doing so. Thus, while (see below) the consequences of the postwar fertility movements will take decades more to play out fully, there is no obvious basis to assume that *future* movements in fertility will be dramatic.

Female workforce participation – and male

However, an obviously closely related phenomenon is movements in female participation in the workforce: especially if supporting childcare services are also more readily available, women having fewer children can more readily enter the labour market. There have been significant trends in this behaviour over the past three to four decades, and clearly these have been quite directly related to economic outcomes. As shown in Figure 16.2, the strong rise in female participation has however been partly offset, in its effect on the labour supply, by a separate phenomenon – declining participation by males (from 84 to 73 per cent of the male population over the period depicted). As will be discussed later, the latter decline relates almost entirely to early retirement by *older* males.

Figure 16.2 shows that between the early 1960s and now, female participation rose from one in three to well over half (55.6 per cent in 2000). While the rate of rise slowed over the 1990s, female participation appears if anything to be continuing to increase, albeit gradually, today.

What the overall female participation figure does not directly reveal is that (as would be inferred) the change is attributable (almost) exclusively to *married* women, whose participation rose from about 25 per cent to about 55 per cent over the period depicted. Participation by unmarried women is just over one-half now, about the same as it was in the early 1960s (although it was a little

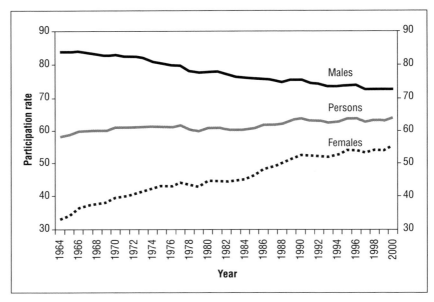

Figure 16.2 Participation rates by gender, Australia
Source: ABS Cat. no. 6291.0.40.001 and RBA (1991) *Australian Economic Statistics 1949–50 to 1989–90*, Occasional Paper no. 8.

lower than this in the 1970s, when married female participation was rising particularly rapidly).

Net effects on participation

The freeing of married women from some of their parenting activities is not of course 'explained' by the change in fertility. As noted, the latter change most likely reflects changes in attitudes and expectations by the community – notably (but not only) on the part of women, as well as in contraception, and the development of working arrangements and support services to facilitate increased participation; that is, part-time work, childcare, and so forth. The result is undeniably a moderate rise in *total* participation, from 58 to 64 per cent of the population – even after the partly offsetting decline in older male participation.

This can be inferred to have lifted absolute productivity levels per head of *population* (as distinct from a per *worker* measure) over the past few decades by about 10 per cent, even allowing that the phenomenon partly amounts to recognising in the market sector labour that was formerly contributed outside that sector.

Given that fertility appears to have no pronounced trend, this source of productivity increase per capita also cannot be assumed to persist into the future. In fact, a more marked phenomenon over recent years has been the early retirement of older males.

Falling male participation

As Figure 16.3 shows, it is *older male* participation that has been falling. Participation by males in the 55 to 64 age bracket has fallen from nearly 90 per cent in 1960 to under two-thirds in the 1990s. As the figure also shows, declining participation is indeed purely a male phenomenon: female participation is rising even in the 55–64 age bracket.

Early retirement – or retrenchment

Early retirement has risen markedly among males, from under two-thirds in the early 1980s to nearly 80 per cent in the late 1990s. Over that time there has been virtually no change in the proportion of females retiring early (see FitzGerald and Rooney 1999).

There is of course a positive side to early retirement – earlier enjoyment of increased leisure – but against this there are negatives:

- evidence that, for some early retirees at least, the increased leisure does not turn out to compensate for the loss of the relationships, stimulus, and so on, that go with work
- abundant evidence of inadequate financial self-provision for retirement – with implications for overall saving in the economy
- premature loss of productive and experienced labour from the economy, with implications for labour supply and productivity improvement. As Figure 16.4 shows, estimates of personal productivity implied by relative pay rates suggest that on average it peaks in the 50s age range and then declines only slowly (albeit that older and younger workers may be productive in different ways). Of course, there are seniority effects on relative pay, and so on, to consider – and 'survivor bias': those still at work at older ages may be on average somewhat more productive than those who have left or been 'pushed' – albeit less pronounced than in the past, but nevertheless the data do show the relative value placed by the market on labour by age.

Indeed the issues here would not be so pointed if we could be confident that the early retirement phenomenon has been a matter of increased exercise of choice. But on the contrary, the evidence is that 'early retirement' by males has often been code for 'given the push'. The 1997 ABS *Retirement and Retirement Intentions* survey showed that two-thirds of male early retirements were involuntary (FitzGerald and Rooney 1999: 29). In other words, this phenomenon has largely been driven by what appears to be poorly based prejudice on the part of employers (and unions, and indeed workers themselves).

The main economic consequences are to worsen the 'dependency ratio' (ratio of those not working to those working or to total population – see below) and hence to raise the difficulty of providing for income, health and aged care. The issue of how to pay for these needs is, however, more a function of the

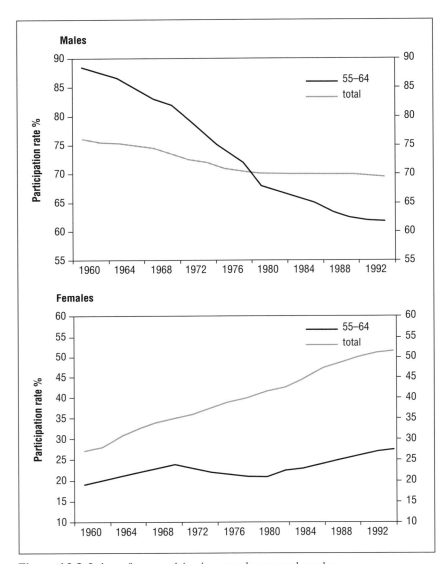

Figure 16.3 Labour force participation rates by age and gender

Source: D. Carey (1999) 'Coping with Population Ageing in Australia', Economics Department Working Papers no. 217, OECD.

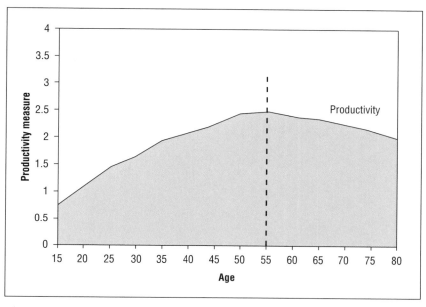

Figure 16.4 Relative productivity by age implied by incomes of the employed
Source: B. Bacon (1995) *Ageing in Australia: Some Modelling Results and Research Issues*, Retirement and
Income Modelling Unit.

overall age composition of the population (driven by the 'baby-boom bulge')
than of the exacerbating contribution of early retirement.

There are other dimensions of the economic consequences, including on
the quantum of gross saving and dis-saving flows and the balance between
them. This is discussed in FitzGerald and Rooney (1999), and was recently the
subject of a very interesting macroeconomic analysis by Ross Guest and Ian
McDonald (1999).

The age composition of the population

The baby-boom 'bulge' or wave

The other major consequence of the big swings seen in fertility postwar is
indeed the marked 'bulge' in the *age distribution* of the population, representing the 'baby-boom' already discussed. 'Baby-boomers' are the Australians
who were born between World War 2 and the early 1960s – 15 years or so
of births (almost a generation) at rates half as high again (or more) than is
usual now.

The wave-like movement of this baby-boom 'bulge' through the age range or
life-cycle as time goes by has been (after migration, perhaps) the most discussed

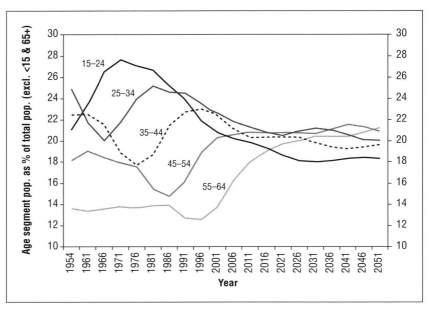

Figure 16.5 Working age population – excludes <15 and 65+

Source: ABS Cat. no. 3222.0 and RBA (1991) *Australian Economic Statistics 1949–50 to 1989–90*, Occasional Paper no. 8.

demographic phenomenon of recent decades, and certainly the most discussed in terms of future consequences. Yet it has probably *so far* had effects that have been less influential on Australia's overall economic performance than the rise in married female participation (or for that matter the decline in older male participation). This is attributable to the 'bulge' being largely *within* the working age range for the past two decades (see Figure 16.5).

It is now widely understood that since the *further* movement of the 'bulge' will take it out of the working age range as the 'baby-boomers' progressively retire (the oldest 'boomers' being already at around age 55), this wave movement poses very significant future problems for meeting the cost of income support, health care, and so on.

As will be discussed below, the prospective increases in costs for these are large, implying (if other responses are not developed) large increases in taxes in the future, which must fall largely on Australians of working age, and that in turn imply significant effects on incentives for labour supply, saving and investment.

'Dependency' and costs of public services

This brings into the discussion the concept of 'dependency', measured either as the proportion of the population outside the working age range – conventionally, those below 15 or over 64 – or as the ratio of those not of working age to those within the working age range. Two component ratios can usefully be distinguished – the 'young dependency ratio' (the proportion aged 0–14) and the 'aged dependency ratio' (the proportion aged 65+). These capture the notion that those in these age categories pay little or no tax (typically) but disproportionately consume public services or transfers (see McDonald and Kippen 1999, Creedy 1999; and most of the other papers in the same volume), including:

- (for the young) schooling, as well as other education and training
- (for the old) income support, health care – which tends to be concentrated in old age, especially in very old age – and other aged care.

Figure 16.6 appears to show that the issue of meeting future costs need not be too concerning. The total dependency ratio (those not of working age as a proportion of the total population) will decline highly over the next few years and then rise relatively slowly.

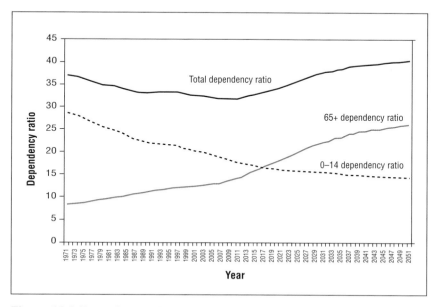

Figure 16.6 Dependency ratios
Source: ABS Cat. no. 3222.0 and RBA Occasional Paper No. 8.

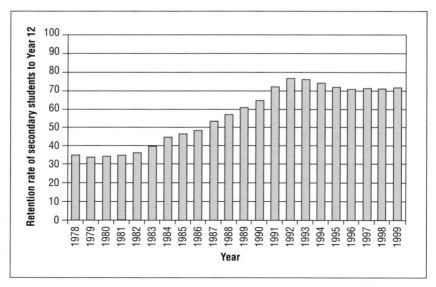

Figure 16.7 School retention rates to Year 12
Source: ABS Cat. no. 4221.0.

Costs for the young

However, this is a misleading view. Costs of public services for the young are substantially lower than those of services for older people; per capita usage of them is not increasing rapidly; and they have a pronounced investment character – that is, yield long-lasting benefits, including economic benefits. Figure 16.7 shows that school retention rates (to Year 12) actually rose *after* the 'baby-boom' cohort passed through, and have been fairly stable over the 1990s.

Student numbers have been increasing most at post-secondary levels (see Figure 16.8) – again largely *after* the passing through of the 'baby-boom' super cohort and therefore not due to it, but still relevant to gauging the effects of dependency movements. However, along with spending on school education, spending at those levels is not to be viewed as an outright drain on the public purse. On the contrary, while education spending may have partly a consumption character, in very narrowly defined economic terms (that is, ignoring its general civil benefits for society), it is increasingly recognised as a critical form of investment for national competitiveness in the information age – that is, as positive for growth.

These comments point directly to the conclusion that it is the *aged* dependency ratio that poses the greatest issues for future performance in per capita economic growth, via the consequent increased needs for *publicly funded services and transfers* in, for example:

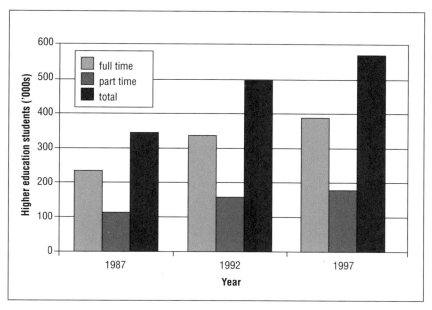

Figure 16.8 Higher education student numbers
Source: ABS Cat. no. 4221.0.

- health and community services
- income support
- aged care.

Future expenditure implications

Costs for the aged: the age pension and health care

Hitherto, a major focus of concern has been the future cost of the age pension. However, the most authoritative estimates, by the government's Retirement Income Modelling Unit, suggest that the extra cost to the taxpayer of the age pension in the 2030s and 2040s (relative to now) has been reduced by what has been done in superannuation to less than 1.5 per cent of GDP (National Commission of Audit 1996: 138–40, and discussion following). Obviously, the breadth and depth of self-provision through superannuation has been a major factor in this (with the relatively tight targeting of the pension also contributing) – longstanding areas of substantial occupational superannuation covered in both the public sector and some industries in the private sector have in fact been the main factor, but the extension to near-universal coverage via the Superannuation Guarantee will be increasingly important going forward.

However, it is becoming increasingly clear that the biggest area of concern for future affordability or *fiscal sustainability* (and hence for tax levels, incentives and growth) is health and related expenditure, rather than expenditure on the age pension.

Health expenditures

Health expenditures have long been concentrated on the aged. Not only do they use the most expensive medical treatments (in hospitals) more often than other age groups, but their stays tend to be longer and their treatments more complex. Of more concern is that, over the 1990s, rates of usage have gone up significantly among the old – a trend that seems unlikely under present arrangements to be reversed (see Figure 16.9).

There are strong drivers of health care costs other than ageing. In a system in which providers dominate, price signals are almost non-existent, and new technologies and treatments are rapidly adopted into community expectations; ageing has not, over recent decades, been a very important factor in *increases* in health costs. Those other drivers (including increased utilisation of services per capita) have dominated, as reflected in Figure 16.9.

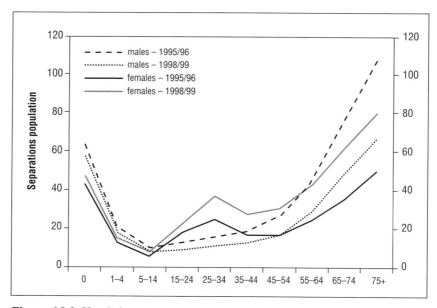

Figure 16.9 Hospital use
Source: Australian Institute of Health & Welfare, *Australian Hospital Statistics*.

The effect of ageing per se

Analyses of the pure effect of ageing (on its own) that may emerge over future decades seem to suggest that it may be a 'manageable' factor for future budgets. For example, a recent study in depth by the Commonwealth Department of Health and Aged Care concluded that:

Given the size of the Australian population as it is today, if its demographic composition were the same as it is projected to be in 2051 then, very nearly, an extra $17.07 billion in today's dollars would be needed to maintain the same level and quality of the three health services as they exist today. This view of the costs due to ageing is isolated, deliberately so, from the tricky issues that have been side-stepped by the assumptions underlying the analysis presented in this paper, particularly those issues related to possible increases in costs due to a larger number, greater variety and complexity of future procedures (1999: 45).

It might be noted, however, that the above estimate of an increase of $17 billion is over 3 per cent of GDP, while the projected future increase in cost to the budget of providing the age pension is now put at 1–1.5 per cent of GDP by the government's Retirement Income Modelling Unit (Rothman 1998). In other words, the pure effect of ageing alone on health costs is more than twice as big an issue as the prospective rise in the public costs of providing retirement income – thanks largely to the extent of private provision through superannuation that is now in train. As previously noted, a major part of this private provision preceded the advent of the Superannuation Guarantee; but the combined effects of voluntary and obligatory superannuation provision have on the face of it now reduced the budgetary issue of retirement income provision to 'manageable' proportions. Can that really be said to be true of the ageing effect on health costs?

In considering the issue of future health costs, it is important to appreciate that the real issue is not what effect ageing will have on its own, but what effects ageing *and* the other strong drivers alluded to above will have *in combination and interaction.*

Work by EPAC, the Retirement Income Modelling (RIM) Unit and the National Commission of Audit has highlighted this, but although their respective assessments imply major budget pressures ahead (rather bigger than the $17 billion estimate above), these assessments have received little public discussion so far.

There are uncertainties in any such assessments, especially about the extent to which health care costs per capita will continue to rise faster than the general CPI, as they have persistently done for some years now, and if so by how much. On the range of RIM analyses put forward by the National Commission of Audit (1996: chapter 6): *health care costs (public and private combined) are likely to rise by 6 to 8 per cent of GDP over the next 30–40 years.*

In 40 years' time, on these analyses, health care costs could reach 17 per cent of GDP, or about double the present figure, with the *aged* health care component being almost 10 per cent of GDP. While health care costs are met privately, currently around 70 per cent are met by government. Health care costs to the Commonwealth could rise by 4 per cent of GDP, with the aged share of health outlays rising from under 40 per cent now to over 55 per cent (see Figure 16.10).

Projections of future health costs are considerably more uncertain than those of future age pension costs, depending in particular on assumptions about future growth in *relative* health costs (cf. other costs in the economy) due to the various drivers mentioned above, such as new treatments, rising community expectations, more intensive use, and so on. Nevertheless, plausible estimates for total health costs in the 2030s and 2040s range from 13 per cent of GDP upwards – implying an increase in aged health care costs of *at least 3 per cent of GDP* to the Commonwealth budget alone.

Saving

Saving patterns by age

When an issue arises concerning how a projected large future expense is to be met, attention logically turns to making provision for that expense ahead of time – that is, saving to provide for it. Saving is in fact an aspect of behaviour that has

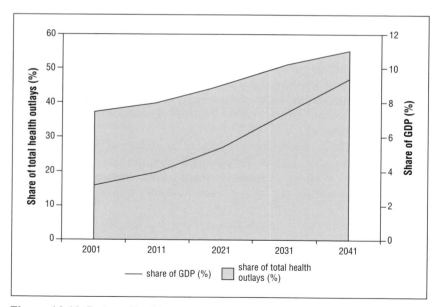

Figure 16.10 Projected health expenditure on the aged
Source: Retirement Income Modelling Task Force, reported by National Commission of Audit (1996).

a quite distinct pattern by age, although data on saving are notoriously imprecise (being derived as the difference between large consumption and income
aggregates that are prone to measurement errors and biases); and data on its age
pattern doubly so. An encouraging feature is that over the life cycle, saving tends
to be concentrated around late working age where the baby-boomers now are,
as illustrated in Figure 16.11, which presents data from FitzGerald (1993).

Declining household saving rate

Unfortunately, the strong saving flows, and increases in saving *rates*, that one
would accordingly expect to see are not visible in the conventional measures
of saving over the past decade or so. The Household Saving Ratio (essentially
capturing net financial saving out of current disposable income) has continued
to test new lows over recent years – despite the increasing levels of compulsory
superannuation saving – as Figure 16.12 shows.

Fortunately, net financial saving is not the whole story. As has been widely
discussed, in the 1990s Australian households made increasing use of debt.
Some of this, especially increased credit card debt (which rose rapidly from a
relatively low base), was undoubtedly used to finance consumption – implicitly
offsetting the restraint on consumption that rising compulsory saving would
otherwise have exerted.

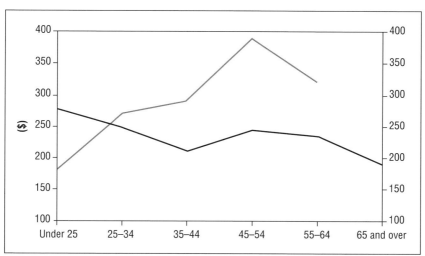

Figure 16.11 Weekly income per capita adjusted for number of children in
household; and consumption by age group (lower line)
Note: Adjustments for household composition were made by Treasury staff assisting the study.
Source: ABS, *Household Expenditure Survey*, and ABS, *Population Projections*; adjustments made for
study reported in FitzGerald (1993).

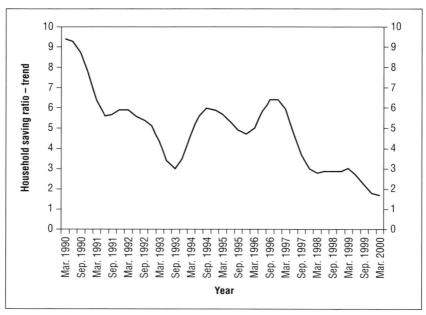

Figure 16.12 Household saving rate
Source: ABS Cat. no 5206.0.

Alternative perspectives on saving

But some savings were used to acquire assets – both the housing assets traditionally most popular with households and, increasingly, financial assets,
notably direct and indirect equity holdings. An alternative measure of saving
can be constructed from the household balance sheet data now published as
part of the national accounts, specifically the real increase in net worth (assets
less liabilities) of households, expressed as a percentage of disposable income,[3]
as shown in Figure 16.13.

While the data shown in Figure 16.13 are volatile, they suggest a 'real
saving rate' of roughly 20 per cent of disposable income over the 1990s, and a
general upwards trend – albeit no doubt due significantly to rising asset prices
over the late years of the decade.

It can be presumed that the net wealth accumulation depicted in Figure
16.13 is being undertaken disproportionately by those in the latter part of their
working careers. If the data on the evolution of the age composition of the
working age population shown in Figure 16.5 are re-expressed as indexes
based in this present year (2001), it can be seen that numbers of Australians in
these categories will rise strongly for some years ahead (see Figure 16.14).

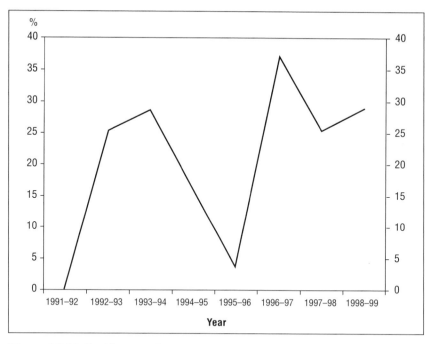

Figure 16.13 Real increases in net worth, % of gross disposable income
Source: ABS Cat. No. 5241.0, *Australian National Accounts – National Balance Sheet* and 5204.0, *Australian System of National Accounts*.

Prospects for stronger saving

As earlier discussed, however, relatively fewer and fewer males in particular are remaining at work beyond age 55, and that is indeed reflected in Figure 16.11 – suggesting that saving is strongest in the 45–54 age range. This is precisely where most baby-boomers are now. Combining the data of Figures 16.11 and 16.14 produces a somewhat artificial projected picture of future savings flows, depicted in Figure 16.15.

The errors, biases, and so on, of the data on which the above figure is constructed can hardly be over-estimated. But it does serve to illustrate that intrinsically, a significant group in the population (from a demographic perspective) will be disposed to maintain saving – or to be more precise, net wealth accumulation – at relatively high levels, or even to increase it, over the next decade or two. Moreover, over much of that horizon, the numbers in the relevant age group will be growing relative to other groups.

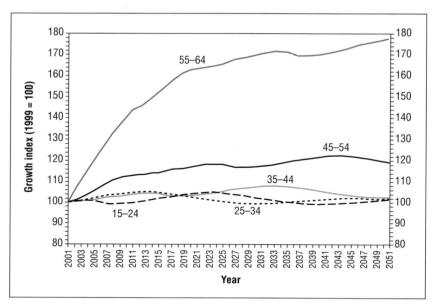

Figure 16.14 Working population: indexes of age group growth
Source: ABS Cat no. 3222.1, *Population Projections*.

Saving as the response to looming future cost increases

The projected rise of public costs for health care in the future poses similar
problems to those involved in the issue of provision for retirement income. The
obvious response is to accumulate provision in advance through savings –
savings ultimately invested in real net additional physical capital – and thereby
to minimise the extent of increases in taxes on labour (or reductions in government spending on the non-aged).[4]

The appropriate approach in respect of retirement income is now widely
agreed to be a balance between support from the *taxpayer* of the day, *compulsory*
self-provision through superannuation beforehand, and *voluntary* saving beforehand. The compulsion is essentially justified on inter-generational equity
grounds, but surprisingly perhaps is shown in opinion surveys to be widely
accepted. Is a similar response appropriate for health care?

It is important to note one difference *vis-à-vis* the issue of ensuring provision
for future income. On health costs, at least part of any advance provision
through saving should desirably be accumulated in *risk pools* to deal with unfore-
seen catastrophic health costs for those covered. Of course, there is some risk-
sharing inherent in the fact that future public budgets will inevitably still meet
a substantial part of the costs. In effect, much of the risk of catastrophic health

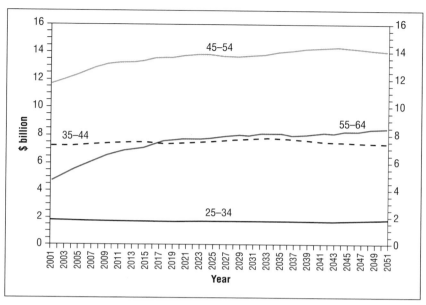

Figure 16.15 Projected saving by age group ($ billions p.a.)
Source: Author's analysis and ABS Cat. no.3222.1, *Population Projections*.

costs for retired people will inevitably, and desirably, be borne by the future Australian taxpayer (collectively).

In the absence of funds built up in advance, the sharing of the costs between taxpayers and the retired will be essentially a 'zero-sum game'. The retired who are members of private health funds will continue to receive some cross-subsidy from younger people, moderated by the new 'lifetime community-rating' arrangements, but the cross-subsidy's viability depends on the maintenance of the present levels of membership and in turn of the private health insurance rebate.

A saving scheme could be neutral between those in private health insurance and those choosing the public system if, for example, it were used to pay the Medicare levy and/or some other future contribution to public health care. If substantial funds were built up in advance, the taxpayer share *and* the share paid for out of retirees' other finances for health care could *both* be moderated.[5]

Saving and growth

One of the key messages of *National Saving: A Report to the Treasurer* was that for many public policy purposes, it is *national* saving – the sum of public and

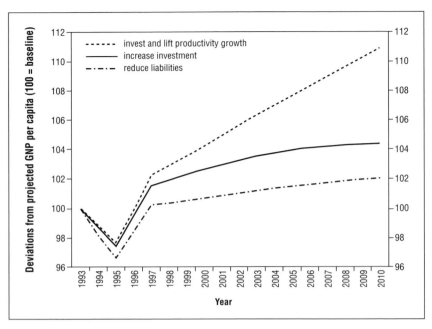

Figure 16.16 Alternative increased saving scenarios: growth implications

private saving – that counts. The question of lifting saving in order to provide for the future without leaving a legacy of growth-inhibiting higher taxes can be addressed in part by increased *public* saving. New Zealand is going this way, planning to use part of budget surpluses to help pre-fund New Zealand Superannuation – a more liberal and costly (non-means-tested) counterpart to our age pension. Some scepticism about whether the policy will endure over future electoral cycles seems in order, and it is just one example of such measures; others include some (public) social security systems overseas that accumulate reserves.

The key for assessing the implications for future economic growth of increased saving is what the savings are used for. This was explored in *National Saving: A Report to the Treasurer* through a range of economic scenarios modelled by EPAC. A selection of the scenarios is depicted in Figure 16.16. They all show a saving rate being lifted first by reducing the early 1990s Commonwealth budget deficit to 1 per cent of GDP or less than lifting saving by a further 0.5 to 1.5 per cent of GDP (sustained) over more than a decade. The figure shows the proportioned effect on GNP per capita relative to a baseline outlook.

The points that the figure makes are essentially as follows:

- To the extent that the increased saving goes to reducing external liabilities, the effect on growth of our living standards is positive but modest.

- To the extent that the increased savings are invested in increased capital within the Australian economy, there is a process of 'capital deepening' (increased capital per worker). This has considerably greater effects on per capita income growth, but without other measures to lift intrinsic factor productivity on an ongoing basis, it is subject to diminishing returns.
- Most powerful of all is a combination of the middle path above and sustained measures to lift productivity growth. The report argued that a lift in productivity growth by 0.5 percentage points was feasible through ongoing microeconomic reform – and subsequent outcomes demonstrate the realism of that scenario. The *combined* approach is capable of lifting the per capita growth rate permanently (without a marked diminishing returns effect).

Of course, such scenarios do no more than illustrate the choices the community faces. But they have sufficient realism to show that we do indeed have real choices – in saving, in our investments in both physical capital and skills, in our reform efforts for higher continuous productivity improvement, in our approach to work and retirement, and in how we provide for the needs of an ageing population – which are capable of addressing those issues effectively while lifting growth.

Other issues

Mortality, morbidity, longevity

There are puzzles in the third component of population change (other than natural increase and migration) – *mortality*, or equivalently, longevity. Longevity has been increasing in recent times (see Higgins 1998), the causes for which are not perfectly understood. Ahead, there is at least the possibility of significant change (for example, arising from the development and application of gene technology). An associated aspect that is of comparable importance for assessing the future impact of demography, especially via the demand for public services, is *morbidity*: the incidence of illness. More precisely is the propensity of people not just to be sick but to utilise health care services and related services. This propensity has been increasing in recent years; for example, increased frequency of hip replacements by older people (sometimes more than once) – while the retired proportion of the population has been relatively static.

Clearly, these aspects heighten the tension between the rising demand for health care as the proportion of old people rises, and the fiscal sustainability of meeting that demand from public budgets – unless some of the approaches to lifting saving and growth discussed in the previous section are pursued.

Conclusions

Looking forward, the main threat posed by the issues discussed in this chapter is that tax rates may have to rise to levels that are inimical to incentive and to

Australia's competitive position unless the kinds of responses canvassed above are pursued more effectively.

Those potential responses include a range of very positive opportunities, such as:

- With the young, a smaller proportion of the population, it should be easier to fund a lifting of the quality of education and training and related activities (research, and so on) that are increasingly critical to productivity improvement and economic competitiveness in the new century.
- There are grounds to be optimistic that the trend to early retirement will be reversed, and that a more sophisticated model will emerge around flexible phasing out of work. This will retain longer in the economy valuable resources of experience, judgement, people skills, and so on, that older workers tend to have relative to the attributes of younger people. Again this will be positive for productivity, saving and reduced dependency.
- While it may cost more, spending that improves the health of older people will also improve the prospects of extended economic contribution – which could help materially in providing for the gamut of needs that ageing will increase: income, health and other care needs, as well as needs for all the goods and services involved in a good lifestyle for future elderly Australians. The economic benefits will be greater if more sustainable funding arrangements – necessarily involving increased provision in advance (that is, increased saving) – can be developed.

In short, the threat to growth from demographic change can be made into an opportunity. The choice is ours.

References

Commonwealth Department of Health and Aged Care (1999) 'The Ageing Australian Population and Future Health Costs: 1996–2051', Canberra, mimeo.

Creedy, J. (1999) 'Population Ageing and the Growth of Social Expenditure', chapter 10 (pp. 229–50) in Productivity Commission and Melbourne Institute of Applied Economic and Social Research, *Policy Implications of the Ageing of Australia's Population*, AusInfo, Canberra.

Dowrick, S. (1995a) 'Demographic Change, Investment and Growth in the Asia–Pacific region', *Asia–Pacific Economic Review*, vol. 1, no. 1, April, pp. 20–31.

Dowrick, S. (1995b) 'The Determinants of Long-Run Growth', in *Productivity and Growth*, Proceedings of a Conference, Reserve Bank of Australia, pp. 7–47.

FitzGerald, V.W. (1993) *National Saving: A Report to the Treasurer*, Canberra, AGPS.

FitzGerald, V.W. and Rooney, C. (1999) *Rethinking Work and Retirement: Better Balance, Better Choices for Australians*, study commissioned by National Australia Bank, The Allen Consulting Group.

Guest, R. and McDonald, I. (1999) 'The Effect of Later Retirement on Optimal National Saving in Australia', in Productivity Commission and Melbourne Institute, chapter 6, pp. 107–34.

Higgins T. (1998) 'Australian Mortality: Improvement and Uncertainty in an Ageing Population', Sixth Annual Colloquium of Superannuation Researchers, University of Melbourne.

McDonald, P. and Kippen, R. (1999) 'Ageing: The Social and Economic Dimensions', chapter 4 (pp. 47–70) in Productivity Commission and Melbourne Institute of Applied Economic and Social Research, *Policy Implications of the Ageing of Australia's Population*, AusInfo, Canberra.

National Commission of Audit (1996) *Report to the Commonwealth Government*, Canberra, AGPS, June.

Pope, D. (1999) 'The role of Immigration in our Economic Development', BCA Papers, vol. 1(1), May pp. 30–5.

Rothman, G. (1998) 'Projections of Key Aggregates for Australia's Aged', Retirement Income Modelling Unit Conference Paper 98/2, The Treasury, Canberra.

Withers, G. (1999a) 'Australia's Need for a Population Policy', *BCA Papers*, vol. 1(1), May: 21–9.

Withers, G. (1999b) 'Creating a dynamic Australia', *Immigration and Multiculturalism: Global Perspective*, CEDA Growth 47, CEDA, November 1999, pp. 47–57.

Notes

1 There have been a number of conferences on these issues and multiple articles in some issues of publications, including the Business Council of Australia's *BCA Journal* (some references to which are cited below), *IPA Backgrounder* (for example, vol. 10, no. 5, December 1998); and the Business/Higher Education Round Table's *BHERT News* (Issue 8, July 2000, entitled 'Populate or stagnate: Australia 2050').

2 For a good recent discussion of alternative population projections for Australia and their sensitivities (without discussion of the relationship with economic growth), see P. McDonald and R. Kippen 'Population Projections for Australia', *BCA Papers*, vol, 2, no. 2, September 2000: 96–104. See also their paper 'Ageing: The Social and Economic Dimensions', chapter 4: 47–70) in Productivity Commission and Melbourne Institute of Applied Economic and Social Research, *Policy Implications of the Ageing of Australia's Population*, AusInfo, Canberra, 1999.

3 Strictly speaking, this increase in wealth should be taken in as part of comprehensive income, as well as being counted as saving, but in keeping with the common practice of referring saving to *disposable* income this has not been done in the data presented here.

4 An extremely important reason for considering advance provision is the sheer power of compound interest. For example, to deliver $1 in real terms in 30 years requires only a single contribution of about 8 to 13 cents now, if well invested. The arithmetic is even more favourable than that, since there are more years of accumulation than of draw-down if accumulation is over the whole of the working life.

5 A scheme pursuing these ideas is outlined in the author's 'Ideas for the Funding of Health Care in the Context of the Ageing of the Population', paper presented to Australian International Health Institute Symposium, November 1999. The paper has since been published in R. Galbally and J. Krupinski (eds), *Reform, Re-design or Revolution: Health Agendas for the 21st Century*, Australian International Health Institute, Melbourne University Ltd, 2000. A version appeared in *The Geneva Papers on Risk and Insurance*, vol. 26(1), January 2001: 1–12 and a brief version of the ideas in a guest editorial in *Australian Health Review*, vol. 23(3), 2000.

Index

Page numbers followed by *n* indicate endnotes; those followed by *fig* indicate figures; those followed by *tab* indicate tables.